SPORT Magazine's Book of Major League Baseball Clubs

THE AMERICAN LEAGUE

SPORT Magazine's Book of Major League Baseball Clubs

THE AMERICAN LEAGUE

THE NEW YORK YANKEES by Grantland Rice

THE CHICAGO WHITE SOX by John Carmichael

THE WASHINGTON SENATORS by Shirley Povich

THE BOSTON RED SOX by Bill Cunningham

THE KANSAS CITY ATHLETICS by Harry Robert

THE DETROIT TIGERS by H. G. Salsinger

THE BALTIMORE ORIOLES by Bob Burns

THE CLEVELAND INDIANS by Gordon Cobbledick

Edited by ED FITZGERALD

The Big League **Baseball Library**

GROSSET & DUNLAP *Publishers* **NEW YORK**

CONTENTS

		Page
	INTRODUCTION	1
Grantland Rice	THE NEW YORK YANKEES	3
John Carmichael	THE CHICAGO WHITE SOX	37
Shirley Povich	THE WASHINGTON SENATORS	58
Bill Cunningham	THE BOSTON RED SOX	88
Harry Robert	THE KANSAS CITY ATHLETICS	122
H. G. Salsinger	THE DETROIT TIGERS	157
Bob Burnes	THE BALTIMORE ORIOLES	190
Gordon Cobbledick	THE CLEVELAND INDIANS	213

SPORT Magazine's Book of Major League Baseball Clubs

THE AMERICAN LEAGUE

INTRODUCTION

Sometimes it must seem, to the general fan as well as to the working sportswriter sweating to inject variety and pace into his dispatches, that there is only one team in the American League. This is not so.

Ty Cobb was not a Yankee.

Tris Speaker was not a Yankee.

Lefty Grove was not a Yankee.

Mickey Cochrane was not a Yankee.

Bob Feller was not a Yankee.

Ted Williams was not a Yankee.

Of course, Babe Ruth, Lou Gehrig, Bill Dickey, Red Ruffing, Joe DiMaggio and Phil Rizzuto *were* Yankees. So were Earle Combs, Lefty Gomez, Red Rolfe and Tommy Henrich. Admittedly, these gentlemen and their talented associates helped the Yankees drape the Stadium with souvenirs of 18 American League pennants and 14 world championships. There can be no caviling that the mighty Bronx Bombers play a dominating role in the story of their league. This book proves that. But it also proves there have been momentous contributions to the saga of the younger major league by every one of the seven other clubs—most definitely including the Baltimore Orioles, nee St. Louis Browns.

Here, as originally published in SPORT Magazine, is the complete history of each of the American League clubs. The

1

ambitious series of which they are part was conceived early in 1950 and all the assignments were given out at once. Eight famous writers produced eight carefully researched and wonderfully readable articles. The result of their labor of love is a unique reference manual which combines the factual wealth of a record book with the liveliness of a novel.

Our all-star team of authors, headed by the late beloved Grantland Rice, has adhered faithfully to a policy of using the chronological progress of the team as the bones of the story, then packing in dozens of anecdotes and personality sketches as the meat. The result is that they have adroitly avoided the pitfall of grinding out repetitious columns of fact, fact, fact. Instead, they have recreated the golden hours of some of the greatest ballplayers ever to pitch a no-hitter, to smash a home run, to make a double play, to steal home in the last of the ninth.

You don't have to be a figure filbert to enjoy these histories. You just have to be a baseball fan.

Ed Fitzgerald
Editor, SPORT Magazine

THE NEW YORK YANKEES

BY GRANTLAND RICE

It was in the spring of 1904 that I first saw the New York Yankees, or Highlanders as they were known then. A fairly nondescript outfit, or so they appeared at the time, they were in Atlanta, Georgia, during their spring training period. I remember particularly Clark Griffith, their manager and a veteran pitcher at the time; the little sharpshooter, Wee Willie Keeler; and Jack Chesbro, the smiling, right-handed pitcher who went on to win 41 games that year. As I watched them work out under the warm Georgia sun, I of course never realized I was watching the formation of the greatest baseball dynasty of them all, one that would reign as world champion 16 times and American League leader 20 times in the next 50 years.

Call the roll of Yankee greats, past and present, and you name so many of baseball's all-time heroes—Babe Ruth and Lou Gehrig and Joe DiMaggio and Herb Pennock and Bill Dickey and Tony Lazzeri and others. Even now, you get a special tingle of excitement when you read over their names and picture them as they were in their many hours of triumph at Yankee Stadium—and in all the other parks around the league.

It is easy to say that they alone made the Yankees, but it is not that simple. The great Yankee record and the pride and tradition that go with it is the product of many years of

3

effort, mixed with anguish and success. No one man is responsible for the achievement; many great ballplayers, managers and front-office executives have contributed their share to baseball's proudest success story.

The American League first started boasting about the Yankees 52 years ago. They weren't the Yankees then, of course. In that first year of their history, 1903, the newspapers referred to them as the Greater New York Club of the American League. But Ban Johnson, the enterprising ex-sportswriter who founded the new group of baseball teams to compete with the well-established National League, was understandably proud and happy with the New York franchise. The success or failure of his project depended a great deal on getting a club in the nation's biggest city. It had been no easy job. The New York Giants had a firm stranglehold on the town's baseball patronage and owner John T. Brush wasn't anxious to share it with anyone. Brush and the former millionaire owner of the Giants, Andrew Freedman, an influential man in town, continually threw up road blocks in Johnson's way. For two years, his attempts to move the Baltimore team into New York and lease property for a ball park were thwarted. But in January, 1903, representatives of the two leagues got together and came to an agreement of sorts over the admission of a New York American League club into the majors. Brush continued his private fight against the plan, but Johnson found two men with the necessary money and influence to push the deal through. One, Frank Farrell, was a big-shot gambler and racing-stable owner and the other, William S. Devery, was an ex-chief of police and a successful realtor. In those days, there was no Judge Landis to fuss about a magnate's private business associations. Farrell and Devery were just what Johnson had been looking for. They paid $18,000 for the Baltimore franchise, selected coal dealer Joseph Gordon to act as their president, and named Clark Griffith manager.

They had only three months to find a suitable park site and build the grandstands. A lot in the Washington Heights section of Manhattan, toward the northern tip of the island, was finally obtained. Despite some eleventh hour efforts by the Giants' owner to have a street cut through the property, work got under way in mid-winter and the 15,000-seat stadium was virtually finished for the first home game, May 1, 1903.

The greatest of all major-league baseball teams certainly had a humble beginning. On a bright May Day afternoon, 16,243 fans crowded into the wooden grandstands and lined up around the outfield to watch the new American League team in action. The right-field area was still somewhat rough and rock-strewn, but special ground rules were made. Before the game, Bayne's 69th Regiment band played "Yankee Doodle" and other lively airs while the crowd waved tiny American flags that had been distributed at the gate. Most eyes were on the Highlanders, as the New Yorkers were called, in their shiny new white uniforms and white flannel caps with black lacing. They watched Willie Keeler, the team's one big-name star, as he warmed up. Willie was on the downgrade then, but he still could punch out hits. The visiting Washington club boasted big Ed Delahanty, who had led the league in batting the previous year and had hit four home runs in one game in 1896.

The Highlanders got off on the right foot before the home crowd and beat Washington, 6-2. Jack Chesbro, the strong arm on the pitching staff that included manager Griffith, was the winner. Farrell and Devery were elated with the performance and so, apparently, was the crowd.

Griffith brought the Highlanders in a respectable fourth that first season. And before the spring of 1904, Ban Johnson was sure he had supplied the New Yorkers with enough ammunition to battle the Giants on even terms for the city's patronage. Jack Chesbro had been persuaded away from

Pittsburgh the year before. Johnson rigged a trade that brought the classy shortstop Norman (The Tabasco Kid) Elberfeld to the Highlanders from Detroit. Pat Dougherty and Dave Fultz were other standout players who joined the team.

Griff's hand-picked crew, often referred to as the "All-Stars," chased the Red Sox right down to the wire in the 1904 season. On the final day, the Highlanders were one and a half games behind the Red Sox and a doubleheader between the two clubs was scheduled for Hilltop Park. A sweep would mean the flag for New York.

The records say 28,540 people pushed their way into a park built for half that number. They packed the stands and crowded around the outfield, standing on benches and boxes. They saw one of the most famous games in American League history.

Happy Jack Chesbro, who won a total of 41 games that year (still a modern major-league record), was locked in a 2-2 pitching duel with Bill Dinneen going into the ninth inning of the first contest. In the ninth, with a Red Sox runner on third, Chesbro wild-pitched to shortstop Fred Parent. The run beat the Highlanders and won the pennant for Boston. New York took the anti-climactic second game, 1-0, in ten innings.

That was as close as the New Yorkers were to come for 17 years, although they finished second in 1906 and again in 1910. In fact, if it hadn't been for the presence of some exciting personalities in the lineup, particularly Hal Chase, the great defensive first-baseman, the club might have dropped right out of the public's sight during the next few seasons. There was little reason why the fans should go to Hilltop Park instead of the Polo Grounds, home of the highly successful and popular Giants.

Chase was one of the few bona fide stars to play for the Yankees in the early years. (I'll refer to them as the

Yankees from now on, because that nickname became popular around 1908, especially with the newspapermen who had a hard time fitting "Highlanders" into one-column heads.) Chase, a cocky, brilliant ballplayer, was probably the greatest of the pre-Babe Ruth Yankees. Of course, you won't find his name in the record books today and baseball people speak of him most frequently in the same breath with the infamous 1919 Chicago Black Sox. Hal got involved in some serious gambling charges and there has been a dark cloud around his name ever since he slipped out of the major leagues in 1920. But with those early Yankees he was all class and color, a gifted, graceful fielder who made plays around first that have never been duplicated.

Whatever small progress the Yankees had made in their box-office battle with the Giants disintegrated in 1908. Farrell and Devery took more active interest in the club and it wasn't long before they were feuding with manager Clark Griffith. The team started to slump in mid-season after a fair start and Griff, loudly resenting front-office interference, quit. The owners promoted shortstop Elberfeld to the pilot's job but their troubles only increased. The Kid was a belligerent, hard-talking player whose normal actions would be enough to get him bounced out of any game today. He had a playful habit of stomping on an umpire's feet when he was disputing a call.

There was considerable bitterness between Elberfeld and Hal Chase. The feeling increased as soon as the appointment was announced. It wasn't exactly a secret that Hal had wanted Griff's job, too. On September 4, Chase packed up and left for San Jose, California, his hometown. Before leaving New York, Chase told newspapermen that the club management circulated stories "detrimental to his character and honesty."

If you could get a look at the league standings in September of 1908, you'd never believe your eyes. On Labor

Day, shortly before Orville Wright astounded military observers at Fort Meyer, Virginia, by staying aloft in an "aeroplane" four minutes and 15 seconds, the Yankees were in the cellar, 16 games behind the seventh-place Washington Senators! In a four-game series with the Nats, the lowly New Yorkers were shut out three times by Walter Johnson. At the same time, the Giants were leading the National League and drawing crowds up to 30,000 at the nearby Polo Grounds. Yankee fortunes were at their lowest ebb.

Farrell and Devery had to do something to pump a little blood into their impotent team. They weren't making enough to pay laundry bills, and neither of the magnates was in a position to throw any more money into the operation. Chase was persuaded to rejoin the team and George Stallings, who made baseball history with the 1914 Boston Braves five seasons later, was named manager. The Yankees pulled up to fifth in 1909 and finished second the following year. But before the close of the season in 1910, Stallings, like Griffith before him, had run out of patience with his second-guessing bosses, Farrell and Devery. He resigned.

Like most unstable, tottering baseball organizations, the Yankees went through managers as quickly as they did uniforms in the next four years. Because of his tremendous fan appeal, Chase was picked to lead the club after Stallings. But as talented and shrewd as Hal was, he couldn't handle a big-league team. A minor-league manager with big-league color and theatrics, Harry Wolverton, was tried out. But after a last-place finish, Farrell and Devery decided on another switch. In 1913, they called on Frank Chance, the great Chicago Cubs hero, to lead them out of the woods. As capable as Chance was, he never should have managed the Yankees, or any other big-league team, that year. Frank had been hit by so many baseballs in his career that his hearing and eyesight were failing.

New York advanced one notch to seventh under Chance.

But an undercurrent of trouble and resentment that ran through the club gained momentum the next season. Chance argued long and heatedly with Farrell and Devery over the need for new players and they complained of his field tactics. Chase revolted against his manager by refusing to carry out orders and playing comedian at Chance's expense in the clubhouse and dugout. The situation became intolerable for manager, owner and team. Chase was traded to the White Sox and Chance, after nearly tangling with Devery, departed for California without finishing the season. A young shortstop named Roger Peckinpaugh filled in as manager of the disorganized band.

The future of the Yankees was obviously limited under the Farrell-Devery banner, and no one knew it better than Ban Johnson. Farrell was in the habit of betting heavily at the race tracks and neither he nor Devery was a good financial risk. Club debts increased and there was no prospect of more revenue at the gate. In 1913, they became tenants of the Giants at the Polo Grounds.

Johnson became more and more anxious to have a solvent, successful American League entry in New York. He talked to Colonel Jacob Ruppert, who had inherited a profitable brewery from his immigrant father and was one of the city's most prominent—and best-heeled—sportsmen, about the Yankee franchise. While serving in Congress in 1900, Ruppert had made a $150,000 offer for the Giants, but had shown little other interest in baseball.

Johnson got Ruppert together with Captain Tillinghast L'Hommedieu Huston, a self-made millionaire and a close pal of John McGraw. The two quickly became interested in purchasing the club. They were as different as two millionaires could possibly be. Ruppert was an impeccable example of the rich, society-minded sportsman, a man of aesthetic taste. Huston was a roughhewn old Army man who had made his fortune as an engineer in Cuba after the Spanish-

American war. He liked a good drink and enjoyed the rough, coarse-talking sports crowd that hung around the ball parks.

Their first look into the status of the American League club was discouraging. The property was overburdened with notes and obligations that had accumulated during the losing box-office battle with the Giants. But both were excited by the possibilities of running a major-league franchise in the biggest city in the country. On January 11, 1915, the deal was completed and Ruppert and Huston paid $400,000 for the New York ball club. They went in 50-50, an arrangement that Ruppert was soon unhappy about.

The new owners found that, among other things, they needed a new manager. They picked Bill Donovan, once a star pitcher with the Tigers and then a successful minor-league manager, to replace Roger Peckinpaugh, who had filled in for Frank Chance during the last season. They made their first important player acquisition when they influenced Frank (Home Run) Baker, property of the Philadelphia A's, to come out of his self-imposed retirement.

But Baker wasn't enough to lift the team into the class of a pennant contender. After a fifth-place finish in 1915, the Yankees pushed into the first division the following year, only to drop to sixth in 1917. Cap Huston had taken a far more active interest in the club's fortunes than his partner, Ruppert. The threat of war was growing darker in those days and, as a result of Cap's military mind, the Yankee players were the first to hold squad drills with bats substituted for rifles at spring training. He even had some of the newspaper crowd marching around with Louisville Sluggers over their shoulders—an experience that Bill McGeehan, Damon Runyon and myself, among others, never forgot. But Huston went off to France with the Army Engineers in 1917 and Ruppert was left to worry about the team and its rapidly decreasing patronage.

Jake liked Bill Donovan personally but had little faith in him as a team builder, so his first post-season move was to look for a new manager. He went to his friend and adviser, Ban Johnson, and asked for suggestions. Johnson didn't hesitate to name Miller Huggins, the dwarfish fellow who was then leading the St. Louis Cardinals in the National League. In France, Huston had his own ideas about a manager. He was determined to get Wilbert Robinson, a good friend of his and the manager of the Brooklyn Dodgers. Ruppert agreed to talk to Robinson, but neither he nor Robby was impressed by the interview.

Jake went ahead with Johnson's choice, even though he was skeptical about Huggins. He had met him once and was a bit startled at his appearance and manner. But a formal meeting with Huggins changed Ruppert's first impression. The Colonel liked the little man's straightforward speech and was impressed with his thorough knowledge of the game. He signed Huggins to a two-year contract, the first and only formal agreement the two had in Miller's 12 years as manager of the Yankees.

Ruppert was satisfied that he had made a wise choice, but when word got to Huston overseas, there was an explosion that broke their partnership wide open. Angered because Ruppert had by-passed Robinson, Cap Huston (soon to become a Colonel) carried on a long-distance campaign against the managerial choice. He wrote letters and spoke bitterly about it to Army friends.

Huggins' first Yankee team struggled through the abbreviated 1918 season with a patchwork lineup that was constantly being changed by the demands of the armed forces. The club finished a creditable fourth.

If you must pick a single turning point in Yankee history, the moment when the team shed the cloak of mediocrity and started its triumphant climb to its place of domination in baseball, it would be January 5, 1920. That was the day the New York Yankees purchased Babe Ruth.

I'm sure no ballplayer had so much to do with the swift, sure success of a team as did Ruth with the Yankees. And yet, at the same time, I feel the Babe was indebted to New York for providing him with an appropriate stage for his tremendous heroics. The greatest figure the game has known needed baseball's greatest team, and vice versa. The Yankees probably would have become the fabulous success they are now without the Babe, but, I'm certain, the road to the top would have been much longer and much less exciting.

When the Yankees purchased Ruth that winter, he was 25 years old, a well-constructed, six-foot, two-inch left-handed pitcher-outfielder who had a fine reputation as a hurler and had just astonished the baseball public by hitting 29 homers in 1919. Ruth's sale to New York was headline news. As announced by Harry Frazee, the Red Sox owner, the Yankees paid $100,000 for Babe—the biggest deal the game had seen. The sale of Ruth caused a near mutiny among Boston fans. Newspapers ran cartoons showing "For Sale" signs on the Boston Common and some people threatened to boycott the Red Sox. Frazee quickly countered with the statement: "It would be an injustice to keep him with the Red Sox, who were fast becoming a one-man team." Later, he said, "Ruth had simply become impossible and the Boston club could no longer put up with his eccentricities." But the truth was that Frazee, hounded by baseball and theatrical debts, desperately needed money. The transaction for Ruth also included a $350,000 loan from Ruppert, who took over the mortage on Fenway Park.

The Babe made a smashing success out of his first season in Yankee uniform. He hit .376 and a total of 54 home runs for the third-place club.

Less than a year after the coming of Ruth, the Yankees made another important acquisition that had a great influence on their future success. Some critics feel that the Yankee

story was written by Ed Barrow, who became business manager on October 28, 1920, more than anyone else. Until he retired as president in 1945, Barrow saw the Yankees
win 14 of their pennants and ten World Series. Under his
direction, the club went from tenants at the Polo Grounds
to owners of the greatest baseball plant in the world: from a
struggling organization surviving on the accumulated wealth
of two sportloving millionaires to the most successful franchise in the majors; from just one of eight American League
clubs to the epitome of everything that is class and "big
league" in baseball.

The Yankees' first pennant in 1921 came a lot harder
than most of those that followed. The Cleveland Indians,
defending champs in the AL, battled the New Yorkers right
down to the wire. The clincher came on October 1 at the
Polo Grounds when the Yanks whipped the A's in a double
header. The Yankee lineup in those days was not filled with
many of the names that were to become famous a half-
dozen years later on. The batting order usually ran something like this: Elmer Miller, cf; Roger Peckinpaugh, ss;
Babe Ruth, lf; Bob Meusel, rf; Wally Pipp, lb; Aaron
Ward, 2b; Frank Baker, 3b; Wally Schang, c. The front
line of pitchers included Waite Hoyt, Carl Mays, Bob Shawkey, and Jack Quinn. But it was a well-rounded combination of youth and experience and it had the mightiest hitter
in the game batting third.

On the final day of the season against the Red Sox,
Ruth belted his 59th home run into the upper right-field deck
at the Polo Grounds—the climax of a terrific year for the
Yankee outfielder.

Because of Ruth's prodigious homerun feats, the Yankees were slightly favored over the Giants in the World Series. It was baseball's first five-cent—or Subway—Series and
New York was steamed up over the prospects of a showdown

battle between the landlords and the tenants of the Polo Grounds.

The newspapers played up the clash between the city rivals to such a degree that fans stayed away from the park, fearing they couldn't even buy standing room. All-night lines formed for the rush seats, but at game time the first afternoon, there were nearly 8,000 empty seats in the upper stands and only 30,203 people attended. They saw Carl Mays pitch airtight ball and beat the Giants, 3-0. After Hoyt shut them out by the same score the next day, there was talk of a sweep for the Yanks.

But in the third game, the silent Giant bats suddenly exploded, sending in eight runs in the seventh inning, enough to win a 13-5 decision. The next day, Mays weakened in the eighth after allowing but two hits and the Giants beat him, 4-2. Ruth thrilled the fans with a tremendous homer that struck the upper right-field tier and bounded into the bleachers. The fifth game went to the Yankees when Waite Hoyt, not far removed from the classroom at Erasmus Hall, Brooklyn, beat the Giants, 3-1.

The Yankees suffered a bad blow when the Babe was forced to the bench with a badly swollen elbow. He didn't appear in the lineup again until the eighth game when he was used as a pinch-hitter. The Giants took the seventh, 2-1, and clinched the five-out-of-nine Series by taking the final, 1-0. An error by Peckinpaugh leaked in the run, but the Yankees put on a dramatic ninth-inning rally that failed to score.

Something of a shock to their prestige, the Series nevertheless gave the Yankees a big financial boost. Each player took home $3,510; the Giants realized $5,265 apiece.

Following their first pennant success in 1921, the Yankees comported themselves like a bunch of champion prima donnas the next spring. Ruth and Bob Meusel had started out by defying Judge Landis and engaging in a long barnstorming tour in the fall soon after the Series. The law-breaking venture cost them their World Series money, a month's pay, and 38 day's suspension at the start of the '22 season. Ruth spent his term playing golf while teammates growled about his attitude and the front office fretted over the loss of his batting.

Huggins' task of running the club on the field was nearly overshadowed by the problems he encountered riding herd on his roisterous, cocky crew after business hours. The management even hired a detective to report on the late hour shenanigans of the players. But the Yankees won again, out-lasting the Browns by a slim margin at the finish. And once more, the Giants and Yankees met at the Polo Grounds.

For the first and only time in their history, the Yankees were shut out without a single victory in the World Series. They played a ten-inning, 3-3 tie in the second game, called because of darkness, but that's as close as they came to Mc-Graw's outfit. Ruth got only two hits in the set and batted a disheartening .118. Performances of other club members were nearly as dispirited as Ruth's.

Fred Lieb tells about riding downtown to the old Commodore Hotel after the final game. Colonel Huston shared the cab with him and was speechless the whole journey. But once in the hotel, Huston suddenly gave vent to the rage that had been burning within him all afternoon. He slapped the top of the bar, rattling glasses and spilling some on the floor and shouted: "Miller Huggins has managed his last Yankee team!"

But instead of Huggins managing his last Yankee team, Huston was spending his last year as part-owner of the New Yorkers. On May 21 the following spring, Ruppert bought out Huston's interest in the organization for $1,500,000. He then proceeded with plans for building a new ball park.

The Yankee Stadium was finished for opening day of

the 1923 season. An estimated $2,500,000 was poured into the structure. It was, beyond challenge, the most magnificent baseball plant in the world at the time. A lot of people referred to it as "The House that Ruth Built" and that was a very accurate description of the Stadium. Some of Ruppert's friends advised him that New Yorkers wouldn't patronize a club housed in the Bronx section, across the river from Manhattan. But on opening day, April 18, 1923, an announced crowd of 74,217 filled the new stadium, even though it was as cold and windy as it gets in New York in April. A few days later, the Yankees published a revised estimate on the crowd and the second figure was closer to 60,000. But it was still a major-league record throng and it saw Babe Ruth hit a home run—an appropriate start to a new era in Yankee history.

Although no one was remotely aware of the significance at the time, it's interesting to note that on the afternoon the Stadium opened, a Columbia University pitcher named Lou Gehrig struck out 17 Williams College batters in a game played at nearby South Field.

Two months later, Gehrig was in Yankee uniform and caused a lot of raised eyebrows among the champions by hitting the ball hard and safely in 11 of 26 pinch-hitting and substitute appearances before he was sent to Hartford. The Yankees of '23 were fast company, too, the best in baseball. Bob Meusel, Ruth and Whitey Witt played the outfield. Wally Pipp was at first, Aaron Ward at second, Everett Scott, the iron man of baseball at the time, was the shortstop, and the talented Joe Dugan played third. Wally Schang did most of the catching for a crack hurling staff that included Herb Pennock, Sam Jones, Bob Shawkey, Joe Bush and Waite Hoyt. Pennock, incidentally, had been purchased from the Red Sox, another handsome addition to the Yankee fold, from Harry Frazee in Boston. No one could stop the Yanks from racing to their third straight flag, which they took by a margin of 16 games.

The 1923 Series provided the same old Giant-Yankee match, but the locale changed and so did the outcome. The games didn't get under way until October 10. The Giants won the opener, 5-4 before 55,307 at the Polo Grounds when outfielder Casey Stengel cracked a ninth-inning homer. But the next day, Ruth hit two and the Yanks and Pennock took a 4-2 decision. The Series shifted to Yankee Stadium, site of so many future October classics, and the Giants (with Stengel) spoiled the occasion for the hosts. The ubiquitous Stengel slapped one of Sam Jones' screwballs over Ruth's head for a home run and a 1-0 victory. A record 62,430 saw the game.

On Saturday, the Yankees evened the Series with an 8-4 win. In the Series finale at the Polo Grounds, the Yankees worked out from under a Giant lead in the eighth and won, 6-4. Ruth hit his third homer in that one.

New York fans charged the Yankees' second-place finish in 1924 to overconfidence, complacency and the inevitable letdown after a run of triumphs. If nothing else, it was a glorious year for Ruth, who hit .378 and led the league in batting for the first and last time in his career. Maybe it was too much of a year for the Babe. Because the next season all he hit was trouble.

It started April 7 in Asheville, North Carolina, where the club was making an exhibition appearance on its way north from St. Petersburg. The Babe suddenly collapsed in the railroad station, falling against a radiator. He was quickly taken to the hospital. The first bulletins announced he was suffering from a severe attack of the grippe and indigestion. The whole country was alarmed by the news.

Babe recovered from the illness but his trouble had only started. His batting dipped far below his 1924 pace—and stayed there. In late August, he was batting .260 and his relations with Huggins were at a new low. So were the Yankees, who floundered around the second division. Ruth was in the habit of popping off to Huggins and disregarding his orders. He carried his rugged individualism too far in St. Louis one day. The Babe came into the Hotel Buckingham hours after Miller's one A.M. curfew and reported late to Sportsmans Park for the game that afternoon. Huggins was waiting for him. The actual exchange of words between the two has become distorted in retelling, but there were plenty of fireworks. The fact remains that Huggins, who had swallowed his pride so many times in "showdowns" with Ruth, called the big fellow's bluff, slapped a $5,000 fine on him and suspended him indefinitely.

The Babe immediately ducked out of town, but eventually showed up in New York where he went into conference with Jake Ruppert. Ruth roared into his employer's office like a lion. He came out like a lamb a half hour later. Newspapermen packed into the hall, waiting for Ruth, were unbelieving. The Babe admitted he had gotten "a bit hotheaded." He was ready to apologize to Huggins. Yes, he wanted to play again right away. Ruppert announced the fine of $5,000—baseball's all-time high—would stick. It did until after Huggins died, when Ruppert returned the sum to Ruth.

There is one other event in 1925 that needs recording. Unlike the other highlights of the season, this is remembered as a bright spot in Yankee history. On June 1, Lou Gehrig, back from training at Hartford, was used as a pinch-hitter for Peewee Wanninger. The next day, he replaced the ailing Wally Pipp at first base and started his remarkable streak of consecutive games that spanned 15 seasons. He was a big, awkward youngster in 1925, but from the day he took over at first, he began to improve himself.

From the dismal end of the 1925 season, the Yankees quickly took the shape of contenders early in 1926 and showed unmistakable signs of coming greatness. The outfield of Meusel, Combs and Ruth was unmatched in the game. The infield was short on experience but bursting with talent and enthusiasm. Mark Koenig, the shortstop, and Gehrig, at first base, didn't have a complete major-league season between them. Joe Dugan was a veteran third-baseman. At second was a rookie from San Francisco by the name of Tony Lazzeri.

The 1926 Yankees did not breeze to a pennant as their immediate successor did. They won only after a last-ditch battle with Cleveland. The World Series that year is still remembered as a personal triumph for the aged St. Louis Cardinal pitcher, Grover Cleveland Alexander. Old Pete's storied feat of striking out young Lazzeri with the bases loaded in the seventh inning of the seventh game is, of course, one of baseball's most famous episodes.

If the Yankees were shaken by that close defeat in the World Series, they showed no signs of it when 1927 rolled around. When you mention 1927 in baseball chronology, you have to say the Yankees, too. Was there ever a more awesome combination of naked batting power, pitching talent, and plain and simple class in the game? This was a matchless collection of ball-players, led by the most lethal one-two punch baseball has known—Ruth and Gehrig. The Babe set the home-run figure they are still shooting at by knocking 60 out of American League parks, and Gehrig, who followed him in the batting order, hit 47. Ruth hit .356; Gehrig .373. But that wasn't all by any means. There was the cold, emotionless Bob Meusel who batted a stout .337 and could fire bullet-like throws from his post in left field. There was tall, gray Earle Combs who led off and had 231 hits during the season. His average was .356. There was Koenig and the dangerous Lazzeri, who hit .309 and had 102 RBI's. The catchers—John Grabowski, Pat Collins and Benny Bengough—knew how to use a bat. So, of course, did third-baseman Joe Dugan. Key men on the best pitching staff in the league were Herb Pennock, Waite Hoyt, George Pipgras, ace reliefer Wilcy Moore and Urban Shocker.

The conservative Miller Huggins once said this was the only team that didn't need luck to win. I think he was right.

The '27 Series was the one in which the Yankees, who had taken the AL pennant with a record total of 110 victories, swept right through the apparently awe-struck Pittsburgh Pirates in four games. Although the Yanks did not exactly crush the Pirates with their bats, they did whip Donie Bush's men at every turn, with sharp pitching, timely hitting and the old Yankee ability to cash in on opportunities, which the National Leaguers supplied in abundance. Pittsburgh errors and a single gave the Yankees three runs and a 5-4 triumph in the first game, much to the disappointment of 41,567 fans at Forbes Field. Pipgras and Pennock took the next two in impressive fashion, and when Miljus wild-pitched with the bases loaded in the ninth inning of the fourth game, the Yankees had a 4-3 victory and their first World Series sweep.

A proper conclusion to the great Yankee success of 1927 came when 24-year-old Lou Gehrig was named the league's most valuable player.

Everyone expected the Yankees to come down to earth in 1928. They did, but they didn't reach the level of the other clubs in the league right away.

If the '28 team was less invincible than its famous predecessors, it was nevertheless a superb club. Ruth produced 54 homers and the great man in his shadow, Lou Gehrig, batted .374. Their spectacular hitting performances in the Series shattered the St. Louis Cardinals and gained a revengeful four-straight triumph over the National League champs. Ruth knocked Cardinal pitching for a record .625 average and Gehrig smacked four homers, a double and a single in compiling a .545 mark. Waite Hoyt three-hitted the

Redbirds in the opener at the Stadium and the Yankees
turned on 41-year-old Grover Cleveland Alexander, hero of
the 1926 set, to pile up a 9-3 margin in the second game.
At St. Louis, the Yankees took the last two by identical 7-3 scores. The Babe, who had thrilled a Sportsmans
Park crowd in the 1926 Series by hitting three home runs
in a single game, duplicated his stupendous feat in the
fourth game—another great Ruthian record.

The first period of Yankee domination came to an end
in 1929. The heroes of 1926-27-28, or most of them, at
least, simply ran out of gas. There were obvious weaknesses
at third and short, Bob Meusel was much slower, and the
pitching of Pennock, Pipgras and Hoyt failed to measure up
to previous years. If time was beginning to tell on some of
the Yankee players, it was taking a serious toll from their
little manager, Miller Huggins. He worried and fretted and
sweated his way through the summer months of 1929, realizing that his club would not make it again. By the middle
of September, he was at the breaking point. After a losing
game on September 20, Huggins went to the hospital with
what was diagnosed as a carbuncle on his face. Five days
later, he died.

There was a brief interlude in the Yankee success story
between the passing of Huggins and the coming of Joe Mc-
Carthy. The hopeful start and failure of Bob Shawkey as
pilot came in 1930 after Ed Barrow and Jake Ruppert had
offered the job to three other men. Donie Bush was a first
choice but the former Pittsburgh manager signed a contract
with the White Sox hours before Barrow contacted him. Eddie Collins and Art Fletcher both refused the offer.

Shawkey, a likable veteran on the Yankees who had
turned to the coaching lines after he retired as a pitcher,
took the job knowing that Babe Ruth was sharply disappointed because he had not been picked. At 36, Ruth knew

his playing days were nearly over and he wanted nothing more than to become manager of the Yankees. Ed Barrow has said that Ruth never was considered for the job. "After all, Ruth couldn't manage himself," Barrow said.

The Yankees finished a respectable third under Shawkey. That wasn't good enough for a team accustomed to league championships. Bob, who lasted only a couple of months longer than one season, found his long association with many of the players a tough handicap.

That the Yankees, in search of a new manager, and Joe McCarthy, looking for another job in the majors, should get together was inevitable. Joe had built a strong reputation as an efficient, sound pilot with the Chicago Cubs, whom he had led to a pennant in 1929. Ed Barrow, who had kept a close eye on McCarthy's progress, was sure he was the right man for the Yankees.

The Yankees' new manager was not long in coming up with a winner. With the considerable help of two recent additions to the pitching staff, Red Ruffing, a big right-hander obtained from the Red Sox in May, 1930, and an angular young lefty named Vernon Gomez, the Yankees won another flag in 1932. McCarthy's satisfaction in his early success in the American League was redoubled in the Series when the Yanks knocked over the Chicago Cubs, his old employers, in four straight.

The Series would be recorded as just another rout of a National League foe by the Yankees except for a famous Ruthian episode in the third game at Chicago. With the score tied at 4-4 in the fifth inning, a Wrigley Field crowd of 49,986 was whooping it up as Babe Ruth, who had homered in the first, came to bat. What happened next belongs to baseball legend.

I was there and I saw the Babe point toward center field. Only he knew what, if anything, the gesture meant. But the crowd interpreted it as meaning one thing—he was going to knock the next one out of the lot. He did, too. As Ruth trotted across the plate with that hippopotomic grace of his, Gabby Hartnett, the Chicago catcher, said to him: "You incredible——!"

That night, I saw Ruth in his hotel room. He was beaming from ear to ear. "Got the ball, too," he said. "The damned thing's lop-sided."

The Series ended in anti-climax the next afternoon as the Yankees trounced the Cubs, 13-6.

After the 1932 success over the Chicago Cubs and their fifth world championship, the Yankees slipped into one of those short-lived interludes during which they regrouped their forces before swaggering to the front again. Some of the club's key players were at the end of their careers and it was necessary to plug some big gaps. When Herb Pennock, a veteran of 39, was unconditionally released in 1934, the Yankees said goodbye to one of their all-time pitching stars. "He's the only pitcher I never gave a signal to," Bill Dickey said later.

But even more important than Pennock's departure was the close of Babe Ruth's career in Yankee uniform. The Big Fellow had tailed off rapidly after 1932, slipping down to a .301 batting average and a homer output of 34 the following season. In 1934, he dropped below .300 for the first time since the disastrous year of 1925. It was clear to everyone that the Babe, at 39, was through as a player.

A happy solution to the problem of disposing of Ruth, from a Yankee standpoint anyway, came in the mid-winter of 1935 when Judge Emil Fuchs of the Boston Braves made a bid to obtain Ruth in an effort to put a little gate sock into his rather drab team. He offered Ruth a job as player and vice-president. The Yankees immediately gave Babe his unconditional release, receiving no money for a ballplayer who had been a priceless commodity for years.

The loss of Ruth came as the Yankees were set to launch a drive that would sweep them into power for another lengthy period. The 1935 team lacked the solid hitting and pitching strength of a championship club, yet it had enough to chase Detroit through the summer and finish second.

While the Yankees were experiencing what could be termed an off season, a young outfilder, who was to play an historic role in future years at the Stadium, was burning up the Pacific Coast League. He was Joe DiMaggio, a 21-year-old Italian ballplayer, hitting at a .398 clip in 1935 and making some of baseball's top scouts bitterly unhappy.

Joe was a product of the San Francisco sand lots, the son of a Sicilian fisherman. His interest in baseball had been kindled by an older brother, Vince, who was playing for San Francisco at the time. A trial with the Seals in 1932 resulted in a three-game turn at shortstop at the end of the season. The next year, he was a regular outfielder, having edged his brother out of a job, and he hit safely in 61 straight games. Scouts from most major-league teams were hot on Joe's trail until a freak, off-the-field accident to his knee cooled them off. Yankee scouts Bill Essick and Joe Devine took time to check into the rumors that young DiMaggio suffered from "chronic knee trouble." They found nothing to scare them off, and the Yanks got DiMag for $25,000 and five players, instead of the $75,000 or more that the Seals had originally anticipated.

DiMag fitted brilliantly into the Stadium scene in 1936. The Yankees grabbed the lead on May 10 and pumped up such an advantage that they clinched the pennant on September 9, the earliest date it had ever been won. Joe justified the faith Essick and Devine had shown in him by batting .323 in his freshman year.

DiMaggio was the junior member of a cast of standout players in 1936. The apparently indestructible Lou Gehrig was at first, maintaining his streak of playing in every game and swinging the most feared bat in the majors. The tried and true second-base combination of Tony Lazzeri and Frank Crosetti gave the Yankees real class in that vital area. Red Rolfe was developing into the league's best third-base-man. The outfield started with Selkirk, DiMaggio and Ben Chapman, but early in the campaign, McCarthy traded the temperamental Chapman for Jake Powell of the Washington Senators.

Not since the Yankees of 1927 had baseball seen such brute batting power as was displayed by the 1936 Bronx Bombers. Five members of McCarthy's wrecking crew batted in 100 or more runs: Gehrig (152), DiMaggio (125), Lazzeri (109), Dickey (107) and Selkirk (107). The team total of 2,703 total bases is still a record and their mark of 182 home runs has not been touched by an American League team.

For the first time since 1923, baseball had a "Subway Series." The Giants had taken the National League flag after a gruelling, season-long battle. They had made it chiefly on the pitching mastery of Carl Hubbell, who won a grand total of 26 games and lost but six.

What little solace the Giants got out of their fourth world championship match with their rivals from across the Harlem River came from Hubbell's trusty left arm. In a steady drizzle at the Polo Grounds on September 30, he opened the Series with a well-fashioned 6-1 triumph over the Bombers. The second game was postponed a day because of wet weather, delaying the record carnage perpetrated by the Yankees against five Giant hurlers. The score of that one was 18-4. Tony Lazzeri hit a grand slam in a seven-run third inning. President Roosevelt was one of the 43,543 who watched the unprecedented scoring spree. The next day, the Yankees were held to four hits by Fred Fitzsimmons but won, 2-1. It was all over for the Giants, although they did win the fifth game. The Giants came to the same conclusion that the seven other American League clubs had during the season—there was no successful way of checking the Yankee power for any length of time. This was to prove true for a four-year period.

In 1937, for instance, the Yankees came through with a season almost identical with the preceding one. They won 102 games again, taking the flag in early September. Everywhere they went, they were expected to win—and they usually did. Gomez and Ruffing were 20-game winners, Gehrig and DiMaggio batted .351 and .346, respectively, and the veterans and newcomers came through in Yankee style. Personnel changes were few, although the club did come up with a promising young free agent in Tommy Henrich, who was used as a replacement for Selkirk and hit .320 in 67 games.

Unanimous choice to win the Series, they did just that with ease. The Giants again supplied the opposition and the Yankees slugged through them in five games, losing only a fourth-game, 7-3 decision to Carl Hubbell. Lefty Gomez won two of the Yankee victories and veteran Tony Lazzeri, playing his last year with the team, batted .400.

Ed Barrow and manager Joe McCarthy were in the habit of standing pat with a championship club, unless there were some obvious repairs to be made. After the '37 Series, the Yankees released Tony Lazzeri so he could accept an attractive offer from the Chicago Cubs. His departure left only one member of the famous 1927 team on the active roster— Lou Gehrig.

The replacement for Lazzeri, Joe Gordon, was no ordinary ballplayer. A dangerous long-ball hitter, Gordon was spectacular in his fielding. With Frank Crosetti, he promised to give the Yankees the best double-play combination in the game. Other changes in 1938 saw Henrich move to a regular outfield post and team with DiMaggio and Selkirk. The pitching strength came from reliable Red Ruffing (21-7), Lefty Gomez (18-12), Monte Pearson (16-7) and Spud Chandler (14-5). Johnny Murphy, a right-hander, was a good relief man. On August 27 at the Stadium, Pearson shut out Cleveland without a hit or run, facing only 27 batters. He walked two and fanned seven.

Oddly enough, the Yankees got off to an unpromising start in the spring that year. Joe DiMaggio was a stubborn holdout during the training season. He sat out the entire exhibition schedule in San Francisco, refusing to weaken in his demand for a contract of about $40,000. His delayed start obviously hurt the team's performance for a few weeks.

By mid-July, however, the Yankees were out in front. The pennant—the club's tenth in the last 18 years—was celebrated on the night of September 18.

The Yankees polished off the National League champs, the Cubs, with familiar ease, winning in the shortest time possible. The only exciting moment in the four games occurred in the second contest at Chicago when a sore-armed Dizzy Dean stopped the Yankee bats for seven innings before weakening. Dean and the Cubs lost, 6-3. Huge crowds turned out at Wrigley Field for the first two games, but the below-capacity gatherings at Yankee Stadium indicated that the New York baseball public was only mildly interested in seeing the Yanks outclass another Series foe.

The Yankees' line of success remained unbroken in 1939, yet two widely separated happenings cast a pall of tragedy over the Stadium.

First, on January 13, Colonel Jacob Ruppert died at his home at 1120 Fifth Avenue, New York. There was concern about the future of the Yankees. It was soon alleviated by the appointment of Ed Barrow as president and the announcement that Ruppert's stock had been divided among his nieces and a friend.

Another blow fell on May 2 when the Yankees were in

Detroit for a series with the Tigers. Lou Gehrig dropped out of the lineup for the first time since June 1, 1929, his amazing streak of consecutive games ended at 2,130.

All of us who watched the Yankees during spring training at St. Petersburg that year were puzzled and concerned about Lou. It was obvious that he was fading rapidly and we knew that, sooner or later, he would have to take a rest. But none of us was prepared for the news that came from the Mayo Clinic in Rochester, Minnesota, where Lou went for an examination in June. It was announced that he was suffering from amyotrophic lateral sclerosis—a form of chronic poliomyelitis—and that it was necessary for him to give up his baseball career.

A few weeks later, Yankee fans and many of us who were friends and admirers of Gehrig gathered at Yankee Stadium to pay tribute to him who had served his club—and baseball—so well. Many of us knew we were saying goodbye to Lou for the last time.

The Yankees, without Gehrig, raced to another pennant in relentless, monotonous fashion that summer of 1939, finishing 17 games ahead of the Boston Red Sox. They were in first place 156 days of the season and ended up with a staggering total of 106 victories against 45 defeats. Lou was gone but Joe DiMaggio, who batted .381, newcomer Charley Keller with a first-year mark of .334, and veterans Selkirk and Dickey supplied more than enough offensive punch. Reliable Red Ruffing won 21 games and Atley Donald, Marius Russo and Steve Sundra contributed a big share.

It mattered little to the Yankees that Cincinnati had won its first pennant in 20 years in the National League and that the city on the banks of the Ohio was in a state of frenzy over its championship team. The Series opened under the shadow of a European war and the newspapers were full of the ominous details of Hitler's triumphant march into Warsaw as the two clubs squared away at Yankee Stadium.

The Yankees revealed all aspects of their greatness in this short Series. They captured the tight ones with the help of superb pitching, blasted the opposition with a typical Yankee homerun barrage, displayed an impregnable defense anchored by Gordon and Crosetti, and exploited Cincinnati weaknesses whenever possible. Cincinnati didn't win a game.

It was just as well for baseball that the Yankees slipped down to third place in 1940. The club was the same, except for a few new faces on the bench and some signs of old age in such stalwarts as Ruffing, Selkirk, Dickey and Gomez. Joe McCarthy had first-base trouble. He said he was no longer satisfied with Babe Dahlgren. In '41, he experimented with Joe Gordon at first and Jerry Priddy at second. It didn't last long. Johnny Sturm was given the job, and although none of the pitchers won over 15 games, the Yankees took another pennant—their 12th—by 17 games.

High note of the season was the record-smashing streak of Joe DiMaggio, who hit in 56 successive games from May 15 through July 16. Joe's string, which bettered Willie Keeler's old mark of 44, was finally broken on the night of July 17 before 67,468 at Cleveland. Al Smith and Jim Bagby were the Indians' pitchers. As DiMag's bat grew hotter in early July, so did the Yanks. They reeled off 14 wins in a row at one point to build up a big advantage in the league standings.

The year was not without its sorrow for Yankee fans. On June 2, Lou Gehrig died at his home in New York. Lou had been sinking rapidly since 1940, yet his death was a blow to the Yankees, past and present, and sent the entire baseball world into mourning.

The result of the 1941 World Series was just what it had been on eight of the 11 previous times the Yankees had played in the October classic. The Yanks beat their NL rivals in five games. But this was no ordinary Series. The event was super-charged with color and excitement simply because

the Brooklyn Dodgers were representing the National League
for the first time in 21 years. The whole nation was intensely worked up over the Dodgers' success. In fact, the
public, including most New Yorkers, forgot all about the
Yankees during the last weeks of September. All that mattered was that Brooklyn had edged St. Louis in a ding-dong
race and was champ at last.

The Yankees and Dodgers split the first two games at
Yankee Stadium, Ruffing winning his sixth Series game in
the first and Whit Wyatt taking the second for the Dodgers.
The third went to New York when the venerable Fred Fitzsimmons was literally knocked out of the box by a Marius
Russo line drive that bounced off his leg. Hugh Casey lost
the game in relief of Fitz.

The ninth inning of the fourth game had to be seen to
be believed. Remember? Two Yankees were out in the top
of that inning and the Dodgers were leading, 4-3. When
Tommy Henrich cut at a Casey pitch and missed it for a
third strike, the Dodger fans were up whooping and yelling.
Police dashed out on the field to protect the diamond from
the happy mob. The Brooks had tied the Series! But had
they? The third strike had bounced off catcher Mickey Owen's
mitt and was rolling toward the stands. Henrich streaked
for first. There was no chance to get him. The Yankees were
still alive.

The rest was a nightmare for Brooklyn—and a superb
example of the Yanks' traditional talent for making the
most of enemy mistakes. DiMaggio, the next up, lined out
a single. Charley Keller had two strikes on him when he
smashed a double off the right-field screen. Henrich scored
the tying run and the swift DiMaggio slid across the plate
with the fifth. Two more Yanks scored before the hapless
Casey could retire the side. It killed the Brooks. The next

afternoon, Tiny Bonham restricted them to four hits and the Yanks won, 3-1.

The world was in chaos in 1942 but things were normal in the American League. The Yankees won again. It was not a great Yankee team, but even with obvious imperfections it was stronger than the rest of the field. The Yankees met a brash, free-wheeling team in the St. Louis Cardinals, and for the first time since 1926, were whipped by a National League entry. The Cards did it with amazing ease in five games.

Like most major-league clubs, the Yanks were nearly unrecognizable in 1943. Spring training was held in Asbury Park, instead of St. Petersburg, and McCarthy spent a lot of time with unfamiliar players like Nick Etten at first base, rookie Billy Johnson at third, Bud Metheny and Tuck Stainback, outfielders, and infielder George Stirnweiss.

The team that successfully defended the Yankees' 1942 flag was a hodge-podge of old Yankee pros, farmhands and replacements from other clubs. No one pretended it was a very good Yankee team. The only regular to hit over .300 was Bill Dickey, who appeared in 85 games. But veteran Spud Chandler, who had an earned-run average of 1.64, and Tiny Bonham gave McCarthy strong pitching.

In the Series, the Yankees got back at the slightly deflated Cardinals, beating them decisively in five games.

The Yankees' string of pennant victories came to a temporary end in 1944. Service calls had left but a skeleton of the once invincible Bombers. Chandler, Gordon, Johnson, Keller and Murphy all went into the armed forces and the usually dependable pipelines from Newark and Kansas City were unable to furnish adequate replacements.

Although the club stopped making big news on the field, it was involved in a headline story in late January 1945.

That was the announcement that the heirs of the late Jake Ruppert—Mrs. Joseph Holleran, Mrs. J. Basil Maguire and Miss Helen Weyant—had sold their interests in the Yankees for the sum of $2,800,000. In a separate negotiation, president Ed Barrow, who had been with the club for 25 years and had seen it win 15 pennants and ten world championships, disposed of his ten per cent share for an estimated $300,000. The new owners were Larry MacPhail, recently retired from the Army as a Lt. Colonel and a man who had made quite a mark running teams at Cincinnati and Brooklyn in the National League; Dan Topping, an Army captain and owner of the Brooklyn pro football franchise; and Del Webb, a prosperous contractor from Phoenix, Arizona.

Under the new directorship, Joe McCarthy brought the Yanks home fourth in 1945, the lowest finish for the team in his 15 years as manager.

Meanwhile, MacPhail was busy streamlining the Yankee organization and modernizing Yankee Stadium in a manner that brought a few growls of disapproval from old New York fans and writers. Light towers went up and the Yanks played their first after-dark game at home on May 28, 1946. Capitalizing on the easy flow of money at the time, MacPhail built a plush "Stadium Club" behind the grandstand for subscribers to the new season boxseat plan ($600 for four). But the new appeal wasn't aimed exclusively at the carriage trade. For the plain fan, there were fashion shows, foot races, clown acts and other sideline attractions. Oldtimers expressed their dismay with MacPhail's operations but crowds poured into the park in such numbers that new attendance records were made.

Yankee turnstiles played a merry tune but there were occasional bursts of disharmony within the organization. One of the dissatisfied employees was manager McCarthy. The ill feeling between him and MacPhail was an open secret. No one was particularly surprised when, on May 24, 1946, Joe announced his resignation. The most successful manager in baseball history, winner of eight pennants in 15 years, left with his team five games behind the Boston Red Sox.

Bill Dickey was moved up from his catching job to replace McCarthy. But Dickey resigned as manager on September 12, when MacPhail refused to assure him that he would be retained in 1947. Coach Johnny Neun finished the season as field boss. Three managers in one season set a Yankee record. The three previous pilots—Huggins, Shawkey and McCarthy—covered a 29-year period.

Bucky Harris was MacPhail's choice to lead the Yankees in 1947. And after three years without a championship, the club drove to its first flag under the new regime. A streak of 19 consecutive wins in July gave the Bombers the momentum they needed to finish 12 games in front of Detroit.

The '47 Series with the Dodgers went seven games, was the richest ever, and was one of the most exciting of all October classics. It was highlighted by the never-to-be forgotten fourth game at Ebbets Field when, with right-hander Bill Bevens pitching no-hit ball with two out in the ninth, Cookie Lavagetto lined a double off the right-field wall, scoring the two runs which gave the Brooks a 3-2 triumph. Then, too, there was Al Gionfriddo's amazing catch in front of the 415-foot sign in left-center at Yankee Stadium that robbed DiMag of a homer and shut off a Yankee rally. The big seventh game went to the Yankees when Joe Page, making his fourth relief appearance in the Series, stopped the Dodgers for five innings.

It seemed as if there had never been a victory celebration like the one that followed the Yankees' 1947 success. In the midst of all the yelling and whooping in the jampacked Yankee Clubhouse, a teary-eyed Larry MacPhail announced that he was quitting. The news took the edge off the happy celebration, of course, and a lot of people blamed MacPhail for muscling his way into the headlines that deservedly belonged to the team. Asked why he was pulling out at the time, MacPhail blurted, "Because I want to . . ."

That night, while champagne corks popped in the festivities at the Hotel Biltmore, MacPhail took a wild punch at John MacDonald, former Dodger road secretary. Before the evening was over, he had nearly tangled with the new Yankee president, Dan Topping. In all the furor and excitement, it was somehow determined that George Weiss, the director of the farm system, would be the new general manager.

MacPhail had ended his 33 months as president of the Yankees with some typical MacPhailian fireworks. Whether or not they were glad to see him go, Yankee fans had to admit he had brought a period of prosperity never before realized by the richest of all baseball teams. During the 1946 season, for example, the Yanks became the first major-league team to attract more than two million customers when 2,265,512 fans paid their way into the Stadium.

1948 was not a particularly happy year for the Yankees. They finished behind Cleveland and Boston in the pennant race and in midsummer they lost the greatest ballplayer they ever had when Babe Ruth died. From the wet June afternoon when New York paid its respects to the Babe with a "day" at the Stadium until August 16, the day he died, we were all grimly aware that Ruth was fighting a losing battle with the sickness that had plagued him for some time.

The Yankees have won so many championships by sheer weight of power, talent and class that the pennant victory in 1949 rates as a special achievement in the club's bright history. It, more than anything else, proves that the Yankees boast an indomitable spirit, too.

You will remember that the '49 team was not ranked very high. It didn't figure to stand much of a chance when the great DiMaggio missed the first 65 games of the season with an ailing heel. A new manager, Casey Stengel, was directing play from the bench, Bucky Harris having been fired at the end of 1948. Casey, of course, had a reputation for being a droll wit and for his comical stunts as the skipper of second-division teams. A lot of people said he just wasn't the Yankee type. Tommy Henrich was also on the injured list that grew to an enormous length during the season.

Apparently, enough of the great Yankee character had rubbed off on guys like Yogi Berra, the fast-improving catcher; Jerry Coleman, a rookie second-baseman; and Hank Bauer and Gene Woodling. For the Yanks stuck right up there despite their troubles in fielding a healthy nine. As the season came to a close, the Yankees were a game out of first place and had two to play with the leading Red Sox at the Stadium. They took both of them, tying the race with a 5-4 comeback triumph on Saturday and clinching the pennant the last day with a 5-3 decision. No Yankee team ever came through so heroically in the last ditch as did this one. It was one of the most popular of all Yankee triumphs and it was appropriately crowned with a world championship when Stengel's spirited gang flattened the Dodgers again in a five-game Series, with the pinch-hitting of Johnny Mize, obtained from the Giants, playing a major role.

Stengel went on to carve out a special place for himself in the gallery of great Yankee managers when he upset the experts' dope in both 1950 and 1951 to make it three pennants in a row—and each pennant decorated by a handsome world championship. In 1950, the Yankees took the Whiz Kids of Philadelphia in four straight, and in 1951, with the incomparable Joe DiMaggio making his last appearance in Yankee flannels, they bested the game Giants, four games to two, in another renewal of the ancient Subway Series. Strong pitching from Vic Raschi, Ed Lopat and Allie Reynolds, brilliant shortstopping by little Phil Rizzuto, potent slugging and astonishingly capable catching by squat Yogi Berra, highlighted those Yankee triumphs. But perhaps the biggest story of all was the way the Yanks kept replacing faded veterans with red-hot rookies.

Tommy Henrich retired as an active player at the end of the 1950 campaign. Joe DiMaggio, meeting his bosses in front of a tremendous battery of reporters and cameramen, announced his retirement after the 1951 season. But the loss of these heroes did not suddenly check the Yankees' domination of baseball. Youngsters Billy Martin, Gil Mc-Dougald and Mickey Mantle helped Stengel to his fourth straight pennant in '52. Then, in one of the most exciting World Series ever played, the Yankees turned back the Dodgers, four games to three. When the two rivals met again the next fall, the baseball world eagerly anticipated another nerve-wracking Series. But the Yankees made their record fifth consecutive world championship look easy. Their combative little second-baseman, Billy Martin, batted .500, and the Dodgers succumbed rather meekly after six games. No one in baseball history, not even Joe McCarthy, could match the record of ex-comic Casey Stengel—five world championships in his first five seasons as Yankee manager.

The Yankees finished second in 1954 but most people considered it a temporary detour in their victory run. For the Yankees are still the Yankees and who is there in the baseball world to stop them from going on to more victories, more pennants and more world championships?

THE CHICAGO WHITE SOX

BY JOHN CARMICHAEL

Almost 18 years ago, the City Council of Chicago was concerning itself with a problem which had to do with hon-
oring the late Charles A. Comiskey, founder of the baseball
dynasty which is now in its third generation. Somebody had
suggested that 35th Street, site of the present home of the
White Sox, be changed to Comiskey Road.

A brash young sportswriter, more interested in getting
off a *bon mot* than with the propriety and dignity of the gesture, suggested in print: "If, perchance, the council cannot
agree on Comiskey Road . . . may we suggest Seventh
Place?"

Whether that suggestion played any part in shelving
the proposal is of no matter today, but the thought never has
officially crystallized since. As the years rolled on and the
once proud Sox continued to haunt the American League
second division, any revival of the idea would not have
caught public fancy.

On the afternoon of August 31, 1920, the Sox were
in first place in the American League. They finished second.
They've never been in first place that late in the season
since, although they spent 44 exciting days there in 1951.
And they've never finished as high as second in the last 30
years.

37

Perhaps any recapitulation of the White Sox half-century presence in the American League should be divided, after the manner of all Gaul, into three parts. There were the formative years from 1900 through 1906, when the Sox won three pennants, one of them official. Then came the span of 13 years which culminated in the famous "Black Sox" scandal of 1919 (not unearthed until 1920) when one of the greatest teams of all time had to be broken up in comparative infancy.

The doldrums set in after that and they weren't shaken until recently, when the aggressive combination of Frank Lane and Paul Richards began to hit its stride.

President William McKinley was busy with the Spanish-American War hangover and "Swamp Root," a mysterious healing potion, was carrying three-column ads in Chicago papers for kidney relief when the 20th century also dawned upon a new baseball park at the corner of 39th Avenue and Wentworth, Chicago. This "modern" 1900 baseball site featured a roofed grandstand that covered 5,000 seats and bleachers in right and left fields to accommodate 2,500 additional customers.

That was the tumbledown home of the humble-born White Stockings, owned by the first Comiskey. Their birth was only semi-legitimate because, at the time, they weren't permitted to have "Chicago" as part of the name. But history is a wonderful equalizer of great and small origins and even the party of established National League officials among the 5,200 who saw the first game on April 21, 1900, foresaw the makings of what has been long since called the "old Roman Empire."

The White Stockings lost to Milwaukee, 5-4, in ten innings. In the lineup were outfielder Ed Lally, shortstop Frank Shugart, pitcher John Katoll and catcher Joe Sugden. A reporter (presumably mustached) chronicled one phase of this inaugural battle as follows: "Centerfielder Hoy, in the ninth, made a great catch. Milwaukee batter Burke sent a short fly to center. Hoy, running to meet it, slipped and fell down, got up, fell down again, rose to his feet and caught the ball, falling down again in the mud as he snapped it to second."

The fans didn't know it at the time but Katoll, Sugden, et al, were destined to help Chicago win its first flag by four games over Milwaukee in a 135-game stretch. It didn't count, of course, and the Stockings had to do it all over again in 1901—for the records. The league, which had numbered Milwaukee, Indianapolis, Detroit, Kansas City, Cleveland, Buffalo and Minneapolis in 1900, had been rearranged with Philadelphia, Boston, Washington and Baltimore the second time around.

So, for purposes of an official opening, that game of April 24, 1901, will carry more weight. Robert Emmett Burke represented Mayor Carter Harrison, but he wouldn't throw out the first ball. He explained that maybe he wouldn't be able to get out of the way of the thing if it was hit in his direction, so he just sat smoking a cigar and clapping his pudgy hands at anything he thought exciting. A field crowd of 9,000 watched the White Stockings beat Cleveland, 8-2, behind the six-hit pitching of one Roy Patterson. Tommy Connolly, later chief of American League umpires, was behind the mound, handling the whole affair.

For the next five months, behind the expert pitching of manager Clark Griffith and Jimmy Callahan and the sterling play of outfielder Sam Mertes, catcher Billy Sullivan and first-baseman Frank Isbell, the Stockings won a ding-dong flag fight with Boston. But there was no World Series in those days, so glory, like virtue, had to be its own reward.

By that time, however, Comiskey and his sidekick, Ban Johnson, were making the tormented National League very unhappy. Johnson was then sports editor of the Cincinnati *Commercial-Tribune* and had helped form the Western League in 1893. It was Johnson (later to become president of the American League) who aided Comiskey in establishing a beachhead in Chicago, although James A. Hart, then president of the Cubs, pushed through an amendment forbidding the use of "Chicago." It wasn't until 1903 that he gave in.

Young Comiskey (he was only 41 when he became boss of the Sox) had been owner-captain-manager-first-baseman of St. Paul in 1895, a project he abandoned to help form the second major league. Before the St. Paul venture, he had managed and played for the St. Louis Browns and with the Cincinnati team, as well as one in the old Brotherhood League in Chicago.

He had broken into the game with Dubuque in 1880 and, as a sideline, hawked candy and newspapers aboard the Dubuque-Chicago run of the Illinois Central Railroad for T. P. Sullivan, who owned the concessions.

Under the successive handling of Griffith, Callahan and Fielder Jones, the Sox, after 1901, finished fourth, seventh, third and second, in that order, and came to the threshold of 1906 already tagged as the "Hitless Wonders." Despite first-division finishes, the team batting average dropped from .275 in 1901 to .237 in 1905.

It was the White Sox pitching staff, constructed over those years when the two leagues were ironing out their difficulties, eliminating player raids and getting together on the World Series (first played by Boston and Pittsburgh in 1903), that brought the third flag in 1906. Thirteen American League hitters batted .300 or over that season and not one was from Chicago. The team batting average dipped to .228, lowest by far in the circuit.

Floundering in the second division in late July, the club won 19 in a row from August 2, a streak in which Sox pitchers turned in eight shutouts. The team won 93 games against 58 defeats to take the title by three games. Twenty-nine of those triumphs were by a single run. Isbell, Jones,

Hahn, Jiggs Donahue and George Davis stole 147 bases. The entire team swiped 209.

What a pitching staff the White Sox had! Ed Walsh, whose spitball was beginning to be deadly effective, had been a Pennsylvania coal miner with the physique of an Apollo and the grace of a wheelbarrow. He first reported to the Sox in 1904 and was anything but impressive as he doggedly worked on the freak delivery which was to paralyze so many outstanding hitters. By 1906, he was ready. He had perfected the pitch which Elmer Strickland, a refugee from Brooklyn, had to give up because of a lame arm. Walsh won 17 games in '06 and went on to pitch in 427 games for the Sox, setting records which still stand. (In 1908, for instance, he won 40 games and never complained about a sore arm until the autumn of 1913.)

Along with those 17 Walsh victories, Doc White won 18, Frank Owen contributed 22, Nick Altrock got 20 and Patterson 10. This quintet took up the slack in the Sox attack and led the club to victory over the Cubs, four games out of six, in the World Series. The Cubs had won 116 games in their own league and bagged the championship by 20 games.

Thus, the first really outstanding White Sox team passed into enchanted history. The "Hitless Wonders" never made the grade again. Indeed, when the next pennant floated above Chicago's South Side, it was gained by the slugging of the famous 1917 and 1919 teams. By then, the fans were flocking to the current park of the Comiskeymen, erected in 1910 at a cost of $500,000 and self-styled the "baseball palace of the world."

Four bands played at the Comiskey Park inaugural on July 1, 1910. There were 30,000 people in the stands and a new mayor, Fred Busse, gave a speech of welcome. The Sox wore new-style uniforms, all white with a blue trim. But

when they lost, 2-0, to the Browns, it was as if a bad-luck
omen finally had called a halt to a long period of success.
After six years in the first flight, the Sox fell that season to
sixth.

Sox fortunes stayed low for quite a few years after that,
but the Comiskey knack of doing the unexpected did not. No
matter where the Sox finished in the next ten years, they
traveled first class. The Old Roman was the first owner to
use special trains for cross-country jaunts. These were out-
fitted luxuriously, loaded with food and drink for "Commy"
and his entourage. The trains ran on hit-and-miss schedules,
permitting unlimited stopovers.

Then came the trip around the world. It was engineered
over a couple of drinks in Stillson's famous Chicago saloon
when Comiskey suddenly turned to John McGraw, the fiery
major-domo of the Giants, and said, "Mac, let's go around the
world." McGraw nodded agreement and they shook hands. In
November of 1913, the tour began, and after 142 days on
foreign lands and seas, the Sox had won 24 games and lost
20 to the National Leaguers.

They played in Japan, China, Italy, Manila, India,
Egypt, Australia, France, England . . . and Dennison, Texas.
In Yokohama, Osaka, Shanghai and Hong Kong they drew
thousands of fans. In Ceylon, the natives came in droves to
marvel at a game they didn't understand. At Cairo, the
Bedouin removed himself to a safe distance, squatted on
his haunches and silently commended himself to Allah for
looking at this strange pastime.

From fifth place in 1913, the Sox fell to sixth in 1914.
There had been short managerial terms for Sullivan and
Hugh Duffy and Callahan, but by 1915 Comiskey deemed it
time for still another change. He plucked Clarence Rowland
(now president of the Pacific Coast League) from Peoria
and put him in charge of what was to be the draft of another Sox milestone.

Up to now, the Sox hadn't needed the lift of proven players. The teams which had carried the colors to early success had been fashioned from minor-league talent. But now Comiskey felt that he had to step into the major-league marts. For an estimated $150,000, he got second-baseman Eddie Collins from the Athletics, Joe Jackson from Cleveland and Oscar (Happy) Felsch from Milwaukee. Finally, he had an excellent supporting cast for such dependables as pitcher Eddie Cicotte, catcher Ray Schalk and infielder Buck Weaver, who had come to the club two years before.

The 1915 Sox finished third. Then outfielder Nemo Leibold and first-sacker Chick Gandil were obtained from Cleveland. A great shortstop prospect named Swede Risberg was picked up, along with infielder Fred McMullin and pitchers Dave Danforth and Claude (Lefty) Williams. At the close of the 1916 campaign, the Sox were second, only two games behind the panting Boston Red Sox.

If the 1917 White Sox team wasn't the most spectacular of them all, it will do in the memories of many old-time Chicago fans until another one comes along. It was virtually the same club that eventually covered itself with shame against the Cincinnati Reds. But in '17 it was brilliant, gallant, unbeatable. It reeled off 100 victories and won the flag by nine games. Cicotte's pitching was phenomenal, his celebrated "shine ball" accounting for 28 wins. Before the race was over, the pitch had become the subject of hundreds of protests and even a chemical analysis.

The Giants of that year captured the National League championship by ten games, but they were no match for the Sox, who won four out of six games and outplayed McGraw's warriors in every department. It was in the final game of this Series that Collins out-ran Heinie Zimmerman to the plate as the Giant third-baseman was forced into committing a famous "skull" because the Giant catcher failed to cover home.

The first World War cut short the 1918 season and the Cubs and Red Sox met in an early Series. But when 1919 rolled around, the Sox forces were regrouped and they won the pennant by three and a half games. Fans were wondering if they weren't better than the 1917 club and eagerly awaited the World Series outcome.

This sordid chapter, the only such ever written into the archives of the national pastime, has been re-told and re-written until it is threadbare in all its ramifications. The Sox startled the world by losing the Series, five games to three. Disbelief grew to doubt which, in turn, wavered toward suspicion. Finally, the finger of guilt wrote the epitaphs of eight White Sox stars—Gandil, Risberg, Jackson, Weaver, McMullin, Felsch, Cicotte and Williams.

Judge Kenesaw Mountain Landis had come upon the scene as baseball's first commissioner, and even with all his sleuthing, backed by Comiskey's time and money, it wasn't until the late days of 1920 that the scandal was completely uncovered.

The Chicago courts eventually acquitted the involved players and many of them still deny their culpability, if they talk at all about that past. Down in Greenville, South Carolina, graying, corpulent Joe Jackson steadfastly denied any wrongdoing as long as he lived. But his role in the scandal has been italicized in the legendary anecdote of the little boy standing outside the Criminal Court Building in Chicago, who said: "Say it isn't so, Joe. . . . Say it isn't so . . ."

Shoeless Joe couldn't say then that it wasn't so. The evidence, which nobody wanted to believe in its fragmentary state, had piled up in such irrefutable volume over almost a full year that there could never be any question of what had happened. Although the actual conspiracy indictments brought against the offending players never stood up in court, that was largely because the fans who comprised the various

juries didn't care about jailing the men. It was enough for
everybody that they had been banned from organized ball
for life. They couldn't possibly be visited with greater pun-
ishment.

Although the whole crooked story didn't burst upon the
public until the late days of the 1920 season, the seeds of
distrust in his club were sown for owner Comiskey at the
end of the first game of the 1919 Series when the Reds
won, 9-1. The following morning, Comiskey voiced vague disbelief in the outcome to president John Heydler of the National League.

Heydler said later: "Commy was all broken up over
that first game. He felt that something was wrong. To me, it
didn't seem as if there could be anything wrong with that
game and I told Commy that the Sox likely had underestimated the strength of the Reds and had been taken by surprise."

The Reds won the second game, 4-2, although south-
paw Williams held Cincinnati to four hits while the Sox
made ten. But while Williams was virtually unhittable, he
walked six men, including three in the fourth inning when
the winners got three of their runs and half of their hits, including a two-run triple. This was the same Williams who
walked only 58 men in 297 innings during the regular season.

It is generally believed that the gamblers who engineered
the scandal won about $500,000 on those first two games and
that they thought so little of Dickie Kerr's chances to stop
the Reds in the third game that they went ahead and pyra-
mided their winnings.

But Kerr won, 3-0, and out of the triumph came a story
involving a gambler who had not been taken in on the original fix. He lost a bundle on the first two games and came
charging out to Chicago for the third game. He learned that
Kerr hadn't been taken in on the plot, figured the little guy

would be leveling, and covered a lot of the fixed dough. He won himself $50,000 and scuttled back to Broadway with a smirk on his face.

The Reds won the next two games. But back came Kerr with his second triumph and then, wonder of wonders, Cicotte won the seventh game and it was 4-3 in games. It was a best-of-nine Series then. Manager Gleason, wishfully thinking that maybe Cicotte had come back into the fold and hoping that Williams would do likewise, started Lefty in the eighth game. But he was batted out early and it was all over. All over, that is, except for the 11-month investigation which even then was getting under way.

The case broke in September of 1920 over, of all things, an inconsequential game between the Cubs and Phils of the rival league. The Cubs, behind Grover Cleveland Alexander, were defeated, and a few days later, a story broke in Detroit alleging an attempt to fix the game by bribing Claude Hendrix, Cub hurler, who was scheduled to pitch that afternoon.

Immediately, talk of the White Sox-Cincinnati World Series was revived and Fred Loomis, a prominent businessman, appealed for a probe that would also include the White Sox. Chief Justice McDonald of the Criminal Court called for action and the wheels of justice began to turn.

It was during this period that the scandal broke wide open in a series of cataclysmic revelations. The night of September 27, the late Jim Isaminger, Philadelphia sportswriter, put a story on the wire about an interview with Billy Maharg, former fighter, in which he named the Sox players involved and also mentioned Bill Burns, who once pitched for Washington, among other teams.

When this story hit Chicago, reporters rushed for Cicotte, who yelled that he didn't know Maharg, never saw Burns and the whole thing was a lie. But early the next morning came the denouement. The Old Roman was in his office at Comiskey Park when manager Gleason arrived. "I guess the truth is about to come out," said Comiskey sadly. Gleason nodded. Then he asked: "Do you want it right now, boss? I can get it for you today. I feel sure of it."

Gleason continued: "I'm sure Cicotte will break down. I've been working on him all summer. He's the weak one. He'll crack. A confession is the only way to clean it up. Shall I get him?"

"Go ahead," said Comiskey.

The questioning was a mere formality. There was no need of it. Cicotte was all through, on the verge of collapse. "I know what you want," he said with misty eyes. "I was crooked, Mr. Comiskey. I took money to throw games. I didn't . . ."

"Tell it to the grand jury," barked the Old Roman and in that moment the biggest threat to the perpetuation of baseball as America's national pastime was in the process of being wiped out. Cicotte was rushed to the grand jury room. He gave a detailed account of the conspiracy, even to the finding of $10,000 under his pillow, and how he did it to lift a mortgage on his home for the wife and kiddies. Confessions by Williams and outfielder Happy Felsch followed quickly, the latter telling his story to a reporter in Milwaukee.

According to Cicotte, Jackson asked for $20,000 and got only $5,000. "I refused to pitch a ball until I got the money," said Eddie. "It was put under my pillow the night before the first game of the Series. Everyone was paid individually and the same scheme was used to deliver." Cicotte further said the Gandil, the first-baseman, who didn't come back to the Sox in 1920, was the chief go-between and was supposed to have received $20,000 for his part in effecting the swindle.

There was no difficulty in keeping Cicotte talking. He even went into the technique of how he helped throw the first game by purposely intercepting a throw from the outfield which, had he allowed the ball to go on, might have caught a Red runner at the plate. And then he recalled a wild throw, later, which permitted another man to score. He further confessed that catcher Ray Schalk's charges of being crossed-up on signals by Cicotte and Williams were true.

The most immediate indictment of the clique was made by Comiskey. Within minutes after true bills had been voted against the eight men, the Sox owner suspended, indefinitely, every player. He issued a prepared statement, addressed formally to Charles Risberg, Fred McMullin, Joe Jackson, Oscar Felsch, George Weaver, E. V. Cicotte and C. P. Williams which read as follows:

"You and each of you are hereby notified of your indefinite suspension as a member of the Chicago American League baseball club, the White Sox. Your suspension has been brought about by information which has just come to me directly involving you, and each of you, in the baseball scandal . . . resulting from the World Series of 1919.

"If you are innocent of any wrong-doing, you and each of you will be reinstated; if you are guilty, you will be retired from organized baseball for the rest of your lives if I can accomplish it. Until there is a finality to this investigation, it is due to the public that I take this action, even though it costs Chicago the pennant."

The name of Gandil was omitted from the Comiskey decree of banishment because he already had put himself beyond the pale by playing outlaw ball in Idaho, perhaps foreseeing, a year in advance, the eventual discovering of this fraud.

The Sox, rocked by this wholesale defection of talent, lost the 1920 title to Cleveland, but, what was more enduring, they lost title and future to a third-baseman (Weaver), a shortstop (Risberg), a first-baseman (Gandil), two outfielders (Jackson and Felsch), and two pitchers (Cicotte and Williams) who, at today's prices, would be grossly undervalued at $2,000,000 on the hoof.

All of them, except Cicotte, Williams and the missing Gandil, tried to come back. For years, their names kept bobbing up in the news as one or the other made futile bids for reinstatement or a cash form of redress. They were actually re-indicted, along with some gambling figures, and brought to trial in 1921. They were acquitted by a sympathetic jury on one ballot and they pounded one another on the back in the courtroom in the renewed hope that they might get back in baseball.

No sooner was the verdict in than the late Judge Landis, newly-named czar of baseball, declared that "regardless of the verdicts of juries, no player who throws a game, no player that undertakes or promises to throw a game, no player that sits in a conference with a bunch of crooked players and gamblers where the ways and means of throwing games are planned and discussed and does not promptly tell his club about it, will ever play professional baseball."

Comiskey, likewise, was unmoved by the legal absolvence of his one-time greats. "Cicotte confessed he was guilty and implicated others," said Commy. "We have three other confessions. They implicated themselves."

There was nothing left for Comiskey to do, of course, but start all over, which he did right valiantly. But never again could he recapture the magic touch. Not only that, but until the day he died at his summer retreat in Eagle River, Wisconsin, on October 26, 1931, people tried to make him shoulder part of the blame for what had happened. Guys like Westbrook Pegler, writing in October, 1939, charged that Rothstein, among the other gambling figures involved, had taken advantage of the knowledge that the Sox were underpaid.

In the wake of the 1920 collapse, the Sox entered upon

the third phase of their existence. An expenditure of
$200,000 landed outfielders Johnny Mostil, Harry Hooper
and Amos Strunk, first-baseman Earl Sheely, third-baseman
Eddie Mulligan and shortstop Ernie Johnson. In 1923,
Willie Kamm was purchased from San Francisco for a reported $125,000.

Ted Lyons, fresh out of Baylor University, Ted Blankenship and Hollis (Sloppy) Thurston joined Faber on the
pitching staff. It wasn't until October of 1948 that Lyons took
off his Sox uniform for the last time, having served Chicago
faithfully for 26 years during which he won 260 games,
and succeeded Dykes as manager in the spring of 1946.

William (Kid) Gleason, who had replaced Rowland as
manager just in time to lead that ill-fated 1919 crew, was sup-
planted by Frank Chance, the former Peerless Leader of
the Cubs. Johnny Evers replaced Chance. The close of the
'24 season found the White Sox in eighth place for the first
time. They had hit rock bottom. Nobody was hitting, nobody
was pitching. Further changes in management involved Collins and Schalk the next four years when the Sox improved
enough to hold a monopoly on fifth place.

But the competition was getting too tough. In 1926,
the Yankees had rallied Lou Gehrig, Tony Lazzeri and Herb
Pennock, among others, to Babe Ruth's supporting cast and
were off on a spree of three straight pennants.

Things went into a tailspin in 1929, including the nation's banks. Somebody has remembered that the country's
top song hit that year was "The Moon Is Low." It was as
good a time as any to dwell in the past, and secretary
Lou Barbour of the White Sox took the occasion to balance
the 28-year budget. It showed the club had won 2,296
games against 2,031 defeats for a percentage of .533. Even
the up-and-coming Yanks were then five full percentage
points behind.

Thus, when the first Comiskey passed away in 1931, he

went out at, or near, the top after a 30-year struggle. His pioneer heritage was left to J. Louis Comiskey, the only surviving member of his immediate family, who had honeymooned with the former Grace Reidy on that 1914 trip around the world and had been quietly groomed to take his father's place.

Under him, the following season, the Sox skidded to their lowest ebb (before or since) when they lost 102 games out of 151. They finished seventh because the hapless Red Sox dropped 111 games. Injuries and general bad luck, which have stalked the Sox ever since, got in their early licks. Manager Donie Bush resigned in 1931 after saying: "There's no future for anybody managing this club," and Portuguese Lew Fonseca, who had won a batting championship with Cleveland, became the 13th White Sox pilot.

It was an unlucky number for Lew, although in September of 1932 Comiskey bought Al Simmons, Jimmy Dykes and Mule Haas from the Athletics for $125,000. That summer, too, a lean and perpetually hungry young man of 23 named Luke Appling hiked his batting average to a semi-respectable .274 in his second full season with the team.

The Dykes-Simmons-Haas deal goes down as one of the most fortunate in Sox annals. Simmons was eventually sold to Detroit in December of 1935 for $75,000 and in the long run, it cost Lou Comiskey only $50,000 for the three players, two of whom remained as manager and coach throughout the most profitable era the club enjoyed since the palmy pre-Black Sox days.

Dykes took command in May of 1934. That was the year the Sox wrested last place away from everybody without a struggle. That was the summer Comiskey decided to make his first trip east with them. He drove from city to city, and a less stout-hearted individual would have turned back after the first stop. It was in Cleveland, after three successive boots of easy infield grounders cost Sad Sam Jones a 2-1 game, that the huge owner (he weighed 360 pounds) remarked: "I wonder if any jury in the land would call it unjustifiable homicide if I sneaked a rifle into the stands some day and shot some of those guys."

The installation of Dykes was a popular move and it presaged the longest managerial career in Sox history. The "Round Man," as everybody came to know him, was a sound tactician, a good judge of players, a sarcastic boss and a fountain of copy for any writer who could stand the aroma of the 20-40 cigars which Dykes smokes every day of his life.

Dykes claimed castoffs on waivers and prodded them into new-found hustle and ability. He bought and traded with a minimum of money and a maximum of ingenuity. Slowly, but surely, Jim restored public faith in the White Sox. Fans who had soured on the Old Roman for his alleged mean treatment of stars like Kerr, and who couldn't bring themselves back into the fold, began to feel a respect for what Lou Comiskey and Dykes were trying to do. This was reflected in the click of the turnstiles.

But obstacles to improved team standing kept crowding one another into the path of the Sox. Appling had won the batting title with .388 in 1936 and the entire infield of Appling, Dykes, Zeke Bonura and Jackie Hayes hit .329 as a unit. Despite gnawing, pestering key mishaps, the team got into the first division for the first time in 16 years. Then Monty Stratton, the most promising of rookie hurlers, was incapacitated by appendicitis. Dykes' legs went bad on him.

Stratton came up with a sore arm in August of 1937 after posting a 15-5 mark in the first part of the season. In 1938, Appling fractured his leg in spring training and both Hayes and Joe Kuhel were leveled with injuries.

The climax to all the bad luck came after the season

ended. Stratton, who had come back to win 15 games in '38, shot himself on a hunting trip near his Texas home. His right leg was amputated and the big-league career of the man whom Charlie Grimm once called "the nearest pitcher to Grover Cleveland Alexander I ever saw," came to an untimely close.

Dykes was the Leo Durocher, the Frankie Frisch, the Casey Stengel of the American League. He could be truculent and arrogant but he kept the Sox before the public eye and in the prints. He cracked every gazette from coast to coast with his famous appraisal of Joe McCarthy as a "push-button manager." "All he has to do with those Yankees," explained Jim, "is push a button for Joe DiMaggio or Charley Keller or somebody to hit a home run. Anybody could manage that team."

The "Round Man" and the umpires had many a set-to and some of their altercations had repercussions as far as the American League office. One twilight in Boston, the Sox were tied and Dykes, realizing that the six o'clock curfew law was about to terminate the game, stalled brazenly while deciding what pitcher to bring in from the bullpen. His tactics resulted in a $250 fine from president Will Harridge.

On the next trip into Boston, Dykes was called to home plate and presented with a $250 watch by sympathetic Beantown fans as a token of their admiration for his daring and general all-around contributions to the "gaiety" of the national pastime.

It was in Detroit that Jim suffered one of his rare humiliations. He had taken the occasion to give a clubhouse talk on the stupidity of being picked off base. It was bad enough, he informed his players, to get caught off first, but he implied that nobody but a 14-carat mongolian idiot would get nipped off second. "How can you?" he rasped. "The whole play is right in front of you. You can't miss seeing it?" Then he informed them that anybody getting picked off second would be fined $50.

About the sixth inning, Dykes himself was on second with the bags full. Maybe he was deciding whether or not to send in a pinch-hitter. Maybe he was counting his money, as the saying goes. Anyway, catcher Rudy York of the Tigers suddenly fired the ball to second and Charlie Gehringer was there to take it. Dykes flopped like a seal toward the cushion, but umpire Bill McGowan called him out.

"No, no, no," yelled Jim, leaping to his feet with arms waving. "I made it. I got back here!"

McGowan, long used to such antics, let Dykes finish and then quipped: "I know you did, Jim, but what detained you?"

The worst part was the long walk across the diamond to the Sox dugout where his own players sat with towels stuffed in their mouths to keep from laughing out loud. The Detroit players, led by pilot Mickey Cochrane, with whom Dykes starred for so many years on the A's, stood at mock attention. That night Jim fined himself the 50 bucks.

Baseball was enjoying good times and Sox fortunes rose at the gate. On August 14, 1939, the first night game was played at Comiskey Park and 30,000 people came out to see the Browns and White Sox. September 3, 1945, a turnout of 53,953 saw the Sox and Tigers and in 1946, the season's attendance totaled 983,403. Through the early Forties, the players still were capitalizing on bonus contracts. There was some grumbling in '39 when the official attendance was posted at 591,000, thus costing a few of the boys extra dividends based upon a 600,000 year.

Early in 1939, Lou Comiskey passed away. He didn't even live to see the lights turned on for the first time at Comiskey Park. In July of that year, when the will was read, the First National Bank was named trustee for Mrs. Grace Comiskey (the widow) and for the three children, Dorothy, then 22, Gracie Lou, 18 and Charles A. Comiskey II, 13. They shared equally in one-half the estate, with Mrs. Comiskey getting the other half. The estate was valued at $2,325,000.

Before the season of 1940 opened the bank petitioned Probate John F. O'Connell for authority to ask for bids on the franchise, lock, stock and barrel, pleading that baseball was a hazardous business, unsuitable for a trust investment because the heirs are dependent upon a fluctuating income. Furthermore, difficulties in meeting state and federal inheritance taxes might be encountered. Mrs. Comiskey immediately took steps to forestall the threatened sale by renouncing the will in favor of taking her dower rights in the estate as provided by law.

Judge O'Connell finally refused the Bank's petition, his decision, in part, reading, "the club has been part of the fiber of Chicago's life for 40 years . . . and while there are factors which make it a hazardous enterprise, still an even greater value may be attached to the team if the Comiskey name remains in association with it. . . . So long as it is not necessary to sell the stock to meet immediate obligations . . . and so long as Mrs. Comiskey does not want to sell, this court is compelled to deny the petition. . . . It would be an insincere gesture to ask solicitation for bids."

One year later, the official transfer of the White Sox to the family was completed as the First National formally withdrew as trustee.

As time marched on, the Sox continued to ride with the rising tide of interest in baseball as expressed in the turnstile count, but they still played second-fiddle to at least half the other American League teams in the annual standings. Players came and went, with Lyons and Appling the last connecting links from former regimes. Appling won the batting crown again in 1943 with .328 and Lyons continued to pitch standout ball for a lack-luster outfit. The Cubs managed to win pennants in '29, '32, '35, '38 and '45 which crystallized baseball interest on the wrong side of town and drove patriotic Sox fans to cover.

The war years saw many White Sox players in service, among them Appling and Lyons. By the time they returned, there had been a turn for the worse in relationship between Mrs. Comiskey and her manager. It was climaxed in the spring of 1946 when the Sox lost two-thirds of their first 20 games. On the morning of May 26, 1946, Dykes announced his resignation and the appointment of Lyons as his successor.

It was soon apparent that Lyons wasn't the answer to what was the matter with the Sox, that he wasn't going to be around too long. Young Comiskey, over legal age and out of school, was in position to move into the driver's seat. His mother never had been able to assume the proper command because of inadequate acquaintance with the day-by-day problems of a major sports undertaking.

Attempts to buy the Sox always had been rebuffed. Veeck tried to get them before he went to Cleveland, and Mrs. Comiskey is believed to have refused $2,500,000 for the franchise. Others were interested but never got a chance to open their check books. Pitcher John Rigney had married Dorothy Comiskey and advanced to the post of farm director of the organization.

The White Sox took their first important step forward when Frank Lane, president of the American Association, was brought in as general manager of the club. That was in 1948, the same year young Chuck Comiskey was graduated to the Sox from the farm club at Waterloo, Iowa. Lane, with Chuck's consent and collaboration, embarked upon a trading spree. He shuffled ballplayers like so many playing cards. He fought furiously with Jack Onslow, who had succeeded Ted Lyons as manager, and finally succeeded (in

1951) in moving his own man, Paul Richards, into the dugout.

Lane's machinations began to pay off heavily as the 1951 season got under way. The White Sox surprised the entire nation by putting together strong pitching, timely hitting and brilliant defensive play to lead the league for 44 days. Attendance at Comiskey Park boomed. The *pièce de résistance* of Lane's trading activity came when he engaged in a three-way swap with Cleveland and Philadelphia in which he bagged Orestes Minoso, a Cuban who could play third base and the outfield spectacularly. Minoso sparkplugged the astonishing Sox, hitting a fat .326 and running the opposition ragged on the bases. Chico Carrasquel, the lithe shortstop whom Lane had purchased from the Dodger farm at Fort Worth, continued to live up to his early promise. Little Nelson Fox, a Philadelphia castoff, was an aggressive secondbaseman. Two former Detroit Tiger pitchers, Billy Pierce and Virgil Trucks, became big winners under Richards. At 34, Trucks was a 20-game winner for the Sox in 1953. Richards' often unorthodox strategy and the hustle of his players in every inning of every game drew South Side fans in great numbers to Comiskey Park. Attendance went over 1,000,000 in 1952, '53 and '54 and in each of those seasons the White Sox came home third, out of reach, but not out of sight, of the flag.

Paul Richards was lured to Baltimore following the 1954 season to accept the job of field and general manager of the Orioles. Marty Marion was chosen to continue the drive toward first place in the American League. The White Sox deserve to get there. It has been over 30 years since they last won a pennant. No other major-league team can make that statement.

THE WASHINGTON SENATORS

BY SHIRLEY POVICH

A four-alarm fire early in the spring of 1910 brought the horse-drawn engines clanging toward Washington's American League Park, then being readied for the opening of the new baseball season. Hours later, a huge chunk of the rickety wooden grandstand and the weathered pine bleachers was a charred mess, waiting for a $20,000 insurance adjustment. The District of Columbia's mustached fire chief poked into the smoking wreckage, pulled at his upper-lip foliage and expressed the opinion that "a plumber's blow-torch must have started this thing."

Out in Chicago, a former manager of the Washington Senators read of the blaze the next day and instantly agreed with the chief's findings. "The chief's right," murmured Joe Cantillon, "and the plumber was probably playing third base."

It was an understandable reaction by Cantillon, who had been fired as manager at the end of the preceding season after struggling with Washington teams that finished last twice, and seventh once during his three-year term as manager. Based on the brand of baseball being offered Washington fans of that era, Cantillon's presumption was not too far-fetched. Washington's place in War, Peace and the American League was already proving one of vaudeville's staunchest props.

Vaudeville, it developed, couldn't survive but baseball

in Washington did. It was a hardy breed of fans that the nation's capital had spawned. They had to be or else they would have become extinct, the victims of heartbreak years before Clark Griffith came along in 1912 to lift the Senators all the way from seventh place to a dazzling second-place finish. It took the club 24 years, including 12 seasons in the old National League, to get into somebody's first division. In fact, at the turn of the century, the 12-club National League had willingly given up on Washington and dropped the city cold. Lopped off with Washington in the cutback to an eight-club league were Louisville, Cleveland and Baltimore.

By far the tightest little family operation in the American League has been the Washington Senators. On the 11 occasions since his ascendancy to the presidency of the club in 1920 when Griffith was faced with the decision of choosing a manager for his team, he usually promoted one of his own players. First, it was his shortstop, George McBride, in 1921, and then Clyde Milan, the most famous of his outfielders. After that, it was Donie Bush, Bucky Harris, Walter Johnson, Cronin, and then Harris again. The next to get a fling at the job was Ossie Bluege, his old third-baseman, and when Bluege was through, he brought back Joe Kuhel. Two years of Kuhel, and Bucky Harris returned. A "foreigner," Charles Dressen, finally took over in '55.

If Griffith had to operate snugly on the fiscal side—and he did because he was trying to run a big-league team in the smallest town in the American League—he has been an eminently successful operator. Today, his Washington club is completely debt-free, an unusual circumstance in the majors.

If Griffith's teams have not exactly terrorized the American League in the 42 years of his managership-ownership since 1912, neither have they been pushovers. They have won three pennants and a World Series, and in nearly half of those 42 years they have finished in the first division.

Griffith prefers to separate himself from the dismal history of the Senators prior to 1912, when he gave up the direction of the Cincinnati Reds to move to the capital city as manager. Against the advice of associates who reminded him that Washington was the graveyard of all baseball operators, Griffith even demanded a stock interest along with the job. He didn't walk into Washington unacquainted with the town's poor baseball history. In the Nineties, Griffith hit Washington regularly as the star pitcher of Pop Anson's Chicago Colts of the old National League. And from 1901 to 1908, as manager of the White Sox and New York Highlanders, he knew of the lean crowds in Washington. Yet in 1920 his faith in the town was so great he sank his last dollar and pawned his Montana farm holdings to buy 40 percent of the Senators' stock, an equal share of the controlling interest.

To keep the Senators operating, Griffith was forced to manipulate his limited player-talent. Rarely did he make a player-deal without cash accruing to the Senators. Washington fans were not always pleased with those deals. "He'd even sell his son," the fans complained. They were almost right. Griffith did sell his son-in-law, Joe Cronin, in 1934, to the Boston Red Sox. The compensating factor was $250,000 of Tom Yawkey's money, the highest cash price ever paid for one player.

Walter Johnson's drawing power and pitching feats sustained Griffith and virtually kept big-league baseball in Washington during the lean years. Griffith made the most of Johnson as a gate attraction. He carefully spaced the Big Train's appearances, and both at home and on the road would contact sports editors the night before the game and plead over the telephone, "Johnson's pitching tomorrow. Give me a headline."

Until Johnson got the Senators home in the seventh game of the 1924 World Series against the Giants, Griffith's most hectic day must have been that July 5th afternoon of 1920 when the Yankees were at Griffith Stadium for a morning-afternoon doubleheader. That was the day Griffith was going to get some money into the till. Four days before, Johnson had pitched the first no-hitter of his career, against the Red Sox at Boston. The Yankee twin bill was to be the vehicle of his homecoming and Griffith advertised it widely. But Johnson didn't show up at the stadium that afternoon. In the morning, he phoned Griffith that his arm was so sore he couldn't raise it to scratch his head. Griffith was panicked. After Tom Zachary had beaten the Yanks, 4-3, in the morning game before 7,490 fans, a whopping crowd of 18,821 was in the stadium to greet Johnson in the afternoon. Calling a meeting of his pitching staff, Griffith explained the spot he was in and asked for volunteers to pitch against the Yanks. First to apply, and winner of the job, was Al Schacht. He wasn't very famous. Griffith had signed him out of the International League the year before in response to a series of letters signed "A Fan," extolling the praises of one Al Schacht, a righthander. Not until years later did Griffith learn that "A Fan" was A. Schacht.

When announcer E. Lawrence Phillips bellowed through his paper-covered megaphone, "Batteries for Wash-ing-ton—Schacht and Gharity!" the howls went up from the fans who had come to see Johnson. They hurled cushions, papers and other junk onto the playing field. They called Griffith vile names. When Schacht strode to the mound, they booed his every step.

You've probably guessed the rest of the story. Yes, Schacht beat the Yankees. He didn't allow any kind of a hit until Babe Ruth singled in the fourth, and at the finish he had a seven-hitter, a 9-3 victory, and a job with the grateful Griffith for the next 15 years.

Baseball in Washington was two years old before the Confederates fired on Fort Sumter in '61. Government clerks, fascinated by newspaper accounts of the "Game of Base Ball" in other cities, formed a team called the Potomacs in 1859. By 1865, the National Athletic Club was drawing as many as 6,000 fans to the Ellipse, behind the White House, and had President Andrew Johnson as one of their followers. He invited them to the White House, and baseball thus qualified socially. When the Nationals took off on a nine-game, 3,000-mile trip in 1867 that carried them as far west as Missouri, it was the first intersectional swing of any baseball team. At whose expense? Their own, of course. They were amateurs and gentlemen, were they not? To accept pay or guarantees would be profaning the social implications of the game.

By the late Seventies, though, baseball in Washington had slipped somewhat down the social ladder. Mike Scanlon's Ninth Street pool room, to which the sporting blood of the city gravitated, became the hub of baseball. Scanlon, later to go on to fame with the Baltimore Orioles, was an adventurer with an honest affection for the game he first played as a Union soldier after joining the army at 15. He drifted to Washington in 1866 and bought on credit the pool room that was to bear his name until his death 65 years later.

In 1870, Scanlon built Washington's first baseball park with a fence around it, at 17th and S Streets, N.W., constructed 500 seats, and charged an admission fee of 25 cents to watch his Olympics play. In 1871, Scanlon got the Olympics a franchise in the National Association, Washington's first link with organized ball. A year later, the Nationals also gained admittance to the National Association. The result was a fearful blow to Washington's pride in its baseball teams. In the 11-club league, the Olympics finished eighth and the Nationals 11th. When the league broke up in 1875, nobody in Washington cared.

In 1892, the Wagner brothers, George and J. Earl, popped into Washington from Philadelphia to announce themselves proprietors of a Washington franchise in the newly-expanded 12-club National League. And for the next eight years, the city's fans found themselves in the cold clutch of a pair of baseball brokers who talked big, spent little, pocketed nice profits and pulled out before they were kicked out.

During the years of the Wagner control, from 1892-'99, no Washington team finished better than a tie for sixth place. But so eager were the fans that the Wagners left town with a neat profit of $230,000 for their ventures in baseball. In fact, the National League owed J. Earl $35,000 when he left town.

The Wagners had five managers in their first three seasons in Washington. James (Orator Jim) O'Rourke was holding the job at one point in 1893. He was famed mostly for his handlebar mustache and his run-ins with umpires. After being fined by Silk O'Loughlin to the tune of $50 when a Senator was ruled out on the bases, O'Rourke kept taunting the umpire. When O'Rourke caught a pop fly and then turned to O'Loughlin with the question, "Safe or out?" he got a quick answer. "He's out," said the umpire, "but it just cost you $5 for the information."

The unpopularity of the Wagners hit a new high in Washington in July of 1893 when, after the Senators had played to a 15,000 crowd in Philadelphia, the owners announced that three games scheduled in Washington between the Athletics and Senators would be transferred to Philadelphia. Three were also transferred to Cleveland, and after August 5, Washington fans discovered they were listed for only nine more home games. The Wagners got away with the transfers but the league hurriedly passed a new rule that winter preventing that kind of trick.

One of Wagner's pet stunts was to make grandiose announcements concerning the high-priced players he was trying to buy for Washington. For two years he took bows by offering $2,500 for the great pitcher, Amos Rusie, who he knew was unavailable at any such figure. The Wagners, though, did come up with some good ballplayers, notably Win Mercer, a pitcher who won his first eight starts in the mid-Nineties. Gene DeMontreville, a flashy short-stop signed out of the Eastern League; Charles Koenig, the pitcher who went on to fame as "Silver" King; and Roger Bresnahan, an 18-year-old lad out of Lima, Ohio, who was signed as a right-handed pitcher in 1897, were other standouts.

Tommy Brown, who as manager had taken the '97 Senators to their loftiest peak, a tie for sixth place, didn't last two months of the next season. The Wagners fired him and promoted first-baseman Jack Doyle, who had come in a six-player swap with the Orioles. Doyle lasted only 20 days before J. Earl Wagner made the announcement that Jim McGuire would be the permanent manager. Ten days later, he had a new announcement to the effect that he personally would help McGuire manage the team.

Under the co-manager system, the Senators lost 15 of their next 18 games and manager McGuire announced in early August that he wanted out. Arthur Irwin became their fourth manager of the season.

The announcement of Irwin's appointment was accompanied by a new mouthful of Wagner double-talk. J. Earl stated that "Arthur Irwin and his friends have purchased an interest in the Washington Club and will take over September 13. We retire on and after that date and will not be actively connected with the club."

But the Wagners didn't retire, actively or otherwise. In late September, they acquired Buck Freeman, the home-run hitter from the Toronto club who was to wallop 25 home runs for the Senators the next season. In 1899, the Wagners came out of "retirement" to retire Irwin as manager and appoint second-baseman Dick Padden on a temporary basis. Despite Freeman's 25 homers and .318 batting average, the

Senators finished ninth and the Wagners started cashing in their chips, with the National League buying them out for the $46,500 fold-up price before reducing the circuit to eight clubs.

With no stomach for a return to the minors by the local backers, that season of 1900 was a complete baseball blackout for Washington fans. Then came exciting news from Chicago. Ban Johnson was giving the city a franchise in the new American League, which he vowed was a major league. The announcement was made on December 7, 1900. Tom Manning, owner and manager of the Kansas City club of Johnson's old Western and American Leagues, would take over the Washington team, Johnson announced from Chicago, and bring experienced players from Kansas City.

During the winter, though, more of the American League story began to unfold. Manning was to be merely the manager. A Detroit hotel man named Fred Postal bobbed up as president of the Washington team. Individual club ownership was a myth. Johnson was bossing the whole works. All the clubs in the new league had agreed to permit the president to control 51 per cent of their stock. Johnson tried to keep a secret of the fact that he was running syndicate baseball of the worst type.

Washington fans didn't give a hoot about such items as stock-control, however. A franchise even in a league that had yet to prove it was a major league was something to be elated about. Quite forgiven was the fact that Manning's 1901 Washington team looked suspiciously like his 1900 Kansas City club. Manning's team set up shop in a park at 14th Street and Bladensburg Road, northeast, after the National League had refused to give up its lease on the Florida Avenue grounds that later became known as Griffith Stadium.

Early in May, the Senators dropped to sixth place and stayed there. Their hitting faded to a whisper. Over one six-game stretch in July, they totaled only six runs. The absolute nadir was reached in Cleveland on May 23, when they went into the ninth inning leading, 13-5, and didn't win. With two out and nobody on, Cleveland stirred up the necessary nine runs to win, 14-13.

Manning had had enough when the season ended. There had been some apparent friction between Manning and Ban Johnson but the league president continued to call the turn for the Washington club. He found a lion-hearted citizen who would accept the managerial post in Tom Loftus, another old Western Association ally from Columbus. His dummy club president, Postal, wasn't even consulted. He rewarded the faithful attendance of Washington fans in 1901, which totaled 358,692, by raising the grandstand prices to 75 cents.

The admission hike was forgiven, though, during the winter of 1901-'02, when the Senators hit the front pages by staging a sensational player raid on the Phillies of the National League. With money advanced from league funds by Johnson, who now was visioning Washington as one of the league's more profitable franchises, Loftus corraled four of the Phillies' established stars. Ed Delahanty, no less, was one of those who jumped the Phillies to play in Washington. With the big outfielder came third-baseman Harry Wolverton and pitchers Al Orth and Jack Townsend. The gimmick was, of course, more money. Delahanty got a contract for $4,000, a $1,000 hike over what the Phillies had been paying the big fellow who five seasons before had set a record of four home runs in a single game against the Cubs. Wolverton, a $2,100 wage-earner with the Phils, took a $3,250 contract with the Senators. Orth's salary was raised from $2,400 to $3,259, and Townsend's $1,200 pay with the Phillies was doubled. The Phillies' owners screamed, of course. But the American League by that time was ruthlessly raiding its stuffy competitor and paying no heed to the squawks.

There was peril of another kind for the Washington club in 1902. Despite the fact that Delahanty led the league in hitting with .376, the Senators were a sixth-place club, and when their attendance dwindled to 188,158, there were rumors that the franchise would be shifted to Pittsburgh. Happily, the rumors proved to be almost as empty as the Washington park.

At that, the club was able to show a profit at the end of the season, according to the official 1902 statement. Gate receipts, at home and abroad, and concessions brought in $76,037.32. Out-going cash, including player salaries, the highest of which was Delahanty's $4,000, came to $75,023.78. That left a bank balance of exactly $1,013.54.

Tragedy literally hit the 1903 Washington club that finished last and thus gave vaudeville of that era one of its staunchest props. Ed Delahanty was killed.

The sham of non-league ownership of the Senators was finally stripped from the whole business in August of 1903 when Johnson announced that the league had bought out president Postal's stock for $15,000 and now controlled the team. At the same time, he virtually fired Loftus as manager by announcing: "Mr. Loftus won't return as manager next season. He failed to please the Washington people."

A month before the 1904 season opened, Johnson unloaded a controlling interest in the Senators' stock to a local group which included Thomas C. Noyes, of the publishing family that owned the highly-profitable Washington *Star*; Wilton J. Lambert, attorney; and William Dwyer, former Associated Press baseball writer. Lambert was installed as president, with Dwyer the business manager. Loftus was replaced by W. J. (Patsy) Donovan, St. Louis Cardinal star, a week after the schedule started.

It was the Senators' saddest season. They didn't win a game until their 13th start. They were shut out in three of their first four. They lost 45 of their first 55. They set a new record for defeats, losing 113 while winning only 38 games. Attendance dwindled to 132,344 for the home season in a year when the overall league attendance zoomed 700,000. Dwyer hustled out of town in May and left the offices of vice-president and business manager open. Donovan was fired and Jake Stahl named the new manager.

A firm hand finally came to the club in January, 1905. Publisher Noyes accepted the presidency, and for the next 15 years gave the team a dignity it had never known before. For himself, he took only a modest salary of $600, and one of his first acts was to buy outfielder John Anderson from Clark Griffith's New York Highlanders and utility man Charley Hickman from Detroit. For the first time, Washington fans could agree there was no stinginess in the front office.

The first year of Noyes' regime was a radical departure from the bargain-counter policies of former club presidents. His report to the stockholders at the end of the 1905 season showed the team had bought players to the value of $12,910 while selling talent that added up to only $3,125.

For finishing seventh, the 1905 Senators cut up a bonus of $1,000 promised them by Noyes if they kept out of last place. Yet during the first seven seasons of Noyes' presidency, they couldn't climb higher than seventh. Managers came and went in a passing show. Stahl lasted only through 1906 after finishing seventh two years in a row. In that season, the Senators' only distinction was stopping the 19-game winning streak of the White Sox by beating Ed Walsh in both games of a doubleheader and ruining that spit-baller's private winning streak of eight in a row.

Joe Cantillon moved in after Stahl. As a manager, he came high. Noyes had to offer him a contract for three years at $7,000 and ten per cent of the profits. There were no profits. In 1907–'08–'09, Cantillon finished eighth, seventh and eighth, respectively. Noyes and the stockholders took their losses gamely, but Washington fans began to despair at the futility of the Senators. Cantillon was recognized as a sound baseball man, but he couldn't think any runs across the plate.

Cantillon did leave something for Washington fans to remember him by, though. A young pitcher named Walter Perry Johnson was his legacy to the club. The Senators came up with their most famous ballplayer during the Cantillon regime, partly by accident—an accident to catcher Cliff Blankenship, who broke a finger in June, 1907, and was sitting it out on the bench when Cantillon spawned the bright idea of sending him on a scouting trip.

For weeks, Cantillon was being bombarded by letters from a Washington traveling man covering the Rocky Mountain territory, extolling the fast ball of "this boy, Walter Johnson, the strikeout king of Idaho's Snake River Valley League." Cantillon discarded the first several letters but the fellow finally broke him down by insisting that "this boy Johnson has a pitch that is faster than Amos Rusie's and control that's better than Mathewson's . . . He throws so fast you can't see 'em, and he knows where he is throwing because if he didn't there would be dead bodies strewn all over Idaho."

When Cantillon did decide to dispatch Blankenship on the scouting trip, Johnson wasn't the primary objective however. The spring before, Cantillon had been smitten with a young outfielder named Clyde Milan he had seen at Wichita on the Senators' homeward barnstorming trip from Galveston, and Blankenship was told to buy Milan "if he didn't come too high."

Blankenship's must have been the all-time most productive scouting trip. He stopped off at Wichita, and for $1,250 caged Milan for fall delivery, before moving on to Idaho to look Johnson over.

In Milan, Blankenship found the Senators' center-fielder

for the next 14 years, the man who was to wrest the base-stealing championship from Ty Cobb. Blankenship's first look at Johnson was an eye-filler, too. He happened into Weiser, Idaho, on the day Johnson was pitching against the Caldwell club. Before the game started he was able to recognize the fellow he had come to scout. The townspeople had told him about the big boy with the long arms and the behind-the-plow gait.

Blankenship got a 12-inning look at Johnson that day. It would be nice to say that he saw Johnson win, but he didn't. What he saw was fair enough, though. In the 12th inning, after two were out, an infield error beat Johnson, 1-0. And Blankenship discovered that the home folks weren't kidding about the kid's fast ball. It really whistled.

With his eyes still popping, Blankenship button-holed the big right-hander before he was out of uniform, and propositioned him. He flashed $100 as a cash bonus to impress the boy and said he would guarantee him $300 a month for the rest of the season if he would join the Washington club. Blankenship wrote out a quick contract on a piece of wrapping paper, but Johnson hesitated. It was a powerful lot of money, the boy agreed, but how about traveling expenses? Yep, said Blankenship, he'd pay that, too. Johnson said he'd have to ask his dad. Papa Johnson listened by telephone to Blankenship's proposition and gave Walter his permission to sign.

Intrigued by the tales of young Johnson's prowess, the fans clamored to see him in action. Eager fans pointed him out on the street before he had made a start for the Senators. They saw a country bumpkin in a derby hat with arms that seemed to hang to his knees. They went to the park early, hoping to see him pitch in batting practice, and were restless until Cantillon announced that he would start in a double-header against the Tigers on August 2.

The crowd's first view of Walter Perry Johnson was

enough to make 'em gasp. This couldn't be the fast-baller they had heard about. Why, look at him! He's throwing side-arm, almost underhand, with a long sweeping delivery. That's not what fast-ballers are made of!

But there he was, out there whipping the ball past the Tigers. Now it was the Detroit players' turn to gasp. Early in the game, the Tigers were impressed with the futility of tak-ing their regular out against Johnson. Sam Crawford did catch hold of one pitch for a homer, but Ty Cobb twice found it expedient to lay down bunts. It was the Tigers' bunts, not their hitting, that proved the undoing of Johnson. The rookie was slightly tanglefoot. On one bunt, Cobb reached first, and on a bunt that followed, Cobb scrambled all the way to third and later scored. When Johnson went out of the game for a pinch-hitter, he was trailing, 2-1. He had al-lowed six hits, only three beyond the infield. The game wound up with the Tigers winning, 3-2, but Johnson was on his way to fame.

Johnson's second start produced the first of the 412 vic-tories he was to win in the American League for the Senators, the only team for whom he ever was to pitch in the majors. Five days after his loss to Detroit, he started against Cleve-land, gave up two hits in the first inning, two more in the ninth, and won, 7-2, with a four-hitter. He issued only four walks. The next day it was written: "Johnson's speed was so terrific several Cleveland players acted as though they took no particular delight in being at the plate."

There was nothing scintillating about Johnson's 5-9 rec-ord for the Senators in 1908, but in September of the next season, he suddenly vaulted into national fame. At New York, he shut out the Yankees three times in four days. He beat them on Friday, 4-0, with five hits. On Saturday, he pitched a 6-0 three-hitter. New York's Sunday blue laws gave him a day of rest, and on Monday he won, 4-0, with a two-hit shutout. Four days later, he was back on the mound beating the Athletics, 2-1. The next day, he started again and licked the A's, 5-4. On his next shot at the Yankees, in October, he pitched another shutout, his fourth straight against the club. For that kind of pitching, the Senators were paying Johnson $2,700 a year. He won 14 and lost 14 with a team that finished seventh.

It was that year Johnson began to get the help of a new batterymate, a young catcher named Gabby Street, who came along from Kansas City with a slender shortstop named George McBride. Street rode to fame as the man who could handle Johnson's fast ball, and McBride blossomed as one of the slick shortstops of the league, later graduating to the management of the club.

Jimmy McAleer was the new Washington manager in 1910. He had piloted the Browns and was formerly in the Western Association, being another old pal of Ban Johnson, who had had a hand in naming all of the Washington managers before him. McAleer met no success. His teams in 1910 and '11 finished seventh. McBride was doing a smart job for him at shortstop, and Milan was a .300 hitter in the outfield. Johnson zoomed to a 25-game winner and led the league in most complete games and innings pitched.

For the first time, a baseball season was launched with White House blessings. President William Howard Taft attended the season's opener in 1910 along with a crowd of 12,000 and watched Walter Johnson shut out the Athletics, 3-0, with one hit. Taft threw out the first ball to set the precedent that every Chief Executive since has followed.

Before the 1911 season opened, Walter Johnson suddenly struck for a big salary raise. At the Atlanta training camp, Johnson and his roommate, Milan, announced they were holdouts. The tractable Johnson, who had never before asked for a salary increase, now was demanding double the $4,500 wage the Senators had paid him for winning 25 games and leading the league in strikeouts in 1910. "I want

$9,000, just as much as Ty Cobb," he said, in what seemed to be a strange kind of pout for the usually easygoing fellow. Young Milan set his demands at $4,000, an increase of $1,000.

When McAleer couldn't swing Johnson into line and the pitcher threatened to walk out of the training camp and go home, the manager became panicky and asked president Noyes to come to Atlanta and negotiate with both Milan and Johnson. Noyes capitulated to Milan and signed him for $4,000. He offered Johnson a contract for $6,500 for three years. Johnson said "nothing doing" and caught the next train to Coffeyville, Kansas, telling teammates he would stay there as a worker on his dad's poultry farm.

Washington fans were in an uproar at the dispatches from Atlanta and accused Noyes of stingy tactics toward Johnson. There were published reports that the Senators would trade the Big Train to Philadelphia or Detroit. Noyes defended himself by declaring "No other pitcher in the American League is paid as much as the $6,500 we are offering Johnson." He might have added that no other pitcher was capable of winning 25 games with a seventh-place club.

The Johnson holdout collapsed suddenly. He was at his Coffeyville home only 30 hours when he took a train to Washington to sign a three-year contract for $7,000 a season. It was just two days before the opening game.

Johnson didn't pitch the opener but his first start was historic. On April 15, he fanned four men in the same inning, yet was scored on by the Red Sox. Big Walter opened the inning by striking out Collins and Gardner. But his third strike to Gardner got away from Eddie Ainsmith and the batter reached first. Johnson then fanned Harry Hooper. But Gardner stole second and Tris Speaker scored him with a double. Johnson bent to his task again and fanned Duffy Lewis for his fourth strikeout of the inning.

Manager McAleer kissed off the remaining year of his three-year contract before the 1911 season ended. He announced he was moving to Boston as half owner of the Red Sox in partnership with Robert McElroy, until then secretary to league president Ban Johnson.

The Senators were a club without a manager until October 27, 1911, when Clark Griffith applied for the job and began to take root in the nation's capital. The 42-year-old Griffith wasn't happy as manager at Cincinnati. He wasn't happy outside the American League which he had helped found in the winter of 1900-'01 along with Charles Comiskey, Ban Johnson and Connie Mack. Griffith had gambled his own future on the success of the new American League, quitting the Chicago Colts at a time when he was their top pitcher, a steady 20-game winner.

In the league's formative years, Griffith carried the battle to the National League to achieve equal status. He led the player raids, trekked from the swamps and bayous of Louisiana to New England and the Midwest to persuade the old league's stars to jump to the American.

Griffith's reward for helping launch the new American League was the managership of the Chicago White Sox. As pitcher-manager, he led them to the pennant in 1901. When the league decided it needed a club in New York, Ban Johnson asked Griffith to set one up there in 1903. He was given the management of the Highlanders, got Tammany Hall on his side in the battle with the Giants for territorial rights, and was in New York for most of six years as manager before being fired midway in the 1908 season.

Garry Herrmann offered him the job of managing Cincinnati in 1909 and Griffith held it for three years but he never was happy within the National League. When his old friend, Ban Johnson, suggested that he would like him to move back to the AL as manager at Washington, Griffith accepted eagerly and bought ten per cent of the club for

$27,000, also assuming a three-year contract at $7,500 as manager.

In Washington, Griffith wasn't taking over much. In the three preceding years, the Senators had finished seventh twice and eighth once. Griffith proceeded to clean house with the consent of president Noyes. "I want a young team," he declared. But when Griffith traded catcher Gabby Street to the Yankees for infielder Jack Knight, Noyes was aghast. "Who'll catch Johnson?" he demanded. Griffith declared either of his rookie catchers, Eddie Ainsmith or John Henry could do the job. "If not, I'll catch him myself," he added. Noyes was impressed with the spirit, at least, of his new manager.

That 1912 team, which zoomed all the way from seventh to second, was built around Griffith's pitchers, the perennial Johnson, Tom Hughes and Bob Groom; Eddie Foster, the young third-baseman; Ray Morgan, a promising infielder; veteran shortstop George McBride; and four young outfielders, Clyde Milan, Danny Moeller, Howard Shanks and Clarence Walker.

The club's chief lack was a first-baseman, and Griffith got one from Montreal—Chick Gandil—in a deal that cost the Senators $12,000 plus infielder Knight and outfielder Gus Cunningham. The effect of Gandil's presence was magical. Griffith inserted him into the lineup on Decoration Day morning in Boston and Washington won a game. In the afternoon, Walter Johnson shut out the Red Sox, 5-0.

It was the beginning of the most amazing winning streak in American League history. The Senators reeled off 16 straight victories on the road. Johnson pitched and won in every western city. In his four starts, he permitted only four runs. The Senators were only a game and a half out of the league lead. They came back to Washington amid wild acclaim and President William Howard Taft saw them make it 17 in a row. The next day, in Philadelphia, the bubble burst. Tom Hughes couldn't hold a 1-0 lead in the ninth.

On that July 3 afternoon when Johnson started against the Yankees and was lifted at the end of six innings because he had a 10-1 lead, it was scarcely suspected he was launching a record winning streak. It bloomed to 16 in a row, despite the fact he averaged only two days rest between jobs. When he was finally beaten, in his jinx city of St. Louis, it was a brutal break. Johnson went in for a relief job with the score tied at 2-2 in the seventh inning, one out and men on first and second. Compton's single with two out got the runs in, and league president Johnson made the ruling that Johnson was the losing pitcher despite the fact that Tom Hughes had put the runs on base. An attempt to get a reversal of the ruling failed.

Clyde Milan, who stole 88 bases to top Ty Cobb in 1912, had a running mate the next season in Danny Moeller. They stole 74 and 64, respectively, and Washington was the running-est team in the league. It was another second-place finish for Griffith, whose fame as a trader and manager was now firmly established around the league.

Just before the turn of the new year, Washington heard some shocking news. Walter Johnson was jumping to the Federal League. He had signed with the new Chicago club on the North Side; Joe Tinker had signed him. Washington couldn't believe it, but it was true.

Griffith himself went west to talk to Walter. He got an agreement that Johnson would return to the Senators if they matched the $10,000 bonus the Feds had given him for signing. In fact, he had already used the Feds' money to set his brother up in the automobile business. Griffith dashed to Chicago to ask Ban Johnson to put up the ten grand and save Johnson for the American League. The league president refused. Griff then sought out Charles Comiskey.

"You don't want Johnson playing for a North Side club in Chicago," Griff warned Comiskey. "For $10,000 you can keep him in our league." He got the money from Comiskey.

It was 1916 before a Griffith-managed Washington club fell out of the first division. Meanwhile, he had picked up a young pitcher named Sam Rice from the Portsmouth, Virginia, club in lieu of a $600 debt when the Virginia League folded. And at Buffalo he got outfielder Charley Jamieson and first-baseman Joe Judge for $7,500. He was starting to build the team that was to win the city's first pennant.

When Griffith demanded more of a spending program after his 1919 Senators had finished seventh, and the stockholders refused, he casually asked how much money they wanted for the ball team. Connie Mack knew of Griffith's yen to be president of a club and steered him to a backer, William Richardson, a Philadelphia exporter. Together they bought 80 per cent in equal shares that cost them $145,000 each. Griffith got an $85,000 loan from his friend, the president of the National Metropolitan Bank, to make the deal.

For one year, 1920, Griffith was manager-president of the Senators. Then he turned the managerial reins over to his shortstop, George McBride, whose 1921 team finished fourth with the help of a young second-baseman from Buffalo named Bucky Harris and a young third-baseman from Peoria named Osssie Bluege. They were a pair of Griffith's finest buys. He scouted Harris personally at Buffalo on a day when the young man knew he was being scouted. Harris collected eight hits in a doubleheader and Griffith made the deal that night.

Bluege was scout Joe Engel's find. The Peoria club warned Engel that Bluege had a bad knee. "I'll find out for myself about that," said Engel, who was smitten with Bluege's talents. After the game, he called to Bluege: "Here, young feller, I'm scouting you for the Washington club. Wanna find out about that bad knee of yours. If you can beat me to the center-field fence, you're in the big league." Bluege won the race and Engel bought him for $5,000.

The Senators meanwhile had picked up another talented young man who was to be their best outfielder for the next decade, Goose Goslin of the Baltimore Orioles.

When 1924 dawned, Washington fans didn't know who was managing the Senators. Donie Bush had taken them into fourth place in 1923 but he didn't hit it off with Griffith and was released. Griffith stunned the baseball world in January with the announcement that Bucky Harris was his new manager. Nobody had ever thought of the kid second-baseman in terms of a manager. The presumption was that Griff had gone daft.

Harris was the youngest regular on the team. But he quickly demonstrated he had tact. Before the season started, he called the players together. "I didn't know a month ago I was going to be manager of this club. I'm not going to tell you guys how to play ball, but I'm asking a favor of you. Go out there and make me a good manager."

They caught fire for Harris. The veterans, Rice and Judge, and 23-year-old Goslin had the finest years of their careers. The Peck-to-Harris-to-Judge combination set a new major-league record for double plays. Muddy Ruel was handling Walter Johnson, George Mogridge and Tom Zachary like a master. Clark Griffith went down to Little Rock and bought Fred Marberry after scouting him for one day. In July, the Senators were scenting a pennant.

Griffith gave scout Joe Engel a blank check to "buy us a good outfielder; I don't care what he costs." Engel reported two possibilities—Billy Zittman, then with Newark, and Earl McNeely of Sacramento. The price on McNeely was $65,000. Griffith finally bought him for $50,000 cash.

Griffith was traveling with the team in Chicago when McNeely reported. "How do you do?" he said, extending his hand to the player. "Sorry, Mr. Griffith, can't raise my right hand," apologized McNeely. Griffith jumped. He had bought an injured ballplayer for more money than he had ever spent before. He tried to have Judge Landis call off the deal. Landis was sympathetic but suggested he wait and give McNeely a tryout. Two weeks later, McNeely was hitting and throwing and had won a regular job.

With the pressure on, Harris made a notable buy himself. He claimed right-hander Curly Ogden from the A's at the $7,500 waiver price. Ogden won eight straight for the Senators in August and September. The Senators won 16 of 21 games over that stretch and came back to Washington with the league lead. Walter Johnson was on a 13-game winning streak, Goslin was en route to a .344 batting average, and Sam Rice had a 29-game hitting streak going.

On a Monday afternoon late in September, Eddie Rommel of the A's beat the second-place Yankees in Philadelphia while Fred Marberry was winning for the Senators at Boston. That was it and Washington had its first flag in history.

The World Series with the Giants was unforgettable. The Senators were the sentimental favorites. It was Walter Johnson, getting his chance after 17 seasons in the majors. It was Harris, the boy wonder, against Muggsy McGraw. President Coolidge was there for the opener in Griffith Stadium, with 5,000 temporary seats added.

Down to the seventh game it went, with Johnson twice failing in starting roles as the nation wept along with the Washington fans. Before the final game, Harris unfolded a radical strategy to Griffith. "The Giants have all that right- and left-handed reserve power at bat," Harris pointed out. "I'd like to get rid of some of their bench strength. Bill Terry, I'm afraid of mostly. If we start George Mogridge, they'll play George Kelly at first base and keep Terry in reserve. I want to start Ogden, a right-hander, and then get him out of there. That'll put Terry in the lineup, and then we'll switch to Mogridge, the left-hander, after Ogden faces one hitter. I don't care if Terry is in there against Mogridge."

Harris got the nod from Griffith and it happened almost according to Harris' script. When Ogden struck out the first batter, Harris was tempted to leave him in, and did, but only for one more hitter, who walked. Then Mogridge got the job. McGraw went along with Terry against left-handed pitching for five innings, then replaced him with the right-handed George Kelly.

But as late as the eighth inning, the Giants had a 3-1 lead behind Jess Barnes. It was Bucky Harris himself who reprieved the Senators at that point. With two out and the bases full, he tied the score with a single to left.

Harris needed a new pitcher after Fred Marberry went out for a pinch-hitter, and from the stands came the frenzied shout: "We want Johnson!" They blew the roof when the Big Train started moving to the mound. The full significance of it was plain. Johnson could still win himself a World Series game.

And then—horrors! Frankie Frisch tripled to center with one out in the ninth. Harris motioned for Johnson to pass Ross Youngs and bring Kelly up. It took only three wickedly-pitched strikes to fan Kelly. Then Johnson got Bob Meusel on a ground ball and escaped further damage.

In the 11th, pinch-hitter Heinie Groh singled to right with none out and Jackson sacrificed him to second. Now Frisch was up, and Johnson struck him out. Youngs was given a deliberate walk to bring up Kelly. Johnson struck him out, too.

But the Senators were getting nothing off Jack Bentley, the Giant pitcher, and it was still 3-3 at the top of the 12th when Meusel opened up with a single. Johnson dealt with Hack Wilson by striking him out. Meusel hit into a force play at second, Gowdy popped a soft fly to Goslin, and Johnson had pitched himself out of trouble again.

As the Senators came to bat in the 12th, Muddy Ruel, with only one hit to show for the seven games, lifted a pop foul behind the plate. It landed in Hank Gowdy's mitt, but Gowdy's foot was in his mask and he stumbled and dropped the ball. It was a big break for the Senators. Ruel, reprieved, doubled down the left-field line. Johnson batted for himself and Travis Jackson fumbled his grounder. The Big Train was safe at first, while Ruel held second. Earl McNeely came up and hit a sharp bounder toward Freddy Lindstrom. It appeared to be an easy play. And then—a funny bounce! The ball hopped over Lindstrom's poised hands, over his head, into left field. Lindstrom later said he thought it struck a pebble. Anyway, Ruel ran all the way to the plate, and the Senators won the World Series!

Lovable Walter Johnson! How could you help rooting for the guy?

Harris had the team clicking again in 1925, beating the A's to make it two pennants in a row. The shrewd Griffith handed Bucky two big-winning pitchers on a platter—Stanley Coveleskie and Dutch Ruether, both of them claimed for the waiver price. Coveleskie led the league in pitching, with the help of a 13-game winning streak. Goslin and Rice were red hot, and Joe (Moon) Harris was picked up on waivers to lend a home-run bat to the Senators.

With Coveleskie winning 20 games and Ruether 18, the Senators never lost the league lead they took six weeks before the season ended. In the World Series against the Pirates, Johnson won his first two starts. The Senators rushed into a 3-1 lead in games. But at the end of six, it was all tied up.

And then Johnson made his third start, in the rain and mud at Pittsburgh. The Senators gave him an early four-run lead but, slipping and twisting on the slimy ground, he couldn't hold it. There was sawdust available for the Pirate pitchers when they worked, none for Johnson, Harris complained. Roger Peckinpaugh's errors at shortstop plagued Walter. Peck set a new record with eight for the Series. The

Pirates made it 6-6 on a Peckinpaugh fumble in the seventh, but he atoned for that one with a homer in the eighth that put Washington ahead, 7-6.

But Johnson lost the lead. In the Pirate eighth, Carey grounded a double-play ball at Peck, who fumbled it for his eighth error of the Series. With the bases filled, Kiki Cuyler delivered the crusher, a double to right that scored two runs for a 9-7 Pittsburgh victory.

Johnson's exit from the pitching ranks began on a spring day at Tampa in 1927 when a line drive by Joe Judge broke his leg. Late in the season, he tried to pitch with a brace. But the next year he accepted a job managing Newark. It was to groom him for his appointment as Washington manager in 1929. Harris had moved on to Detroit as manager of the Tigers and again Griffith turned to one of his old ballplayers.

Johnson's four-year reign produced no pennants, but only once did the Senators drop as low as fifth. It was notable chiefly for two player acquisitions. In 1930, Griffith bought, for $65,000, first-baseman Joe Kuhel from Kansas City. In 1928, he bought Joe Cronin for $7,500 from the same club. They both were destined to be managers for the Senators.

After Johnson's failure to win a pennant, Griffith resorted to the player-manager setup again, and Cronin was it. Together, during the winter of 1932-'33, they plotted their trading strategy. They needed pitchers. Cronin suggested the names of Earl Whitehill of the Tigers, Jack Russell of the Indians and Walter Stewart of the Browns.

"Whoa," said Griffith. "You just don't go planning on other clubs' pitchers."

"You're the master trader, Mr. Griffith," Cronin said. "You have a way of doing these things."

Griff set about doing it, immediately. To the Indians, he gave first-baseman Harley Boss and catcher Ray Spencer for relief pitcher Russell. He wangled Whitehill by trading off pitchers Fred Marberry and Carl Fischer. Stewart came higher. He had to give up outfielders Sam West and Carl Reynolds and pitcher Lloyd Brown for Stewart, Goslin and Fred Schulte.

Again it was the Senators and the Giants in a World Series. But this time it was no contest. The Senators couldn't get past Carl Hubbell. He beat them in the opener and in the fourth game, winning that one, 2-1, from Monte Weaver in an 11-inning duel. Earl Whitehill's shutout in the third game was Washington's only victory.

In a negative sort of way, the 1934 Senators were a sensation with their drop from the pennant to seventh place in one season. The biggest sensation was reserved for the season's end, though, when Clark Griffith announced a deal. He was selling Cronin, his son-in-law, to the Red Sox for $250,000 cash. "No ballplayer is worth that much money," Griffith declared. "But it might have been embarrassing if my son-in-law had stayed in Washington with a losing team," he added. "I think I did it for Cronin's good and the team's."

The next Washington manager? It was Bucky Harris, who had been fired at Boston to make room for Cronin. He was back for an eight-year term, secure in his job, though finishing only once in the first division. It was under Harris' wing that the Senators brought up two of their proudest kids from Chattanooga, Cecil Travis and Buddy Lewis.

Myer won the league batting championship in 1935 by making four hits on the last day of the season to edge out Joe Vosmik, who had held the lead up to that point. Vosmik sat out the first game of the final day's doubleheader at Cleveland to preserve his average, but hurriedly got into the second game when he heard of Myer's spree in Philadelphia. It was too late. The speedy Myer beat out two bunts for a pair of his important hits.

Harris willingly took on Buck Newsom in 1936 when

there was a chance to buy him from the Browns for $30,000, despite Bobo's doubtful training methods and headache-inducing antics. "I don't care how he behaves as long as he can win us some games," said Harris. Newsom rewarded Harris quickly. In a season-opener against the Yankees, Bobo was felled by a throw from third-baseman Ossie Bluege. Newsom was knocked cold and carried to the dug-out for first aid. He insisted on returning to the game, however, and pitched the full nine innings to beat Lefty Gomez, 1-0.

When Joe DiMaggio broke in with the Yankees, New-som declared he had observed DiMag's weakness and couldn't wait to pitch against him. A week later, it happened. DiMag whaled Newsom for three doubles. "That's his weakness," said Buck, "two-baggers."

Al Simmons landed with the Senators in 1937 on a cash deal with the Tigers and lasted only two seasons. Griff gave him his unconditional release after fining him $300 for curs-ing customers in the box seats at Griffith Stadium. Simmons always said it was a helluva coincidence that his $300 fine exactly equaled the bonus he got for hitting .300.

A chunky, swarthy figure of a man was increasingly in evidence around Clark Griffith's little stucco office in the late Thirties and early Forties. He was Joe Cambria, spe-cializing in digging up Cuban talent for the Senators. He made good with Griffith when he brought in George Case and Mickey Vernon, but had no success with his recommen-dations of such as Joe Krakauskas and Ken Chase. In Cuba, he signed a big pitcher-outfielder named Roberto Ortiz.

Harris was enchanted with Ortiz' speed in training camp, also his hitting. In a hotel room, he asked the Cuban whether he wanted to be a pitcher or outfielder but couldn't make him understand English. Harris called in Cambria and explained his plight. When Cambria asked the same ques-tions in English, only louder, Harris exploded: "Get out of here, Cambria, the kid isn't deaf. Just ignorant like you."

Cambria provided the Senators with a Latin Quarter all their own. He did come up with a fair-hitting kid in Bobby Estalella, but not for a decade was any Cuban really to make good with the Washington club.

When Harris had a chance to take a front-office job in Buffalo, Griffith consented and named Ossie Bluege his 1943 manager. The Senators moved all the way up to second place in a year which saw the Yankees run away with the pennant by 13 and one-half games. Early Wynn blossomed as an 18-game winner. George Case led the league with 56 stolen bases.

After that second-place finish in '43, the next season was a letdown for the Senators. The town and the league were quite unprepared for what happened—a drop into the cellar. It was the first Washington team to finish last since 1909. Travis and Lewis had gone to war, and Griffith was so desperate at one point that he signed Eddie Boland, an outfielder with the New York Department of Sanitation.

Under Bluege, though, the Senators had bounce—in both directions. In the wartime league, they were not too much outclassed. The next season, they came up with a tremendous four-man knuckleballing pitching staff—Dutch Leonard, Roger Wolff, Johnny Niggeling and Mickey Haefner. Buddy Lewis returned from the service in mid-season, and Rick Ferrell was doing the catching. They won nine games from the Red Sox in five days of doubleheaders and were within a game of the league-leading Tigers on September 23. It might have been different had George Binks not forgotten his glasses in Philadelphia and lost a ball in the sun to deprive the Senators of an important victory in the final week. The Tigers were still a game ahead, with the Senators having wound up their schedule and sweating out the Tigers' last four games. Then came the news that Hank Greenberg had hit a home run in St. Louis to clinch it for Detroit.

When Clark Griffith reckoned that Bluege would fit best into the organization as boss of the farm system, he didn't take long to acquire a new manager. It followed custom. Ex-Senator Joe Kuhel, then a minor-league manager in the White Sox chain, was offered the job, took it and held it for two undistinguished years, 1948 and 1949. He could pull no rabbits out of his hat in Washington despite his standing as a card-carrying member of the American Society of Magicians.

There shortly was a new vacancy in the Washington management, and when the Yankees fired Bucky Harris at the end of 1948, anybody could guess that he was coming back to Washington for a third term. He did, at the end of 1949, after slipping back to a minor-league job at San Diego for a spell.

Griffith was desperate when he named Harris manager for 1950. He gave him a three-year contract despite the fact that no manager since Johnson had ever been tendered a pact for more than a single year. Griffith was beset by the fact that John Jachym of Jamestown, New York, had bought the Richardson estate's 40 percent of the Washington club and wanted an active part in the operation. It was the first threat to Griffith's control of the Senators since 1920, or so he thought. Anyway, he hustled up enough stockholders' proxies to give himself nominal control and pleaded with Harris to come back as manager.

When Harris lifted the Senators into fifth place in 1950, the stockholders were appeased, Jachym sold out to Griffith's friend, H. Gabriel Murphy, and there was peace in the official family once more. With what he had to work with, Harris did a magnificent job. He personally advised the purchase of Irv Noren for $50,000 and brought along Gil Coan as a .300 hitter. He had the confidence of the younger players who had wondered at Kuhel's indecision and at long last, some of the Cubans began to make good for him, particularly in '51, although the club could finish no better than seventh.

Conrado Marrero and Sandalia Consuegra, two of Cambria's finds, began to act as though they belonged in the big leagues. The sawed-off Marrero, without a cigar only when he was pitching, unbashfully confessed "Me gude peetch." Sid Hudson's back injury handicapped Harris in his return to the Senators, but he pleased Griffith with his shrewd deals that brought Bob Porterfield and Don Johnson, ex-Yankee pitchers, to the Senators for the waiver price, and swapped Irv Noren for Yankees Jackie Jensen, Archie Wilson and Frank Shea.

Shea won some key games and Jensen proved to be an excellent outfielder and fair hitter in his two seasons with the Senators. Late in 1953 he was traded to the Red Sox for outfielder Tom Umphlett and the erratic but frequently spectacular pitcher, Mickey McDermott.

Bucky Harris' third tour of duty at Griffith Stadium came to a close after the '54 season, in which the Nats finished sixth, 45 games out of first and 81,000 fans behind their 1953 attendance figure. The decline in interest in the club convinced the Griffiths, octogenarian Clark and his son Calvin, the club's vice-president, that it was a time for a major change. Pepperpot Charley Dressen replaced Harris and was given the biggest contract any Washington manager had received and Griffith promised to rebuild the team's modest scouting and farm systems. Now the last remaining active member of the American League's original family, Griffith still looks to the future and the return of baseball prominence to Washington.

THE BOSTON RED SOX

BY BILL CUNNINGHAM

President Theodore Roosevelt and the American League were inaugurated the same year, 1901, and the team that for 47 years now has been known as the Boston Red Sox might well have borrowed the name "Rough Riders" from the tough little gamecock who believed in talking softly but carrying a big stick. Born under the innocuous name, Boston Puritans, it wasn't until 1907 that they adopted the name of the Boston Red Stockings, later shortened to Sox, and then it was only a salvaging operation. The Boston National Leaguers always had been known as the Red Stockings. They discarded the monicker in 1907, and the new American Leaguers fielded it on the first bounce.

Rough Riders, however, would have been far more descriptive and even prophetic. This most colorful of all the major-league dynasties has ridden high, wide, and handsome. It has also ridden low, narrow, and homely. It has stormed the heights. It has bounced around in the depths. Its ride has been rough, but through the starspangled half century of its mortal existence, its men ever have been up in the stirrups, swinging their sabers and charging straight on.

"Colorful" has been the word for them all down the historic years. Even upon the recent occasions when they fell on their faces with the goal in sight, they've made more flaming sports copy through their failures than most teams have been able to make through their triumphs. There's a lilt and a swing, a cocky set of the cap and a consistent challenge, in the attitude of the Red Sox. This is only fitting, because although they have come, through the years, from almost every state in the Union, once in the flannel regimentals of what Oliver Wendell Holmes called "The Hub of the Universe," they have become the sons of a mighty tradition.

Boston has always loved a winner—as who doesn't?—but its fandom has shown loyalty verging upon idolatry through rich years and lean. It loves a winner, but it likewise loves color and power and refusal to quit.

The Red Sox seemed made of it, and for it, and all down through the years, the Sox have generally been the team to read about, to rave about, and to argue and shout about. They were a team of great power. They still are today. From Pat Dougherty and Buck Freeman of the originals down to Ted Williams and Vern Stephens, the Sox have always boasted mighty men of the mace. The Sox were the major-league incubator of the greatest of all, Babe Ruth. James Emory Foxx contributed tremendous blows to their record.

In their time, they have known the greatest pitchers: the immortal Cy Young, Bill Dinneen, Smoky Joe Wood, Hugh Bedient, Babe Ruth again, Herb Pennock, Lefty Grove, and so on across the years to the modern Mel Parnell and Ellis Kinder. Truth to tell, the Sox pitching of late years has been their weakness, but, in their great general average, their hurling stands high.

The Sox have had their great catchers—Lou Criger, Bill Carrigan, and across to Birdie Tebbetts. Their infields have sparkled with Jimmy Collins, Jake Stahl, Freddy Parent, Hobe Ferris, Jack Barry, Larry Gardner, Everett Scott, Dick Hoblitzel, and a dozen others leading down into the era of Bobby Doerr, Junior Stephens, and George Kell.

The outfielders stand with the immortals. Possibly no team in either league has ever matched the Lewis-Speaker-Hooper combination of the great Carrigan teams. You can find Bostonians who will argue today that their peers never lived.

The Sox have known their great years and their lean ones. They have been up and down but they never have been out. Their city has stuck with them despite repeated disappointments these past years, because there is always color when they take the field. There's appeal in the uniform, magic in the name. The Sox are, quite simply, Boston's team. They always have been, and from any distinct evidence to the contrary, they always will be.

For easy reference, the half-century history of the Boston Red Sox, like all Gaul, can be divided into three parts. The first was 18 seasons of historic success, during which the new favorites of the Hub won six pennants and five world championships, and finally stood possessed of one of the greatest ball clubs ever assembled. The second was 14 dismal seasons through which the wreckage of a once-great enterprise rusted mostly in the cellar. The third has been the expensive, exciting, often controversial, always colorful, but strangely frustrated rebuilding effort of the past 22 years under the patient multi-millionaire, Thomas A. Yawkey.

It all began back in 1901 in a climate of raiding, defiance, rebellion, and confusion that now seems to have been prophetic. That was the year of the birth of the American League, and the invasion of Boston by the new organization was considered tantamount to the efforts of the British to take, and hold, Bunker Hill.

National League baseball actually had been established in the city since 1871, although the National League, as such, wasn't officially born until 1876. The exact age of baseball in Boston isn't known, but Dr. Oliver Wendell Holmes was once quoted by an ancient reporter as saying that he played the game while a student at Harvard, and the good Dr. was graduated from Harvard in the class of 1829.

In June, 1870, however, the Cincinnati Red Stockings, universally conceded to have been the first professional baseball team, visited Boston, cleaned up everything in the vicinity, and so fired the imagination of the local sports and civic leaders that they decided Boston should have such a community asset. They put the wheels in motion by hiring the two chief wheels of the Cincinnati nonpareils to renounce their Ohio affiliation and head the local enterprise. These were two reformed cricket players, English-born brothers, Harry and George Wright.

The Wright brothers firmly established what was to become the National League professional baseball team in Boston, calling it, oddly enough, "The Boston Red Stockings," the name undoubtedly being cribbed from their previous affiliation.

Boston had known 25 years of monopolistic National League baseball when the new American League threw its challenge in 1901. The older team was well established. It had been successful artistically and financially.

Ban Johnson once told this reporter that he hesitated considerably over trying to break into Boston. The Beantowners, as they were by then called, seemed too firmly entrenched. But, he said, the refusal of the National League executives even to talk to him convinced him that he would have to fight them to the death in their own territories. Johnson, backed by a well-heeled and fast spending Midwesterner, Charles W. Somers, decided to move in. This Mr. Somers, incidentally, backed four separate clubs in Mr. Johnson's new league. That's syndicate baseball and wouldn't be permitted today, but in this extremity anything went—and practically anything, and everything, proceeded to happen to the smug and successful Boston baseball monopoly.

When the invaders struck, they swung from the heels. The now venerable and venerated Connie Mack was in on the deal. In fact, it was Connie who leased a large plot of land not much more than a loud foul's distance from the South End Grounds where the Boston Nationals played. There, the new organization began the construction of their new field that would come to be known as The Huntington Avenue Grounds. It was Connie, too, who began helping Johnson and Somers assemble a team for the Boston invasion.

They may or may not have known it—Ban Johnson intimated to me in that ancient talk that they didn't know it—but Boston was ripe for a venture such as theirs. The local monopolists, or The Triumvirs, as they were generally known, had ridden their nag pretty ragged. The fans were long since disgusted with their shabby little park. The players, knowing that the owners were waxing rich, seethed helplessly against a $2,400 salary ceiling, but there was no release. There was nowhere to jump. A perusal of the yellowed files of the time reveals that the press was bitterly sarcastic in all sorts of comment.

Into all this came the new enterprise waving fresh money in generous quantities. The new organization's first blow, swung without warning, knocked the old club to its knees. That was the capture and installation as manager and captain of the old club's star third-baseman, the town's idol, James Joseph Collins. Jimmy Collins was but five feet seven inches tall and weighed only 160 pounds, but he was a strong hitter and a brilliant stylist afield. Old-timers still insist that Jimmy Collins was the greatest third-baseman the game ever knew.

The new American Leaguers got Jimmy Collins with $4,000, but his proselytism wasn't all. They armed him with the authority, guaranteed him the funds, and commissioned him to explore all possibilities of encouraging other stars to jump. Collins' persuasive power must have been considerable, and the money may have helped. He rapidly assembled a truly formidable ball club.

From his former team, the Beantowners, he quickly raided Chick Stahl, the center-fielder; John (Buck) Freeman, who played right field and first base; and a general utility man, pitching included, Ed (Parson) Lewis, possibly the only professional baseball player who ever went on to become the president of two state universities (Massachusetts and New Hampshire).

Collins, with $3,500, managed to talk possibly the greatest pitcher of all time, and officially the record winner of all time (511 victories), Cy Young, away from the St. Louis Cardinals. From the Cards, he likewise lured Young's famous battery-mate, Lou Criger.

Collins' first team, known temporarily as The Puritans, boasted the amazing Cy Young and Lou Criger as its principal battery; Buck Freeman at first; Hobe Ferris at second; Collins himself at third and Freddy Parent at short. His outfield consisted of Chick Stahl, Tom Dowd, who had been weaned from Chicago, and Charley Hemphill, from Ban Johnson's American League club at Kansas City. It was equipped with spares, including George Winters, a pitcher from Gettysburg College, who ranked right behind Young as a winner that first year.

The raided Boston Nationals, however, went doggedly ahead, and the first direct showdown between the embattled originals and the swash-buckling invaders for the applause and the patronage of the by-then-thoroughly-excited metropolis came on May 8, 1901, when they played in direct opposition, just across a set of railway tracks from each other.

The new American League team had opened on the road and had lost seven out of nine games to Baltimore, Philadelphia, and Washington. Despite this dismal beginning, 11,500 spectators stormed the new park to cheer its local debut versus Connie Mack's Athletics. They were rewarded when Cy Young pitched a 12-4 victory over the A's.

Meanwhile, the old team was offering a top attraction—a game versus the 1900 pennant-winning Dodgers. The old team had been playing at home and, despite the inroads on its strength, had been doing very well. Neutral observers thought the Nationals would hold their own. Still, their paid admissions for this first showdown contest totaled only 2,000.

The brilliant Jimmy Collins led his so-called Boston Puritans to second place that first season of 1901—four games behind the Chicago White Sox. Boston fandom went wild about them, with good reason. They could hit. Despite the dead ball and freak deliveries, they led the league in team batting with .293. Buck Freeman became the first of a long line of celebrated Red Sox sluggers with a .346 average and 12 home runs.

They could also pitch. The great Cy Young won 32 games and lost 10 as the team's premier moundsman. Winters registered a 16-12 record; Parsons; 16-17. The customers liked them. The box office proved it. They drew 527,-548 paid admissions that season, against 200,000 at the National League ball park. The original Red Sox, although they weren't to wear that name until six years later, were solidly installed and ready for the fight.

They continued to strengthen the next year when they lured pitcher Bill Dinneen from the park across the tracks and acquired George (Candy) LaChance, the first-baseman who wore a handlebar moustache, from Cleveland. Since Charlie Somers also owned Cleveland, this may have been nothing but an intra-organizational switch, but it released the hard-hitting Buck Freeman for outfield duty and was supposed to strengthen the ball club. Possibly it did, but not

enough to win the pennant. Boston finished third that second
year, six and a half games behind the A's.

That second year was a period of readjustment and
the loss of some friends. The new management found that it
had overreached itself in the matter of high salaries and low
admissions. It upped the third-base bleacher pews from a
quarter to 50 cents, with subsequent wailing and some talk
of a boycott. On the other hand, the more reputable burghers gave the new team and the new league a resounding vote
of confidence when Ban Johnson promptly suspended second-baseman Hobe Ferris five days for pushing an umpire.
This was hailed as sterling evidence of a policy of clean
play and fearless administration.

The next year, 1903, the new team hit the jackpot. It
won the pennant from the Athletics by 16½ games, then
took the world championship from the Pittsburgh Pirates in
the first of the modern World Series. It was, however, a tem-
pestuous year locally, and a momentous one generally in the
world of baseball. The most important fact, historically, is
that this was the year the National League threw in the
sponge and admitted Johnson and his Americans as full-
fledged partners in the industry.

How much of what happened in Boston on Patriot's
Day, April 19, a local holiday commemorating Paul Re-
vere's ride, had to do with the general surrender, isn't part
of the record. But on that classic occasion, the Boston Americans and the Boston Nationals went squarely against each
other with morning and afternoon doubleheaders. The result
was a stunning box-office defeat for the Nationals. The Americans drew 8,376 versus the Nationals' 1,800 in the morning,
and 27,658 to the Nationals' 3,867 in the afternoon. The
National League's Mr. Soden is understood to have notified
headquarters at that point that he had had enough.

The Boston Americans of 1903 were a stout team.
They had picked up Jake Garland Stahl, a catcher out of the

University of Illinois, and a powerful hitter in Pat Dougherty, an outfielder. Dougherty, in fact, had batted .332 for the season; Cy Young, who could hit as well as pitch, had a .330 average; Freddy Parent, .304; Jimmy Collins, .296; and Buck Freeman, .285, including 13 home runs.

The pitching had been beautiful. Cy Young, who by this time was 39 years old, had won 28 games and lost ten. Tom Hughes and Bill Dinneen, right-handers like Young, had won 21 games apiece.

Outracing the champion Athletics so decisively had been truly a spectacular feat. The A's had the young Rube Waddell, Eddie Plank, and Chief Bender, plus six .300 hitters led, appropriately enough, by Captain Lave Cross. The Boston team pulled away from them, however, at midseason, and staged one of the few runaways in the early history of the league.

There was tremendous excitement about the new postseason championship series, disrupting all normal life in Boston. This first modern World Series was to be five-out-of-nine, with the first three games in Boston, the next four in Pittsburgh, then two more in Boston if necessary. The clubs were to split the gate receipts evenly.

The Boston beginning was promptly disrupted by a suspected ticket scandal. So far as the playing went, the Pirates, a swash-buckling crew, led by the incomparable Fred Clarke, and including such greats as Honus Wagner, Tommy Leach, Claude Ritchey, and Kitty Bransfield, defeated Cy Young, 7-3, in the opening game before the first World Series crowd of 16,242.

Bill Dinneen turned them back the next day, 3-0, but the Pirates won in what was more a mob scene than a baseball game the following day, which was a Saturday. More than 19,000 people stormed the new park, but many found their seats already occupied by stubborn burghers who insisted they had paid, and who seemed to have the stubs to prove it. The latecomers refused to leave the park and poured out on the playing surface. Ropes were hastily stretched, but the crowd kept breaking through. It was a game of much interference and a plethora of ground-rule doubles. The Pirates won, 4-2, behind the pitching of Deacon Charles Phillippe, a 24-game winner, who spun a four-hitter against the mesmerized Puritans.

The caravan then moved to Pittsburgh for the next four games. It was then and there that the famous Red Sox fight song, "Tessie," occasionally still heard now almost a half-century later, was born. Rather, "'Tessie" wasn't born—she was borrowed. An organization of gay blades calling themselves the Royal Rooters invaded the Smoky City some 200 strong, wearing bright red stockings and Boston badges on their breasts. The combination of a Sunday and a rainy day held up the Series and, as Jimmy Coughlin, long after a famous Boston band leader and the Royal Rooters' band leader upon that immortal occasion, once explained to me, "Tessie" was a happy accident. Because of the rainy day, the bandsmen had time to look around for something new and catchy to brighten up their repertoire.

"Tessie" was merely a new popular song of the hour. The words had nothing to do with baseball. But the melody was new and it was likewise lilting. The band liked it and bought it. From that date, and forever after, as long as they had bands in ball parks, "Tessie" was the battle song of the Boston Red Sox.

But getting back to the Series, the Pirates won the fourth game, the Sox the fifth, sixth, and seventh. This made it 4-3 in favor of the Puritans, and called for the switch back to Boston. The better-rested Bill Dinneen whipped the Pirate ace, Phillippe, in that climactic contest, allowing the desperate Pittsburghers just four hits and two bases on balls. The score was 3-0, the crowd only 7,455, largely because the day was a very cold October 13th.

But there was a hot time in the old town that night. In fact, it started at the ball park with practically all the fans, led by "Tessie" and the Royal Rooters, marching the team around the park on their shoulders. The celebration spilled over downtown and proceeded far into the night.

The total receipts of that first series were but $55,000. Each Pirate received $1,316 because owner Barney Dreyfuss generously tossed his owner's share into their players' pool. The Boston athletes received only $1,182, plus salary up to October 15, which meant for an extra 15 days. The Boston club kept its owners' share, and that became part of an incendiary mess that was already smoldering and that was destined shortly to explode the entire ownership out of office.

Much hard feeling had come from the handling of the Series in Boston. The press was angry over what it called the "niggardly and skinflint methods" of the management, which not only had charged all visiting sportswriters admission, but had also forced every National League executive, including Barney Dreyfuss, president of the participating Pirates, to pay for their seats.

This wasn't anything, however, compared with the burning fury of the fans over the way ticket sales had been handled. There were open and nasty charges of collusion with speculators. This increased, rather than subsided, through the Winter, and the alert Ban Johnson, fearful of losing public support in his new Eastern stronghold, moved in and cleaned house. Just before the new season, be managed to have the club sold to General Charles Taylor, owner and publisher of the Boston *Globe,* and the General's son, John Irving Taylor.

Officially, John I. Taylor was the owner and new president. His reputation was that of the playboy scion of a magnificent sire, and rumor had it that the General had bought the team for his son as a stabilizing influence. The story was that John I. knew little more about baseball than the number of outs in an inning, and some of his deals rapidly enlarged that impression.

The father, however, had bought the son a championship ball club, and nothing the son could do in his first season of ownership could seriously disturb its momentum. It seemed to the fans and the scribes that he did his best to wreck it on June 19 of that year, 1904, when he sold the popular and hard-hitting outfielder, Pat Dougherty, to New York, receiving in exchange Bob Unglaub, a utility infielder of no particular sheen. This was the first Boston American deal really to turn the fans sour, but owner Taylor was saved by the fact that his team won the pennant regardless. Cy Young won 26 games; Bill Dinneen, 23. A new left-hander, Jesse Tannehill, procured from the New York Highlanders, (Yankees), won 21.

The highlight of the season was magnificent pitching. A running feud between the Athletics' amazing, if eccentric, Rube Waddell, and the calm and corpulent Cy Young, came to an early climax on May 5 of that year, when Young, for once enraged at the taunts of Waddell, pitched that rarest of all phenomena, a perfect ball game, retiring 27 Athletics in order. The new man, Tannehill, also pitched a no-hitter that season.

It was a close pennant race, but the Bostons won, for the second year in succession. The margin was a game and a half, and eight percentage points. But the Puritans were robbed of their second successive shot at the world title when, to the amazement of the baseball world, John T. Brush, owner of the National League winners, the New York Giants, declined to play Boston.

Both Brush, and his manager, John J. McGraw, were diehards, so far as the American League "invaders" were concerned. They took the attitude that they were the champions of the only real league. "Why should we play this up-start club, or any other American League team for any post-season championship?" stormed the truculent McGraw.

This did not set well with the fans of the nation. It was equally unpopular with the Giant players, who held a meeting and drew up a petition requesting permission to meet the Boston Pilgrims, as they called them. But the Giant brass was adamant, and there was no World Series in 1904.

There were no more pennants for the Boston Americans, either, for eight weary years. The team dropped to fourth place in 1905, plunged all the way to the bottom in 1906, climbed one notch to seventh in 1907, and kept floundering around until 1912.

Injury, illness, friction, weird sales and trades by Taylor, and similar tribulations ruined what had been a championship ball club. Not the least of the afflictions was trouble between manager Jimmy Collins and the new owner. Collins resented Taylor's second guessing and dressing-room tirades, and he finally barred the owner from the players' boudoir.

Collins couldn't take it past June of that dismal year. He left without even giving notice. Ban Johnson persuaded him to come back. He tried it again, and got as far as August. Then Boston's greatest early hero bowed out for the year. He couldn't endure John I. Taylor. He returned the next year as a private to try to help his old players, but it didn't work out and he departed for good.

Taylor rests in Red Sox lore as a disastrous bungler but I'm not certain that's entirely fair. He did make some astounding moves that angered the Boston fans and puzzled all baseball. These began when he sold Dougherty, the team's leading batter and first World Series slugging hero (two home runs), before he had got his chair warm as president. The next year, 1905, he blundered egregiously again in trading a young, hard-hitting outfielder, George Stone, for the 35-year-old Jesse Burkett.

To make matters worse, his driving Jimmy Collins into resignation inflicted his disrupted ball club with a string of makeshift and often unwilling managers—Chick Stahl, who committed suicide at Spring training camp; Cy Young, who didn't want the job; George Huff, University of Illinois athletic director, who lasted 13 days; Bob Unglaub, who had been acquired in the Pat Dougherty deal; Jim McGuire, a veteran catcher of experience with six other teams; Fred Lake; Patsy Donovan . . . they came and went in a ragged parade.

Boston fandom braced itself for at least one serious shock a year in the matter of trades. It had been Pat Dougherty who went in 1904. The promising George Stone was lost in 1905. Jimmy Collins had been driven out in 1906. Buck Freeman was let go in 1907. But the real crusher that year was the trading of the great Bill Dinneen to St. Louis. The next year, 1908, saw Hobe Ferris shipped to the Browns and Freddy Parent to the White Sox. The real crash came in the Winter of 1908–09, when it was announced that the historic Boston battery of Cy Young and Lou Criger had been split and sold—Criger to the St. Louis Browns in December, Cy Young to Cleveland in February.

Stories following this paralyzing communiqué had Charlie Somers, the original Boston owner, besting John I. in a drinking bout at an American League schedule meeting in Chicago and persuading him to part with the mighty Cy for $12,500 and a couple of mediocre moundsmen, Charley Chech and Jack Ryan. This was all the harder for Boston to swallow because Cy, at 41, the previous season had pitched his third no-hit game, and the entire community had given him a great demonstration of admiration and affection. Every player in the entire league had pitched in to buy him a beautiful cup in honor of the day and the ceremony.

Taylor did all these things, and still he couldn't have been too utterly dumb because he was slowly gathering, while he let these fading veterans go, a group of brilliant youths who were to bring the Red Sox four world championships in seven seasons—the greatest era the Sox ever have known. He was no longer going to be head of the organization when this came to pass—he had "made too many mistakes" and had alienated too many fans—but nobody can erase the fact that he had discovered the talent, scouting much of it personally, had done the talking, and had inked the contracts.

In 1906, for example, he signed a young college catcher named Bill Carrigan, of Holy Cross. That one really belongs to his father. The General had seen Carrigan, a sophomore, catching a game against Harvard, and had recommended him to his son. In 1907, however, John I. personally scouted and then purchased from the Houston team of the Texas League for $750 a deer-footed young centerfielder named Tristram Speaker. In 1908, for $3,200, he picked up from Kansas City a thin, 18-year-old pitcher whose name was Joe Wood. Also in 1908, he personally scouted and signed a young outfielder named Harry Hooper, then a member of Sacramento in the outlawed California State League. In 1909, he signed a 21-year-old outfielder named Duffy Lewis from Oakland in the Pacific Coast League.

With these players in the fold, the Rex Sox were well on their way to the great years just ahead. But the great years didn't start to arrive until 1912, and by that time, John I. Taylor had gone. At least, he had sold 50 percent of his stock to Jim McAleer, manager of the Washington club, and Robert B. McRoy, secretary of the American League and Ban Johnson's right-hand man. Johnson unquestionably engineered the deal. McAleer became president; Taylor slipped back to vice-president.

This was a memorable year. The team had a fine new field, the present Fenway Park. It was now officially known as the Red Sox. That was another contribution of John I.'s. The Boston Nationals had dropped the title "Red Stockings" in 1907, and Mr. Taylor had quickly appropriated it.

The 1912 Red Sox were led by their hard-hitting first-baseman, Jake Stahl, a Chicago banker in the off-season. Steve Yerkes was at second, Larry Gardner, another Jimmy Collins, was at third and Heinie Wagner was an acrobatic shortstop. The immortal outfield of Hooper, Speaker, and Lewis, welded by two seasons' experience, was now perfection. Smoky Joe Wood, with his blazing fast ball, Hugh Bedient, Ray Collins, a stylish left-hander, Buck O'Brien and Sea Lion Charley Hall comprised a great pitching staff. Forrest Cady and the rough-and-ready Bill Carrigan did the catching.

In the successful pennant race, this team won 105 games for a .691 percentage—a record that was to stand for a decade and a half. Smoky Joe Wood was sensational on the mound. He won 34 games, lost only five, and burned 258 strikeouts past the whiskers of the opposition. He had a string of 16 consecutive victories, and the great excitement of the season was the percentage race between Smoky Joe and the incomparable Walter Johnson of the Washington Senators, who likewise was making records. The other pitchers stood up. Hugh Bedient won 20, Buck O'Brien, 18; Collins and Hall, 14 each. Tris Speaker hit .383 for the year. These Sox took first place on June 18 and ran away with the race, winning by 14½ games over Washington.

The 1912 World Series between the Red Sox and the New York Giants was the most hectic ever played. These were strong times in the Polo Grounds—the great McGraw machine, with Christy Mathewson, Jeff Tesreau, and the young Rube Marquard, was in the midst of winning three consecutive National League pennants.

The Sox defeated the New Yorkers, four games to three —but they had to play eight games to do it because the second was an 11-inning tie. The final game went 10 innings and has a place in World Series lore because that's where Giant center-fielder Fred Snodgrass made his famous "$30,000 muff." This was the flub of an easy fly ball that went for a double and set the scene for the Red Sox to win, 3-2, after the Giants had gone ahead, 2-1, in the top of the 10th.

Speaker, Wood, Bedient and Hooper were the big Red Sox heroes. Speaker hit .300 in the Series and fielded sensationally. Smoky Joe, as a starter and in relief, received credit for three victories and one loss.

It was a bad fielding Series. The two teams made 31 errors, of which the Red Sox contributed 14. Yet, Harry Hooper and Tris Speaker made two plays in the Series that possibly never have been surpassed. Hooper's was the spectacular catch of a line drive off Larry Doyle's bat in the sixth inning of the all-important final game. The ball rocketed to deep right center and seemed a certain home run until the lightning-fast Hooper streaked to the spot, leaned far over the low railing and, with the fans bracing his back, made one of the great saves of all Series history.

Speaker's stellar contribution was an unassisted double play in the seventh game. The fleet Texan always played a shallow center field and was famous for his ability to go back under fly balls. In this game, Art Fletcher hit a line drive that was sinking short even of Speaker's normal station. The brilliant and jet-propelled Sox center-fielder took the ball at top speed while racing toward the diamond, and he simply sprinted on to second instead of throwing the ball. This unexpected stratagem doubled up Giant base-runner Art Wilson, who had started for third under the impression that the blow was a hit.

This was the richest World Series to date, and, in fact, the figures stood until the years of the mammoth stadia. Each of the victorious Sox received $4,024; each Giant $2,566. Since the difference between the pools was some $32,000, poor Fred Snodgrass stood tagged for all history as the perpetrator of the "$30,000 muff."

I have brought the saga of the Red Sox this first dozen years more or less chronologically because there are so many *firsts* in those years that deserve to be noted. The ancient citadel of Boston, for example, was the first community to break almost entirely with tradition and accept the new American League completely from the very first day. The Red Sox were the first American League team to move toward the top and stay there. The White Sox won the first pennant; the Athletics, the second. But neither could hold the pace. The Red Sox, on the contrary, finished second, third, first, and first in their first four years.

The Red Sox were the first American League team to win two pennants in succession. The Red Sox were the first American League team to play in the modern type of World Series. They won, and therefore became the first world champions. Jimmy Collins was the first great American League manager, with a possible bow toward Connie Mack. He and Larry Gardner were the first great American League third-basemen. Cy Young and Lou Criger formed the first great American League battery, and the herculean Cy was the first, and the greatest, of the many great pitchers. Hooper, Speaker, and Lewis were the first great outfield, and possibly still the greatest, with a respectful genuflection toward the staunch Bob Meusel-Babe Ruth-Earle Combs combination that was to roam the Stadium gardens some 20 years later.

The Red Sox were the first and only team ever to miss a World Series because the National League winner refused to play. The Red Sox were the first to take really heavy loot from a World Series . . . and now came another first, that was due to be of great importance in the everlasting records.

The Sox dropped to fourth place in 1913, were still trying to build in 1914, and, in the normal course of shopping around, picked up a burly, left-handed, 21-year-old pitcher from Baltimore. His name was George Herman Ruth, and his nickname was Babe. They bought him as part of a package including Ernie Shore, and he was written in at $2,900. The immortality of Babe Ruth as the greatest hitter of the long ball the game has known to this time, has almost completely obscured the fact that he likewise came pretty close to being one of the greatest left-handed pitchers of all time. He still holds one very important World Series record as a pitcher. It's the greatest number of consecutive innings pitched without a run. The Ruth record is $29\frac{2}{3}$ innings. His runner-up is the peerless Christy Mathewson with $28\frac{1}{3}$.

So much has been written about every phase of the home-run king's career, it seems nothing new can be added, but on the chance that his first Red Sox catcher, and manager, Bill Carrigan, might remember something not generally known about the Babe's early years, I recently made a pilgrimage to Lewiston, Maine, especially to talk to him about it.

"Why, yes," said the still ruddy-faced, steel-eyed, and square-jawed Rough Carrigan, "I think there's something that ought to be straightened out. Ruth joined us late in the season of 1914. He pitched in four games for us and was then sent to Providence.

"I've read many times that he was sent down for more seasoning. That's not true. He was already a finished pitcher, good enough for us, or anybody else. His record in the four games with us was two wins and one defeat. But there was a club situation involved. Joe Lannin, who owned the Red Sox then, also owned Providence. We were out of the race mathematically, but Providence had a chance to win the pennant in the International League. So Lannin sent Ruth down to help them, and he did. They won the pennant with the help of his pitching."

"While we're on it," I asked, "how did you handle Ruth on the Red Sox?"

"By rooming with him," was his unexpected reply.

"Did he give you any trouble?"

"No," said Bill, "there was no trouble. He behaved himself, if that's what you mean. But he had no idea whatsoever of money. You've got to remember his background—that orphan asylum and all—and this was his first big job. I think he was getting $3,500, and that was all the money in the world. He didn't seem to think it could ever run out. He'd buy anything and everything. So I moved him in with me."

"Did you handle his money?" I asked.

"Yes," said Bill, "I did through the season. I'd draw his pay, and give him a little every day to spend. That generally lasted about five minutes, and at the end of the season, I naturally had to give the rest of it to him. I cal'lated it wouldn't last long, but that was the best I could do."

Bill Carrigan had become the Red Sox manager in 1913 and had led and driven the team to second place in 1914, a matter of minor consequence in Boston just then because that was the year the Braves rocketed from last place in mid-July to the pennant and a four-straight World Series title over the Philadelphia Athletics. That was the Braves' "Miracle Team," and it was the big news in New England.

But Carrigan, nonetheless, had a team of destiny ready in the wings. It may not have been the most stylish ever assembled, but on the authority of Ty Cobb, who had plenty of experience with it, it was one of the hardest to beat.

It was a blend of the old and the new. Some of the stars who had helped Jake Stahl win the pennant and the world title in 1912 were still there. Larry Gardner, who had replaced Home Run Baker in popular acclaim as the greatest third-baseman, was one. Everett Scott, a fielding genius, had taken over at shortstop. The former great Athletics' shortstop, Jack Barry, had been installed at second base. Dick Hoblitzel was on first. The famed Hooper-Speaker-Lewis outfield, now in its prime, was a monumental asset. Carrigan, Cady, and a new man, Chet Thomas, took care of the catching. The pitching staff had changed completely since 1912. Smoky Joe Wood was virtually useless with a sore arm that resisted every known treatment, but the Sox had two stout right-handers in Ernie Shore and George Foster, and a matching pair of dependable southpaws in Hubert—the first "Dutch"—Leonard and Babe Ruth.

This rugged aggregation reflected the personality of its manager, who was nicknamed "Rough." It had its brilliance, but above all else it was a driving, fighting, never-quitting ball club.

It may astound some of their elder idolators to learn that they also had their cliques and their feuds. Tris Speaker and Joe Wood were roommates and bosom companions. This arrangement was happy for them, but not for some of the others, especially when Speaker would criticize a play he felt had let his pal down.

There were strained relations for an extended period between Speaker and Lewis, although both were considered then, and are considered today, two of the finest gentlemen who ever played baseball. Their trouble began when all the Red Sox decided to have their heads shaved on a blistering Summer trip through the West. There was no penance involved. It was simply in the interest of keeping cooler. Everybody's hair grew back but that of the very dapper Mr. Lewis, who then, as now, in his portfolio as traveling secretary of the Braves, was known throughout baseball as a "snappy dresser." Mr. Lewis was very self-conscious concerning his cranial nudity, but the fun-loving Tris thought it very comical.

At a pre-game batting practice, when the team got back to Boston, Speaker kept snatching Duffy's cap so the crowd could see how bald he was. The normally meek Lewis finally became so enraged that he said to Speaker, "If you do that again, I'll kill you."

Speaker awaited his opportunity and did it again. Lewis thereupon threw his bat at Speaker with all the force he could generate. Fortunately, the bludgeon struck no vital part, but it did crash the Speaker shins with such force that he had to be lifted from the ball field. For a long time, thereafter, the two never spoke except for such terse occupational dialogue as "I've got it," and "You take it" on a fly ball hit between them.

This was the Carrigan team that beat the Tigers for the pennant in 1915, winning 101 games and losing 50 for a .669 percentage. Great pitching was its strength, and the young Babe Ruth, in his first full season, was much of that strength. He won 18 games and lost six. The Sox pitchers mowed down the Philadelphia Nationals in five World Series games. Babe Ruth always remembered that Series. He begged all through it for a chance to pitch, but Carrigan used only three hurlers—Shore, Foster, and Leonard.

These Red Sox gave an exact repeat performance the following year, Brooklyn being the World Series victim, also in five games. They finished second in 1917, as the war began to bite, but won the pennant again in the war-shortened season of 1918, and took the World Series from the Cubs. That latter event is now memorable for one of baseball's sourest episodes—a players' strike for a bigger cut of the receipts. It held up the start of the fifth game for more than an hour.

A truly ghastly thing had quietly happened to the Red

Sox and their idolatrous fandom. There had been some changes in playing personnel, two of them involving great figures. One of these was Tris Speaker, whose salary had rocketed to $18,000 in 1914, to hold him against raiding from the Federal League. After the Feds collapsed, owner Lannin tried to cut the Grey Eagle back to $8,000. Spoke held out bitterly, and Lannin sold him to Cleveland on the opening day of the 1916 season for $50,000, an infielder named Fred Thomas, and Sad Sam Jones, a pitcher who later did pretty well.

Bill Carrigan, his successful career climaxed by two straight world championships, likewise foreswore baseball to enter business after the 1916 season, despite the fact that he was only 33 years of age, and despite the fact that all Boston fans and the Red Sox management practically prostrated themselves at his kite-size feet, begging him to stay.

But those things happen. Stars are sold and managers move on. What never had happened to a baseball property before, and has never happened since, had quietly moved in on unsuspecting Boston in the form of new ownership. The newcomers were a couple of theatrical sharpies from Broadway named Harry Frazee and Hugh J. Ward.

Frazee was the front and the fast talker. He bought on a shoestring and signed notes for most of it. Lannin, who appears to have been a trusting sort, sold the club to him in mid-December of 1916. Possibly Bill Carrigan saw it coming.

Frazee was a fantastic and controversial character whose later years were to be starred with contention and litigation, including a suit of Lannin's to try to collect on his notes and an odoriferous divorce libel flaming with charges of adultery. He seems to have started life as a bell-hop in a hotel at Peoria, Illinois, to have graduated to bill-posting, and from that to the profession of theatrical producing.

He was supposed to have made a million dollars from show business alone, and he later was to have at least one historic hit, "No, No, Nanette," the titillating theme song of which, "Tea For Two," is still with us today. Frazee may have been sincere about wanting to buy into baseball, but the trouble with him as Red Sox owner was that he was in two kinds of business—and his other kind was a gamble in which he could lose money fast. He was a big operator, a heavy gambler in extravagant musicals. He was alternately rich and broke, sometimes in rapid order, but he was the latter too often.

Another seemingly uncorrelated but vital coincidence is that a very rich metropolitan brewmeister, Col. Jacob Ruppert, and an almost equally well-heeled partner, Col. Tillinghast L. Huston, had bought the New York Yankees, nee Highlanders, in 1915, the year before Frazee bought the Red Sox. This team had spent all but three seasons of its entire American League life in the second division and had never won a pennant. The new owners were big sports and heavy spenders.

Just when Frazee began to tie together the two facts that he had some great ballplayers and the Colonels had a lot of loose money isn't known, but he could smell a dollar farther than a fox can smell a goose. So far as could be seen, Frazee was an honest and conscientious owner his first three seasons. He even bought such players as Stuffy McInnis, outfielder Amos Strunk, catcher Wally Schang, and pitcher Joe Bush. He had tried hard to persuade Bill Carrigan not to retire. He had experimented with Jack Barry and Edward Grant Barrow, later long-famed as the general manager of the Yankees, as managers. He seemed to be doing his best, and his best was enough to win the world championship in 1918. It was to develop, however, that an era of

Red Sox history ended with the last out of that year's final Series game.

The year of 1919 was a glad one for the world and for baseball. The war was over. We had won. The baseball players were back. It must have been a bad year, however, for Harry Frazee. A couple of big shows had flopped. He needed money. Nobody paid too much attention when he sold Ernie Shore, Dutch Leonard, and outfielder Duffy Lewis to the Yanks for two pitchers, an outfielder, and $50,000. It looked like just another trade—not a good one, maybe, but no worse than some.

Nor did anyone see the handwriting on the wall when he later sent along his World Series pitcher, Carl Mays, to the Yanks for $40,000 in cash. Mays was a hard man to handle. He had jumped the club. This could be only getting shut of a cantankerous ballplayer.

Everybody, however, saw only too clearly what was being done to their darlings on January 9 of the next year, 1920, when a bombshell hit Boston in the form of an announcement that the new home-run sensation, Babe Ruth, had been sold to the Yankees for $100,000. Barrow had taken the daring gamble of converting a great pitcher into a greater outfielder in 1918. The Babe had hit .322 in 1919 and had blasted the unprecedented figure of 29 home runs, four of them grand slams.

What everybody didn't know, and what some don't know even yet, however, is the rest of the story. Frazee, despite the previous sales, was broke again. The Lannin and Taylor interests were pressing him on his notes, for one thing. He wanted $500,000, and he went to Colonel Ruppert to see if he could borrow it. The Colonel countered with an offer to buy Babe Ruth. He offered cash and players. Frazee was interested only in cash. The Colonel gave him $100,000 cash and a $350,000 loan for the greatest property the Red

Sox had; for a player who was to become the greatest gate attraction of all time.

The Colonel now had the Red Sox owner in his clutches, or possibly his ready money had the Red Sox owner under its spell. From this distance, it looks almost as if Frazee became a Yankee agent. In batches, he shipped everything that was any good along to New York, collecting cash and a few nondescripts each time in exchange. Wally Schang, Waite Hoyt, Mike McNally, and Harry Harper went in one consignment; Joe Bush, Sam Jones and Everett Scott, in another. Joe Dugan was shipped over. So was Herb Pennock. The final touch to the murder was the forwarding f.o.b. of a promising minor-league farmhand—a pitcher named George Pipgras.

Within two years from the time this began, the Yanks were in first place, and they went on to win six pennants in the next eight years. Their unprecedented dynasty was founded upon the blood of the Red Sox, the sweat and tears of their fans.

The press, the public, even the civic leaders of Boston were raging while this rape was being carried out. The entire baseball world denounced it, for that matter. One of the mightiest inveighers against it was Ban Johnson himself, but the mouthy Mr. Frazee inveighed just as mightily against Ban Johnson. In fact, he tried to organize a movement to have Johnson removed from the American League presidency.

Having nothing more to sell, Frazee finally sold the franchise, and to the great joy of the city, despite the fact that the city had never heard of the purchasers.

A Midwestern syndicate, headed by J. A. Robert Quinn, vice-president and business manager of the St. Louis Browns, undertook the rehabilitation job in 1923. Frazee's reign of ruination had lasted seven and a half years. The money man in the new combination was an Indiana glassworks millionaire, Palmer Winslow. Other contributors were based in Columbus, Ohio. Ban Johnson was understood to have engineered the deal, and possibly to have found the money.

No committee of sportsmen ever meant better or did much worse.

Except that they set the stage for a new and generous owner who came along 11 years later, their efforts are scarcely worth the recording. Their team was consistently in the cellar. It was in last place when they bought it. It lifted to seventh the next year, 1924, then clunked dully back to the bottom, to rest there six years in succession. In 1931, it actually got as high as sixth, but the effort was too much and the next year it reclined again on the nethermost level.

Quinn did the best he could on the thinnest of shoe strings, but nothing ever went right. His financial resources were pitifully limited. His players were, of necessity, mostly minor-leaguers and misfits nobody else wanted. When, occasionally, fate seemed to throw him a bright prospect such as the minor-league shortstopping sensation, Dudley Lee, in 1924, the boy didn't have it. In 1926, his bleachers burned down and he almost lost his ball park. Sunday baseball was legalized in Boston in 1929, but it rained almost every Sunday when the Red Sox were scheduled. Quinn persuaded Bill Carrigan to emerge from retirement and try to help with the rescue at the end of the '20's, but the market crashed and Bill had to hustle back to Maine to see what had happened to the banking business.

Bob Quinn did eventually come up with a powerful pitcher, Big Ed Morris, and was preparing to sell him for $100,000, the deal having been signed and sealed, when Morris was stabbed to death in a knife fight at a fish fry in Florida just as he was taking off for the 1932 training season. With all these woes, and his teams so bad that town teams and Twilight Leaguers were out-drawing his games, Quinn had to collide head-on with the depression.

He did get some lifts. Otherwise, he would never have been able to survive as long as he did. Charlie Ruffing, later famed as a Yankee hurler and hitter, was developed by the Red Sox, and was promptly sold to the Yanks for $17,500 to stave off some creditors. Danny MacFayden, a Boston schoolboy pitcher, signed with the Red Sox. He was good for $50,000.

Quinn had a few good men at various times: Tom Olive, a slick outfielder; Jack Rothrock, later with the Cards; Billy Rogell, who went on to the Tigers; Doc Prothro, later the Phils' manager; Ira Flagstead; Charley Berry, now an American League umpire; Dale Alexander, a clumsy first-baseman, but a hitter good enough to lead the league in 1932.

But he didn't have the money necessary to rebuild the ball club. By 1933 he was completely broke, and was supposed to be in debt for some $350,000.

That is believed to be about what the Boston Red Sox cost Thomas Austin Yawkey. There may have been more, but part of the price for the privilege of taking over the exhausted and exhausting white man's burden was the reestablishment of Bob Quinn as a private citizen free and clear. That was practically the sole achievement of the second era of the Red Sox.

The third, and resuscitative, era for the Sox began on February 25, 1933, under 30-year-old Yawkey, a husky baseball-loving heir to a vast industrial empire, Midwestern of origin. Yawkey was Yale educated and New York residence. To understand why he took over Boston's broken-down enterprise, and his immediate procedures, one needs to understand something of his personal history. He did it for love of the game, possibly through love of the memory of the man he called Dad—another wealthy Yawkey, who owned another ball club. The new Red Sox owner was the nephew of Bill Yawkey, one-time owner of the Detroit Tigers. The uncle adopted the nephew, made him his heir, and educated him to succeed him in the management of the Yawkey fortune. Bill Yawkey had a showplace near Detroit, and he frequently entertained his famous baseball employes there. The kid, Tom, grew up in this atmosphere, on chummy terms with some of the greatest stars the game ever knew.

When the time for his education came along, he was shipped East to Episcopal Academy in New York City. This chanced to be the same school Eddie Collins had attended as a kid, and Eddie Collins, their most distinguished baseball alumnus, was naturally the idol of every kid in the school. That included young Master Thomas Yawkey. From this fitting beginning, the young man matriculated into, and in time was graduated from, the Sheffield Scientific School at Yale University. While there, he tried his best to make the Yale baseball team at second base, and while he played enough to keep warm, he rests in Eli annals as a frustrated infielder.

The foster father died, and under the terms of the will, Tom Yawkey didn't come into full possession of his inheritance until he was 30. He had long since determined to become a baseball owner like his uncle, and as soon as he received legal freedom to handle his own affairs, he began scouting for a team to buy. The Red Sox, of course, were more than available.

The deal was easily completed and the papers signed in Boston. Yawkey's next move was to make Eddie Collins his vice-president and general manager, to tell him money was no object, or words to that effect, and that his commission was to get the Red Sox out of the cellar.

Collins started buying where he could. He picked up catcher Rick Ferrell and southpaw Lloyd Brown from the Browns for $50,000 and a catcher named Merv Shea. Then he bought pitcher George Pipgras, once a Red Sox chattel, and shortstop Billy Werber from the Yanks, for $100,000. These weren't all-time all-stars by any means, but it had been so long since Boston had seen anything like it that the entire community almost wept.

Collins kept buying. Connie Mack was having bank trouble in Philadelphia again and was ready to peddle some of the veterans who had won three consecutive pennants for him in 1929-'30-'31. The great Lefty Grove, Rube Walberg, and second-baseman Max Bishop changed to Red Sox uniforms for $125,000 and a couple of nondescript athletes. The Indians were persuaded to part with pitcher Wes Ferrell and outfielder Dick (Wiggles) Porter. Shortstop Lyn Lary was bought from the Yankees, and southpaw Fritz Oster-mueller from a Cardinal farm—all these for good prices. Herb Pennock came back from the Yanks.

This went on to the grand climax at the end of the 1934 season when Joe Cronin, shortstop and manager, was purchased from the Washington Senators for $250,000 and shortstop Lyn Lary—the highest price ever paid for any player. Alumnus Collins turned back to the A's then to snare the celebrated slugging first-baseman, James Emory Foxx, and pitcher Footsie Marcum for $150,000, a pitcher, and a catcher. From the same source, Doc Cramer, the outfielder, and shortstop Eric McNair were pulled loose for $75,000, a pitcher, and an infielder.

In the meantime, owner Yawkey had completely rebuilt Fenway Park at a cost of $750,000, making it probably the prettiest park in the league, and Bucky Harris, the first Yawkey manager, had got the Sox into fourth place within two years after the rebuilding began. That was the first time the Sox had even entered the first division in 16 years.

This was a general policy of "trying to buy the pennant," and it didn't succeed. One reason, whatever others existed, was that it was practically impossible to break through the Tigers and Yanks of the early '30's. But where Yawkey did succeed was in winning back the hungry Boston fans.

The policy of buying established stars stopped at the end of the 1936 season, not because the Yawkey coffers dried up, but for three reasons, only one of which mattered. That was that it wasn't panning out. One of the others was that other teams were now reluctant to deal strength to the "Back Bay Millionaires." They were not far from having enough strength to make trouble. The other was that the Sox now had a sufficient nucleus for real building.

The chief reason, however, was that the plan simply wasn't working. Yawkey had spent over $1,000,000 on talent and his team that season of 1936 had slid from fourth to sixth. It was thereupon decided to develop a farm system— to go after young talent and train it.

That was the real start toward the colorful, controversial, often exasperating, but always exciting Red Sox, as they are at the moment. It took a little time. There was still trading, and there has been some buying. But a 17-year-old part-time second-baseman named Bobby Doerr was brought on from the Coast; Eddie Collins personally went out to San Diego to scout and sign a tall, skinny, 20-year-old outfielder, who originally fancied himself a pitcher and whose name was Ted Williams. They passed up a chance on a big Coast League outfielder named Joe DiMaggio because he was understood to have a trick knee, but they signed his little brother, Dominic. They picked up a kid shortstop named Johnny Pesky, and so on. That was the new system and it began to pay.

By 1938, six seasons after the Yawkey transfusion, the Red Sox were licking everything in the league but the Yanks —and who else was licking the Yanks through that stretch that ran from 1936 to 1943? The New Yorkers won four pennants in succession, missed with a third place in 1940, then won three more in a string.

Throwing out '43 and '45 as war years, the Red Sox may almost be called the annual American League runner-up from 1938 to 1951. Since 1938, they have won but one pennant—in 1946—have been second six times, and third three times. They have appeared eternally fated to chase the leader to the wire. In most of these years, they have been picked to win the pennant. Often, they have been "the team to beat," and always, save for that one time, really a war-weakened year (1946), they have been beaten.

Reams of copy sufficient to pave a four-lane highway to the moon have been written, especially in Boston, upon the classic subject, "What's the matter with the Red Sox? In fact, that phrase has become a gag greeting on the street as friend meets friend.

What in thunderation *is* the matter with them?

There have been some fine ballplayers in Red Sox spangles these last few years—the mighty Ted Williams, graceful Dominic DiMaggio, reliable Bobby Doerr, heavy-hitting Vern Stephens, voluble Birdie Tebbetts. Of course, the Sox haven't had the pitching, everybody knows that. Dave Ferriss, Tex Hughson, Mickey Harris and Joe Dobson came through in the pennant year of '46 but the first three couldn't do a thing after that.

Some people have said Joe Cronin, now the club's general manager, was a poor manager for the Sox because he wore out the pitchers. But Joe McCarthy, universally respected as one of the most brilliant managers of all time, had no better luck during his relatively brief stay in the Boston dugout. McCarthy, however, came close. He carried the Cleveland Indians all the way down to a post-season playoff game in 1948 but Lou Boudreau, managing with his bat and glove as well as with his head, whipped him for the flag.

Has the Red Sox failure been caused by temperament? Who d'ye mean, Ted Williams?

So far as the Red Sox are concerned, no. They have always liked Williams and Williams has always liked them. Most of Ted's difficulties during his hitch in Fenway Park have been with the heckling quotient of the paying clientele and with certain caustic members of the local press. The truly great Red Sox slugger can be put down, psychologically, as a man who likes individuals and hates people. Williams has spat at, and made indelicate gestures toward, an entire park full of fans. He has verbally assaulted sportswriters to their faces in language generally associated with muleskinning. He has refused to tip, or even touch, his cap in response to applause. He has ignored the ancient baseball custom of shaking hands with a teammate who has just walloped a home run. But one thing Ted has always been able to do is pull in the customers. It has never made any difference whether they came to boo him or to cheer him—they came.

In recent years the Red Sox have not even qualified for their familiar role as runners-up but, thanks to a change in top-level policy, there is the bright promise of future pennants. From the old star-buying policy, which resulted in one first-place finish and a number of seasons of frustration, owner Tom Yawkey has switched to a somewhat less expensive, less spectacular, but much more sound program of youth development. Red Sox scouts, armed with bonus contracts, were turned loose in a vast talent hunt. Teen-age pitcher Frank Baumann received $85,000. A Los Angeles schoolboy, Billy Consolo, was given a $60,000 bonus to sign. At one time the Red Sox had 15 bonus youngsters of the $20,000-and-up variety under contract. Young, aggressive Lou Boudreau was brought in to replace the veteran Steve O'Neill after the 1951 season.

The first results of the Youth Movement didn't become

visible at Fenway Park until 1953, although Boudreau did some experimenting with rookies the previous season. A recall to active duty in the Marines took Ted Williams away from the Sox in May, 1952, and the efficient work of George Kell, obtained in an elaborate trade with Detroit, was not enough to compensate for the loss. A late-season slump dropped the Red Sox into sixth, their poorest finish since 1945. Boudreau started the 1953 season with a lineup that averaged 23.6 years. But pitching veterans Ellis Kinder, Mel Parnell and Maury McDermott were chiefly responsible for the club's surprising fourth-place finish. Ted Williams made a dramatic return from combat duty in Korea, hitting .407 in 37 games. One of the products of the Youth Movement, slick-fielding Jim Piersall, thrilled the fans with his ball-hawking feats in the outfield.

The Red Sox were fourth again in '54 but it was not a particularly happy baseball season in Boston. Williams suffered a broken collarbone in spring training and an attack of pneumonia a few months later, yet he played in 112 games and batted .344. After the last game of the season, on September 26, he announced his retirement.

Red Sox fans can't expect to see "another Ted Williams" right away—they waited 30-odd years for the first one—but a new manager and old friend, Pinky Higgins, and a collection of improving young ballplayers should give them something to cheer about. And cheering for the Red Sox has been an old New England custom since the early years of the century.

THE KANSAS CITY ATHLETICS

BY HARRY ROBERT

A genuine white elephant, meaning one without an assist from a coat of calcimine, occurs about once in more than 5,000 of the species. That it happens at all is almost incredible, considering that for an elephant to be white, one of the thickest-skinned beasts extant must be completely devoid of pigmentation. Manifestly, a white elephant is a paradox. This makes it a perfect symbol for the Athletics, now of Kansas City and formerly of Philadelphia.

It will take baseball fans a while to get accustomed to it but they are the *Kansas City* Athletics now and have been since early November, 1954. After 53 years of success and failure in Philadelphia, the House of Mack, divided by a family quarrel and weakened by the financial drain of poor teams, finally collapsed, a victim of the changing times in baseball. When the last of the Macks' trophies and citations were packed for shipment to major-league baseball's newest and westernmost city in January, 1955, only memories of a team that alternated between glorious victory and humiliating defeat remained in Philadelphia. Under Connie Mack, who managed and/or shared ownership of the club from 1901 until the sale of the franchise in '54, the Athletics were indeed baseball's paradox.

Mr. Mack never believed in doing things by halves.

Like the little girl with the curl in the middle of her fore-head, when his Athletics were good, they were very very good. But when they were bad, horrid was hardly the word. At least two of his productions will always be remembered among the greatest the game has ever seen. On the other hand, some of his cellar clubs were less than futile.

Mack directed nine pennant-winners and five World Series champions for Philadelphia. His colors drooped in the basement 18 times, twice as often as he won titles. Oddly enough, the Athletics have finished either first or last, at the two extremities of the standings, more often than in all the other positions combined. Mack's good teams were so strongly constructed that once they gathered full momentum, it took years to halt them. They were accused, like later Yankee clubs, of doing the game more harm than good be-cause of their superiority. Connie had three brilliant squads, two of which have secured their place among baseball's all-time best. The A's were the early power in the American League, from 1902 through 1905. They ran roughshod over it from 1910 through 1914, and again ruled the circuit from 1929 through 1931. In between his two masterpieces, and since the dismantling of the last one, Athletics followers have wandered victory-parched through barren seasons.

The Athletics have some great baseball tradition behind them. First and foremost is Connie Mack himself. One of the most popular figures sport has ever known, he is destined to be unique in the game's annals, for it is unthinkable that the combination of circumstances that enabled him to remain at the helm of one team for 53 years can ever be duplicated.

The World Series achievements of the Athletics rank with the most thrilling. Connie's 1910 "kids," supposedly hopelessly outclassed, broke the back of the famous old Chi-cago Cubs and brought their reign to a finish. The 1911–'14 edition, featuring the legendary "$100,000 infield," crushed McGraw's swaggering Giants twice. And it's hard to conceive of any World Series with greater heroics than the one of 1929 when the A's beat the Cubs. In that stunning triumph, Connie sprang one of the biggest surprises in Series history by starting a "has-been" in the opening game. Howard Ehmke not only set the Cubs on their collective ears but at the same time set a World Series record of 13 strikeouts that stood until 1953. In the same Series, the A's staged that most amazing uprising when, after being shut out for six innings and trailing by eight runs, they suddenly went berserk in the seventh, pile-driving 10 runs across the plate to crush Chicago.

On the other hand, no team has ever been more ignominiously humbled in World Series play than the Athletics. The 1905 club, routed in five games by the New York Giants, were shut out in four of them, three times by the great Christy Mathewson. And the apparently invincible 1914 A's, prohibitive favorites, were swept aside by the Miracle Braves, the first time any team had been shut out in the Series.

The list of famous players Mack has developed or managed would make a respectable Hall of Fame by itself. In addition to Rube Waddell, generally considered the most colorful character in baseball until Babe Ruth came along, he has had two of the most famous pitching triumvirates the game has seen in Chief Bender, Eddie Plank, and Jack Coombs, and the later trio of Lefty Grove, George Earnshaw, and Rube Walberg. His catchers included Wally Schang and Mickey Cochrane, the latter often regarded as the greatest backstop of all time. Baseball is not likely to see again the equal of his $100,000 infield of Stuffy McInnis, Eddie Collins, Jack Barry, and Frank (Home Run) Baker. Such a quartet could hardly be bought for $1,000,000 of today's inflated currency. Among Mack's outfielders was Al Simmons, one of the top hitters of all time, who was named to the Hall of Fame in 1953, and he also developed that slugging first-baseman, Jimmy Foxx.

Yet not even the Pirates or old Browns or any other chronic tailender ever was represented for longer stretches by a more nondescript collection of humpty-dumpties than have played for the A's in their periods of famine, including the one that preceded their move to Kansas City.

It is only natural that such contrasting splotches of light and shade have made Connie Mack one of the most controversial figures in the game. Because of his long list of achievements, the great teams and numerous stars he has turned out, his magnetic personality, his shy and winning charm, and his profound wisdom, he has been affectionately and respectfully nicknamed "Mr. Baseball." All over the country, Mack has millions of rooters and well-wishers, most of whom have never seen his benign features but would know him instantly from the many photographs of him that have been published. I have seen strangers recognize Connie in hotel lobbies and railroad stations, walk up, and accost him; and I have never seen him give anyone less than a cordial friendly reception, not even those who were a few sheets to the wind.

Mack has been accorded honors such as no other man associated with baseball has ever received. He has been given testimonials from high officials of government and from men of science and letters. He has been eulogized by presidents, cabinet members, governors, senators, and business tycoons. To me, however, none seemed to say so much in so few words as one of Connie's own players, Walter French, an outfielder who is better remembered as a dazzling West Point halfback. After the glittering 1929 triumph, the entire A's squad was given a lavish banquet. During the evening, every member of the team was called upon for a few remarks. When it was French's turn, he stepped up to the mike, turned his impish grin upon the diners, and confined himself to one succinct sentence:

"When God made Connie Mack, that's all He did that day."

In order to understand how a team under the leadership of one individual could alternate between such contrasting fortunes, it is necessary to recognize that Connie Mack, in addition to being one of the finest sportsmen the world has ever seen, was essentially a businessman in his capacity as president of the Athletics. It was no accident that he had teams of magnificent power and others that were disgracefully weak. When Mack decided it was good business to have a good team, he got it—and hang the expense. When he decided it was good business to have a bad one, he had it—and hang the fans.

The Old Man (a term which connotes no disrespect when applied to Mack) may have guessed wrong occasionally, but who in baseball hasn't? Connie overlooked some good bets, the biggest of these being a chance to get Babe Ruth. Of course, at the time no one had any idea of the tremendous hitting potential of the Babe, but Connie was aware of his pitching ability when he passed him up. The opportunity happened to come at a time when Mack's plans called for a cheap ball club.

It is my belief that the only times Connie was far off the beam came within the post-war years, and that he was twice deceived by the same ball club. Apparently he at first underestimated the quality of his post-war team and then overestimated it. The mistakes led to the worst financial difficulties in which the A's were ever involved, and ultimately to the sale of the club to Arnold Johnson.

Connie's 1946–'50 team was put together almost as cheaply as the magnificent 1910–'14 squad. It is illogical to believe Mack expected it to be much better than the lackadaisical clubs that had preceded it. It was composed of a draftee here, a waiver player there, and numerous young hopefuls. Suddenly, this assemblage of bargain-counter discoveries caught fire and made two great races in the American League, although hanging in the stretch each time. For more than two-thirds of those seasons and at least half of a third, the team had Philadelphians dreamy-eyed.

All the evidence is that Mack then over-estimated the abilities of his squad, which simply didn't have the class of a pennant winner. He caught the bug from the enthusiastic fans and not only laid out a big price for the St. Louis Browns third-baseman, Bob Dillinger, but planned his season budget on the basis of a pennant contender. And then the team collapsed as unexpectedly as it had crystallized three years previously. Much older than the general public realized, it clattered apart like the wonderful one-horse shay and, with the Phillies winning the pennant and attracting a new record attendance, the Athletics played to melancholy expanses of empty seats. Although few guessed it at the time, it was the beginning of the end of the club's long life in Philadelphia.

As early as 1946 the public became aware that there was disorder in the House of Mack. Connie, who became majority stockholder in 1940, divided his 141 shares among his three sons: Roy and Earle, by his first wife, and Connie, Jr., by his second. This precipitated a family row that caused Mr. and Mrs. Mack to separate for a few months. She was unhappy with the arrangement that gave the offspring of Connie's first wife two-thirds of the stock. The Macks were soon reconciled but the controversy over the stock continued, with Roy and Earle Mack on one side and Connie, Jr., and the Shibe-MacFarland interests, which still controlled a large block, on the other.

The confusion and strife in the front office were reflected

in the team's performance in the field. Coaches Jimmie Dykes and Mickey Cochrane, who replaced Earle Brucker and Al Simmons in a move that was made over manager Connie's objections, hardly knew from whom to take orders. Meanwhile, the sickly condition at the box office put the Macks flat on their financial backs. An apparent solution came in 1950 when Roy and Earle got together and arranged a loan of $1,750,000 from the Connecticut General Life Insurance Co. of Hartford. With it, they bought out the holdings of stepbrother Connie, Jr., and the Shibe and MacFarland families. Mickey Cochrane, who had been made general manager by young Connie, was soon dismissed and Roy and Earle took complete command.

They promised that their father, who was to celebrate his 90th birthday in 1952, would remain as field manager as long as he chose. But no sooner was the announcement made than the pressure on him to retire as field commander was gradually increased. The only conclusion possible is that after the books were finally totaled up on the disastrous 1950 season, in which the A's finished last, Roy and Earle brought the final influence that their father could not withstand.

Briefly the Athletics showed signs of new life under Connie's successor, Jimmie Dykes. A product of the Philadelphia suburb, Bryn Mawr, and an old Shribeshire favorite as a ballplayer, Dykes was a logical choice to become the second manager of the A's. He escorted them to sixth in 1951 and up to fourth the following year, marking only the second time since 1933 that the club had been in the first division. The A's boasted two league leaders in pitcher Bobby Shantz, who won 24 and lost seven, and first-baseman Ferris Fain, who won the batting title.

But the prosperity didn't last. Shantz injured his pitching arm the following season and the Athletics slumped back into the second division. When Jimmie Dykes followed general manager Art Ehlers to Baltimore in 1954, Eddie Joost was given the difficult assignment of trying to check the club's collapse. Eddie's job was made hopeless by injuries to his best players, including Shantz and Gus Zernial, and the A's finished last, 60 games behind the pennant-winning Indians. During the long summer, the crowds grew smaller and smaller and Roy Mack denied one rumor after another that the franchise would be transferred.

That most Philadelphians had long since lost interest in the Athletics and cared little where they went was apparent in mid-season, '54, when a civic rally to save them turned into a dud. From then until November 8, when the sale to Arnold Johnson was approved by American League club owners, the once highly valued and respected old baseball franchise of Connie Mack was tossed and batted around like a warmup ball.

On August 3, with the Athletics already mired in the cellar, Arnold Johnson, wealthy Chicago financier, announced he wanted to buy the club and move it to Kansas City. The news touched off a flurry of proposals by unidentified Philadelphia groups to keep the franchise in the city. But Johnson's offer of cash (the deal totaled $3,500,000), the support of an enthusiastic baseball town and a ball park, which he owned and which could be expanded to major-league size, were not easily ignored, even by Roy and Earle Mack who hoped to find a local "angel." On October 12 the American League approved the switch of the A's to Kansas City. Hardly had the cheering in the Midwest died down when a syndicate of eight Philadelphia businessmen said they had pledged sufficient money to keep the club in town. The tug-of-war continued, to the disgrace of the American League and the confusion of the public, until late October when the club owners, without suggesting a reason, denied the bid of the local syndicate.

Johnson and Kansas City fans had to sweat it out right up to the final hour when Connie Mack, on his sickbed, accepted Johnson's check for $604,000. Separate payments of $450,000 were made to Roy and Earle for their shares.

The last chapter of the Athletics' history in Philadelphia is a sorry one and in it the aged Connie Mack plays a weak and passive role. But the new fan of the new Kansas City Athletics should be reminded that for all but the most recent years the Athletics were Connie Mack and Connie Mack was the Athletics. The two are so inseparably intertwined that it is impossible to part them. It is necessary to know something of this man to understand the story of the Athletics.

Cornelius McGillicuddy was born in East Brookfield, Massachusetts, December 23, 1862. However, he always celebrates his birthday a day early, on December 22. The records were lost in a fire and for years he believed the 22nd was his birthday before discovering in an old family Bible, that it actually was the following day. But he went on observing the customary day. Contrary to popular belief, his name was not shortened to Mack for the convenience of baseball box scores. Connie says his family always used the shorter form.

Connie was the third of seven children. By present standards, he had a hard childhood, although it never seemed so to him. He worked part-time in a cotton mill as a child. When his formal education ended with grammar school, he went to work in a shoe factory. But the tall, skinny kid loved baseball. He put in every spare minute playing it, and became well known locally as a catcher.

Mack's shoe factory was one of many to shut down during the election year of 1884, and he lost his $15-a-week job. Baseball had never before seriously occurred to him as a means of livelihood, but now he tried to get a job in the new Connecticut State League. The managers all thought him too thin. But his East Brookfield battery mate, Willie Hogan, was engaged as a pitcher by Meriden and he refused to report unless Connie, too, was given a job. Connie joined the team for $90 a month, which he regarded as so much money he kept it secret from the other players for fear of arousing jealousy.

Meriden ran second to Waterbury that year. It was a good season for the club but a sad one for Mack. Young Willie Hogan caught pneumonia late in the Summer and died within a few days. Three years later. Connie married his sister, Margaret Hogan, the mother of Roy, Earle, and Margaret Mack. The first Mrs. Mack died five years after the marriage.

The new Connecticut State League had no reserve clause and in 1885, Mack signed with Hartford in the South New England League. Fans were beginning to say the lanky catcher was headed for the big leagues—and they were right. At the close of the 1886 season, Washington made an offer for several players and again Connie's battery-mate, this time Frank Gilmore, proved a good angel. Gilmore, too, insisted Mack be in the deal and Connie was a throw-in with four other players.

According to all the evidence, Mack was not a star player, but he was a good one. A better catcher than a hitter, he was a smart, peppery backstop, and a great jockey without ever having to resort to profanity or obscenity. After catching for Washington for three seasons, Mack, with many another big leaguer, jumped to the Brotherhood and the Players League. Connie not only played for the Buffalo club in the new league; he invested all his savings in it and lost everything when the circuit flopped.

Then Mack was assigned to Pittsburgh in the National League, and late in 1894 he was appointed manager. His 1895 team showed promise but the club reverted the next year to its chronic second-division status and Mack was fired. Actually, it was the real beginning of his success story, for it led to his friendship with Ban Johnson, the aggressive young president of the Western League, and eventually to his career in Philadelphia. Johnson sent for Mack and offered him the managership of the Milwaukee club. Connie spent four educational years there and although he won no pennants, his team was almost always in the first division.

It was there in 1900 that Mack introduced the fabulous Rube Waddell to organized baseball. This eccentric was famous for wrestling alligators, chasing fire engines (and riding them, too), leading parades, and other gleeful clowning, but all Mack knew of him when he tried to get him was that Rube looked like a good pitcher. The south-paw was then pitching for the little Pennsylvania coal town of Punxsutawney. Waddell was deaf to all messages and Connie, not one to give up easily, went after him in person. He got Rube out of bed and after breakfast, Waddell suggested a little walk, as he had "a few things to do." The "few things" proved to be bills at practically every store in town, which Connie settled. Mack was practically out of money when they finally went to catch their train.

Pittsburgh actually had title to Waddell at this time but had made no effort to bring him in. Then, when the Rube proved his worth at Milwaukee, the club reclaimed him and took him away, much to Connie's annoyance. But he was to gain national fame under Mack later on.

Ban Johnson changed the name of his Western League to the American League in 1900. At the close of that season, he met with the more solid members of the circuit and they decided not only to expand but to move into the East and challenge the National League. Mack was chosen as the proper man to take over in Philadelphia, and Johnson advised him to get in touch with Ben Shibe, one of the owners of A. J. Reach and Company. Shibe had always been interested in baseball and had backed earlier Athletics teams, in the American Association and Eastern League.

When the National League decided on war with the up-start circuit, the American accepted the issue and began to raid the National on a wholesale basis. Mack concentrated on the Phillies and hijacked the great Lajoie with the princely offer of $4,000, nearly doubling the $2,400 Larry was receiving. Connie also took pitchers Chick Fraser and Bill Bernard and snatched Lave Cross from the St. Louis Cardinals. Mack also brought from his Milwaukee club Dave Fultz, Mike Powers, and the early home-run king, Ralph (Socks) Seybold. He approached and thought he had obtained young Christy Mathewson from the Giants, but Matty changed his mind and stuck with his club, a decision Mack had cause to mull over at length four years later.

It was at this time the A's got the nickname that so perfectly fits them. John McGraw had occasion to comment: "The Athletics will be the white elephants of the league." Instead of taking offense, Connie accepted the designation and it has been the club's official emblem ever since.

Ben Shibe finally agreed to back the new team. He took 50 percent of the stock, Mack was assigned 25 percent, and the other 25 percent was divided between Frank Hough, Philadelphia *Inquirer* sports editor, and Sam Jones, in the Philadelphia office of the Associated Press—an arrangement scarcely calculated to keep the name of the new team out of the newspapers.

Building a ball park then was by no means the project it is today. A piece of ground at 29th Street and Columbia Avenue, in the heart of Brewerytown, was leveled off, wooden stands were erected, and Columbia Park was ready for business.

The name Athletics was a popular one in Philadelphia from its many forerunners since 1859 and the new edition was well received. Lajoie led the infant circuit in batting with .405. During the season, Mack persuaded Harry Davis, former Girard College boy who had deserted baseball for a clerkship, to return to the game and signed a young college lefthanded pitcher from Gettysburg, Eddie Plank. This youth became one of two southpaws ever to win 300 games. The other was another Mack product, Lefty Grove. Connie's new team finished fourth.

During the following Winter, Mack continued his raids on the Phils, added Topsy Hartsel, and felt he had a real pennant contender. Then, on April 21, he got a stunning jolt. A Pennsylvania Supreme Court decision upheld the Phillies contracts, stripping the team of all the talent obtained from that club. Mack felt as if someone had jerked a rug from beneath him. Gone was the foundation of his title hopes. Despite the blow, his dismantled team won the pennant handily. The new league rallied to his aid with a few players and Mack regained Waddell, who was pitching in Los Angeles, after the usual difficulties in persuading him to report. The A's stole 239 bases, Waddell and Plank were mound aces, and Seybold set a record of 16 home runs that stood until the mighty Babe Ruth hit 29 in 1919.

To Mack's disappointment, the Boston Red Sox beat him by a wide margin for the 1903 pennant and the A's fell to fifth in 1904. But in 1903 he had acquired another gem, Chief Albert Bender, out of Carlisle Indian School and Dickinson College. Bender, by the way, was only one-quarter Indian.

With very much the same club that had won for him in 1902, Mack rebounded to the top in 1905. Connie himself admits, however, he was lucky. Cleveland had the most powerful team in the circuit but was laid low by one injury after another. The Chicago White Sox almost overtook the A's down the stretch but they were beaten off in a crucial series, the last three days of September.

By this time the National League had accepted its new rival as an equal and Connie Mack was in his first World Series. Although in time, winning flags was to become an old story, Mack never became calloused to the thrill of triumph. The success in '05 was particularly hard-earned. For one thing, the A's were deprived of the services of the great left-hander, Waddell. The ebullient Rube, engaging in a scuffle on a station platform at Providence, Rhode Island, injured his left shoulder on September 1 and was out for the rest of the season.

Every game of that World Series resulted in a shutout, and Christy Mathewson pitched three of them for the Giants. Bender scored the only Athletics victory in the second game, and Iron Man McGinnity, his victim, came back with a white-wash job in the fourth. Over a period of six days, Matty held the A's to no runs and 14 hits in 27 innings. The White Elephants batted only .162 for the Series. It was nine years before a National League club would again make such a show of Connie's performers.

The next four years were a period of building. During that time, Mack assembled stars whose names are almost as well known today as they were some 40 years ago.

In 1906, Connie picked up a young New York semi-pro, Rube Oldring. Later in that same season, he came up with a youngster whose name was seen in a few box scores as "Sullivan." This was the peerless Eddie Collins, a great athlete at Columbia University who wanted to retain his amateur standing. (Eventually, the deception came to light and Collins was a non-playing captain of the baseball team in his senior year.) From Colby College Connie obtained one of his most famous pitchers, Jack Coombs. In 1908, he acquired the former Holy Cross shortstop, Jack Barry. Toward the close of that season, he purchased from Greenville, South Carolina, for $325, one of the greatest hitters of all time, Shoeless Joe Jackson. And Connie brought Frank Baker up from the Reading Tri-State League club. In 1909, his short-stop on opening day was an 18-year-old kid from Gloucester, Massachusetts, Jack McInnis, later first-base custodian on the $100,000 infield, and his center-fielder that day was a former Philadelphia scholastic flash, Amos Strunk.

The season of 1909 was a milestone. It saw the opening of the present home of Philadelphia big-league baseball, Shibe Park, at 21st Street and Lehigh Avenue. When its doors were first thrown open, it was one of the show places of the game, made of steel and concrete, with seats for 20,000.

As the 1909 season unrolled, Mack's most glittering production began taking shape. Harry Davis was still on first, but to find a place for Collins, Danny Murphy was shifted to the outfield. An unpopular move when made, it proved one of the smartest Connie ever devised. Not only did Collins become the best second baseman of all time, but Murphy turned out to be a crack outfielder. Barry and Collins developed into an unbeatable combination around second. Frank Baker settled down at third.

Ira Thomas was catching great ball and 1909 also witnessed the most sensational debut ever made by a rookie pitcher. Harry (Lefty) Krause, from St. Mary's College, California, broke in with 10 straight victories, in which he allowed a total of only five runs. Six of his games were shutouts.

The young club ran quite a race, but Detroit hung on for its third successive pennant. The final series between the two in Philadelphia was fought tooth and nail and drew 120,000 for four games. It was in that series that Cobb spiked both Barry and Baker, infuriating the partisans. Cobb got numerous telegrams, letters, and phone calls threatening his life and had to be escorted to and from the park by police.

The 1910 Athletics were a team of youngsters, steadied by an experienced catcher and first-baseman and although everybody recognized their potentialities, they were believed too young to win a pennant. But they ran away with the flag. Jack Coombs scored 31 victories against nine defeats, Bender won 23 while losing only five, and Eddie Collins led the league in stolen bases with 81. However, in that same season, Connie gave up one of the best natural hitters in baseball. He traded Shoeless Joe Jackson to Cleveland, along with Morris Rath, to get an experienced outfielder, Bris Lord. Connie says he knew Jackson was a great hitter but his players never got along with him.

Seasons were even longer then than now and October 5, 1910, was a great day in Connie Mack's life. His players, dipping into their anticipated World Series' shares, bought Mack his first automobile. On the same day, with the pennant clinched, he let his son, Earle Mack, up from Utica, catch. The A's lost, but Earle was the batting star with a triple and single, which probably pleased Mack more than the automobile.

The National League schedule ran until October 15, a week beyond the American, and the A's tuned up for the Series with some exhibitions against a team of American League all-stars. The World Series did not open until October 17. When it did, the great Chicago Cubs, one of the best teams of all time, were expected to win easily.

"So you're the boys who think you can beat us," one of them chided the A's when they came on the field for the first game.

"We don't think it," snapped Barry. "We will."

And the A's made good his word by running the Cubs dizzy and washing them up in five games. Mack has always blamed himself for not taking the title in four straight. His team was nosed out, 4-3, in 10 innings of the fourth game, and thereby hangs a tale.

Having seen their old standbys, Orval Overall and Mordecai Brown, trimmed by the American Leaguers, the Cubs went with a new pitcher, King Cole, in the fourth. Leading 3-2, the A's had a great chance to wrap it up in the eighth. Baker singled, Davis walked, and after Murphy sacrificed, Barry was hit by a pitched ball, filling the bases. Connie was going to send up Topsy Hartsel to bat for Ira Thomas. Topsy had one of the keenest eyes in the game and Mack felt sure he could wangle a pass from the unsteady Cole. But Thomas protested: "No, no, Connie, I can put 'em over," and Thomas was pretty good at slapping hits in such situations. Besides, Connie didn't want to hurt Ira's feelings. So Thomas batted, bounced right to Cole and the Cubs made an easy double play. Then the home team tied in the ninth and won in the 10th, Brown getting credit in relief.

That was a historic decision by Connie, even though he has often rued it. For by not using a pinch-hitter, he preserved an astounding record. The Athletics played the entire 1910 World Series without a single substitution. No other team in history has ever done such a thing and the A's have done it twice! They duplicated the record in 1913.

Mack put Coombs back in the box next day and the A's polished off the Cubs, 7-2. A crowd of nearly 50,000 jammed around the station in Philadelphia to meet the conquering heroes on their return—and among the throng was a kid from Germantown who was later to give his boyhood hero many an unhappy afternoon. It was Joe McCarthy, whose Yankees were to become terrors, not only to the A's, but to all baseball. The champions were honored by a parade and a banquet, but a bigger event in Mack's life preceded that.

Mack was married for the second time on October 27, to Miss Katherine Hallahan, and it has been a long and happy union. They have had five children, Mary, Connie, Jr., Ruth, Rita, and Elizabeth.

Until now Mack had never had a team that repeated. But although he let another fine player get away toward the end of the season, releasing Steve O'Neill to Cleveland, his team remained at the head of the class. At first, it looked like a sad season for Mack. The A's were in the cellar after two weeks while Detroit won 21 of its first 23 games. But the Macks picked up momentum, rolled past the Tigers in August, and won going away. The World Series did not open until October 14. When it did, Mack relished it. His opposition was the New York Giants and Connie had not forgotten the way that team had humbled his 1905 squad.

The Series opener left him downhearted. Bender pitched one of his greatest games, fanning 11 Giants and allowing only five hits. And still the great Mathewson again beat the A's, 2-1. But Baker, starting to earn his "Home Run Baker" sobriquet, broke up the second with a homer and then pulled the third game out of the fire with another in the ninth. The latter came off Matty himself, and the A's won in the 11th. The series returned to Philadelphia and for a while, it looked as if it would never be resumed. For six days it rained, and it was not until October 24 that the teams took the field again. The A's then proceeded to cop the title in six games, blasting the Giants, 13-2, in the final.

Although the A's finished third in 1912, it was by no means a wasted year, though. Mack added three brilliant young pitchers, Joe Bush, Herb Pennock, and Stan Coveleskie, although the last slipped through his fingers when an agreement with a minor-league club went wrong, Mack also brought up two good outfielders from Baltimore, Eddie Murphy and Jimmy Walsh. Later in the season, he obtained Bob Shawkey from Baltimore. And during the previous year, he had completed his now legendary infield with McInnis at first, although Stuffy had missed the World Series because of a broken hand. Davis had been allowed to go to Cleveland to become manager there. Before the 1912 season began, Mack acquired a young catcher from Buffalo, Wally Schang, the best catcher Connie ever had until he discovered Mickey Cochrane.

The A's got back to business in 1913 and again met

the Giants in the World Series. This was one of Connie's happiest experiences. His team mangled his old rivals in five games. The only New York victory was a 3-0, 10-inning shutout by Mathewson.

Connie was now the first manager in history to win three world titles and it was said he could go on winning forever. Almost entirely forgotten now, one of the most vital decisions ever to affect the club happened that Winter. Frank Farrell, who had assumed ownership of the New York Highlanders, made Mack a sensational offer to manage his team. Mack would be the perfect man to offset McGraw in Gotham. Connie was sorely tempted and had he accepted, the entire course of Athletics history would have been altered. He went to Ben Shibe and said: "This offer is too good to turn down, unless you can offer something to offset it."

The something that offset it was the acquisition for Mack of the 25 percent of Athletics stock that had been farmed out to the two newspaper men, Frank Hough and Sam Jones. He and Ben Shibe now had 50 percent each. It was agreed Shibe should have complete charge of the business end, Mack to have full control of the playing end. Had Connie acquired less, it is possible he might have been pushed out of the driver's seat during the ensuing dreary years. But the part-ownership gave him a firm hold with the club.

Connie hung up his fourth pennant in five years in 1914 but has since called it the most unpleasant season he ever experienced. The Federal League had opened in opposition to the established majors and all year long stars were being enticed with juicy offers. Although they won the American League race, Connie says his boys went into the World Series with their minds on other matters.

The Boston Braves had captured the imagination of the country with the most fantastic triumph baseball had ever witnessed. In last place on July 4, the Braves, behind the fine pitching of Rudolph, James, and Tyler, swept past the seven other teams to the title. As a climax, they whipped the star-studded A's in four straight games.

Not only were the A's pondering Federal League offers, they were imbued with the belief they were unbeatable and could handle the Braves just as they pleased. To their dismay, the sensational Boston pitching trio stood them on their ears and Hank Gowdy assaulted everything the A's pitchers had. He hit .545 for the Series. The Macks came out with a sickly batting average of .172. Even Baker hit only .250 and the incomparable Collins a dismal .214.

Connie did a lot of thinking that Fall. Not only was the Federal League a threat, a world war loomed on the European horizon. And it had been demonstrated at the box office that the mechanical perfection of his team had palled upon the Philadelphia fans.

Mack always had his choice of any players developed by Jack Dunn in Baltimore and that Winter, he was offered a promising young left-handed pitcher known as Babe Ruth. But Connie was selling, not buying. So Ruth, Ernie Shore, and Ben Egan went to the Red Sox for a total of $10,000.

It must not be supposed that Mack dismantled his steamroller in one sweep. Just before Christmas, he announced the sale of Collins to the White Sox for $50,000, a staggering price in those days. Connie later explained he did it to save Collins for the American League but the 50 grand was no drawback. At the same time, Connie announced the unconditional release of his famous pitchers, Bender, Plank, and Coombs. Bender and Plank went to the Feds but Coombs signed with Brooklyn and helped the Dodgers to a pennant two years later.

It is hard to understand how the 1915 A's finished last. Mack obtained the veteran Lajoie to replace Collins, and he still had Bush, Shawkey, Pennock, Schang, McInnis, Barry, Murphy, Strunk and Oldring. He had title to Baker, too, but the home-run specialist, mentally disturbed by the continual Federal League offers and a countryman at heart who was tired of being away from home so much, remained out for the entire season. For some reason, the team scored only 43 victories, lost 109 games and was ensconced in the cellar for the first of seven long, bleak years.

Now the enthusiasm with which crowds avoided the A's was boundless and before the season was old, Mack sold Barry and Pennock to the Red Sox, Eddie Murphy and Lapp to the White Sox, and Shawkey to the Yankees. The following Winter he sold Baker's contract to the Yanks for $37,500 and they persuaded him to return to the game.

After the 1917 season, Mack picked up another $60,000 from the Red Sox for Schang, Strunk, and Bush and, before the Winter was out, sold to the same team the last of his stars, McInnis. The Sporting News said: "Connie Mack 100 Percent Efficient as a Team Wrecker. He Has Himself and Home Plate."

The Athletics of 1916 won 36 games and lost 117 for the lowest major league percentage of this century, .235. They were 40 games behind seventh-place Washington. The game offers no parallel for those dark ages of the Mackmen. Hundreds of players tried out; virtually all a youngster had to do was show up and ask for a chance. Often he would be put into the game that same day. It used to be said of those A's that they always had three teams: one coming, one playing, and one going. The park was cluttered each morning with hopefuls swarming over the field, trying to make an impression.

One of the most remarkable records of all time was made by Joe Bush in 1916 when he won 15 games and lost 24 for the weakest team of this century. And one was a no-hit victory over Cleveland! Considering his support, it surely must have been the greatest ever recorded. Bush, by the way, recalls a revealing sidelight on that era.

"We had lost 20 straight in 1916," he says, "tying the

American League record. Then I beat Detroit, 6-1. To my surprise, when I came into the clubhouse, instead of congratulating me, the team gave me hell. They said I'd ruined their chance of setting a new record."

Nevertheless, Mack uncovered some fine players during those years. Among them were Eddie Rommel, Whitey Witt, Joe Dugan, Tillie Walker, Jimmy Dykes, Cy Perkins, Ivy Griffin, Chick Galloway, George Burns, Charlie Grimm, and Charlie Jamieson. Dugan was nicknamed "Jumping Joe" because of his habit of deserting the team at frequent intervals. Homesickness was supposed to be responsible for this absenteeism, but Dugan confided to another player that whenever he went home, he got a little more money to come back.

Mack made a terrible deal at the beginning of the 1919 season when he gave Cleveland Larry Gardner, Elmer Myers and then threw in Jamieson to get a player of little worth, Bobbie Roth, who was gone by mid-season. The team, not too bad in 1918, now flopped back to a percentage of .257. However, Labor Day of that season saw the turn in the road that eventually led up out of the shadows.

On that day, scout Tom Turner brought in nine rookies: infielders Ivy Griffin, Jimmy Dykes, and Chick Galloway; outfielders Doug Welch and Red Wingo; pitchers Bob Hasty, Slim Harriss, and Jack Nabors and catcher Glenn Myatt. They were stones in the foundation of later top-notch teams. But there were no real signs of their worth for years and the Macks continued to drag bottom through 1921. Bugs Baer remarked the A's had reached the state where a base on balls constituted a batting rally and Huston, the Yankee owner, commented: "Mack must have Philadelphia hypnotized. Any other manager would have been run out of town." Mack had no hypnotic powers but he had what was more potent—50 percent of the stock.

Ben Shibe died January 14, 1922, and his sons took

over the business department, Tom as president, and John as vice-president and secretary. When these men passed away in later years, Connie's eldest son, Roy, became the head of the business side while Earle was Mack's lieutenant on the playing field.

A new bleacher had been erected in left field before the 1922 season and the A's led the league with 111 home runs, 37 by Tillie Walker. Eddie Rommel made a phenomenal pitching record, 27 victories against 13 defeats, and the A's at last emerged from the cellar. They were out by only one step, but they moved up to sixth in 1923 and showed strong sign of recovering some long-lost glory.

The boom of the 1920's was getting underway and Mack decided it was now good business to get a winner again. He had at last resigned himself to the fact that super-stars were no longer to be had for the asking. He already had acquired Bing Miller from Washington and Joe Hauser from Milwaukee, and now he bought Sammy Hale from Portland and got Freddie Heimach from Camden and Rube Walberg from the Northwest.

The 1923 Athletics amazed everybody, but themselves most of all, by battling the Yankees for the lead until late June, then fizzling out. The 1924 club reversed the procedure. They got away to a frightful start, but for the last half of the season played the best ball in the circuit and finished fifth. Mack blew $40,000 on a highly-publicized Salt Lake City slugger named Paul Strand but neglected to take into consideration the rarified atmosphere that contributed to his .394 average and 43 home runs. However, Connie had a less ballyhooed purchase, Al Simmons from Milwaukee, who became one of the game's most powerful hitters, especially in a clutch. Mack also paid Jack Dunn a good price for his second-baseman, Max Bishop, leadoff ace, who later became known as "the man with the camera eye."

While Strand flopped from the start, Simmons broke in

whaling the ball, but he was the center of a wild controversy. It was noticed that when Al took his stride to swing at the ball, he pulled his left foot back away from the plate like a timid kid fearful of the pitcher. Simmons knocked the cover off the ball despite his unorthodox style and was tagged with the monicker, "Bucketfoot Al." A raw newspaper cub at the time, I was sent to ask Mr. Mack if he intended to change Al's style. Connie looked at me pityingly. "Young man," he said, "anybody who hits the ball like Simmons can stand on his head at the plate if he wants to."

The deal that made this team was the purchase of outfielder Bill Lamar from Toledo for cash, pitcher Rollie Naylor, and the costly bust, Strand. Lamar was a playboy, but he was a dashing performer and could hammer the ball. And that Fall, the A's paid the highest price ever put down for a single individual, $100,600 to Baltimore for Bob (Lefty) Grove, who proved worth every penny of it and more, too. They also acquired the brilliant catcher, Mickey Cochrane, from Portland, Oregon, for $50,000.

It really looked like the Promised Land was at hand for the A's as 1925 unfolded. Grove was slow developing, but Connie was getting some great pitching from a previously unsung young right-hander, Sammy Gray. When the A's started their last Western trip in August, they were leading the league, the train was loaded with sportswriters, and it was dubbed the "Pennant Special." To their unmitigated horror, the Macks went into a tailspin that resulted in 17 defeats in 19 games, including 12 in a row.

Mack might have won, after all, but for one of the oddest injuries ever known. Starting to cover first on a routine infield grounder in a Spring exhibition with the Phillies, Joe Hauser somehow cracked his kneecap. This long ball hitter was never the same afterward and Mack replaced him with a quick pickup from Portland, Jim Poole, who did a fairly workmanlike job.

Mack had a far greater first-baseman than either on the way. Frank Baker had tipped him off that there was a kid down at Easton in the Eastern Shore League, who could knock a ball out of sight and Connie got him for a song. He was Jimmy Foxx, who eventually hit 534 home runs, more than any other right-handed batter in baseball and second only to the 714 total of Babe Ruth.

About that time, Mack went in heavily for oldtimers and gate glamor. He took on Kid Gleason as a coach, brought back the fading Eddie Collins, outbid everyone for Ty Cobb, cut loose by Detroit, and picked up Zach Wheat after the latter's 18 years in Brooklyn. Connie tried for Tris Speaker, too, but Tris went to Washington, although he joined the A's the next season. Connie laid out more dough for Joe Boley, Baltimore shortstop, who should have reached the majors years before, and in mid-season swung a deal with Boston for Howard Ehmke.

That team could doubtless have made a shambles of the American League of the last few years but it was confronted with one of the mightiest aggregations of all time, the 1927 Yankees of "Murderers' Row" fame. The Yanks set an American League record of 110 victories and the A's, winning 91, were 19 games back.

The Yankees were still all-powerful in 1928, but this time they got all the argument they were looking for. By July 4, they had a lead of 13½ games. But the A's had taken final shape with the addition of George Earnshaw and Mule Haas, and they suddenly began to run riot through the league. The Yankee lead dissolved until on September 7 and 8, the Macks won two successive doubleheaders in Boston and went on top by half a game. Then they invaded New York for the final series of the season between the two contenders.

More than 82,000 jammed Yankee Stadium for the

opener Sunday, but it was a sad day for Mack. George Pipgras, pitching one of his best games, shut out the A's, 5-0.
Then the Yanks reared up with one of their famous rallies,
climaxed by Bob Meusel's bases-full homer, to win the
second, too, 7-3. The last two were split but the Macks went
West a game and a half from first place.

That was one of the most exasperating trips any club
ever made. The A's won game after game, yet every time
they won, the Yankees won, also. When the Yanks did lose,
the A's lost. At last, came a Saturday in Detroit when the
scoreboard showed the Yanks already beaten and the A's
leading, 5-2, in the ninth, with Grove fireballing the Tigers
back on their heels. In the last half inning, the Tigers
pushed a run home and with two on base, Harry Rice, a left-
handed batter, tagged Lefty for a game-winning homer.

The Yanks hung on to win that pennant but it was the
end of an era. A new king was about to ascend the throne.
The A's made a cakewalk out of the 1929 race, ringing up
104 victories and leading the Yankees by 18 games. Their
.693 percentage was even higher than any recorded by the
1910-14 teams.

The Athletics' 1929 World Series triumph was as ro-
mantic as the 1914 Braves dash to glory. Now the Cubs
were led by the Germantown boy, Joe McCarthy, who had
been in the welcoming mob when the A's returned from defeating the Cubs of 1910. He had an awesome collection of
right-handed hitters: Rogers Hornsby, Kiki Cuyler, Hack
Wilson, Riggs Stephenson, and Woodie English. The only
left-handed hitter was Charlie Grimm. Gabby Hartnett had
a lame arm and Zach Taylor caught in the Series.

A few weeks before the season ended, Connie had called
Howard Ehmke to his office and said: "Howard, I hate to do
it but I'm going to have to let you go."

"I'm not surprised," replied Ehmke. "I haven't been

much help this season. But I've always wanted to pitch in a World Series and I'm sure I've got one more good game left in me.'

"All right, maybe you have," said Connie. "Now, instead of making our last trip, you stay East and watch the Cubs. See what they like to hit and don't like. And I'll pitch you in the first game."

When Mack called the team together before the first game in Chicago, they expected to hear an analysis of the Cubs and a ringing exhortation to victory. This is the speech they heard:

"You'll go out the side entrance of the hotel and a bus will be there to take you to the park. When you come out of the park after the game, the bus will be there to bring you back. After that, you can go where you like, but you must take the bus to and from the park. That's all."

Out at Wrigley Field, when it came time for a pitcher to warm up, Ehmke stepped out. The Athletics looked at him aghast. Most of them only mumbled, but the intrepid Simmons belled the cat. "Are you going to pitch that guy?" he demanded.

"Yes," said Connie. "Don't you like him?"

"If he's good enough for you, he's good enough for me," replied Al.

Howard proved good enough for anybody. He had that one good game left and he set a World Series record by fanning 13 of the hard-hitting Bruins. He defeated Charlie Root, 3-1, in a bitter duel. Much has been written about his befuddling the Cubs with slow stuff and "nothing balls." That anybody can strike out 13 big league hitters with "nothing balls" is a manifest absurdity. Howard had sharp side-arm and overhand curves and a stinging fast ball that he kept down on their fists. Mack calls that game his supreme thrill.

The A's followed up with a 9-3 victory and the two

scores almost duplicated the start of the 1910 Series, when the A's won the first two by 4-1 and 9-3.

The Cubs won the third game in Philadelphia and next day they shelled Quinn, Walberg, and Rommel and after six and a half innings, had an 8-0 lead with Root going great guns. They were back in the Series and if they took this one, they would be hard to stop.

The A's had made only three hits in six innings when Simmons opened the seventh with a home run to polite but restrained applause. Mack was preparing to take his regulars out to give some substitutes a chance to play in a World Series. But Foxx followed Simmons with a single and in rapid succession came three more by Miller, Dykes, and Boley and the A's now had three runs. Burns batted for Rommel and popped to English, but Bishop smacked another single to center for a fourth run and the fans began to sit up and take notice as Art Nehf replaced Root.

What happened next turned them into wild-eyed maniacs. Mule Haas sent a drive to center, a well-hit fly ball but apparently a routine out. Hack Wilson came after the ball, suddenly was blinded by the sun and as he ducked away, the ball skidded on into the deepest corner of center and the Mule raced around behind Boley and Bishop for a home run. It put the A's only a run behind and Dykes, in his glee, slapped the back of his nearest bench-mate. It proved to be Connie Mack, who was knocked to his hands and knees in front of the bench. Jimmy was contrite but as Connie brushed himself off he said: "It's all right, Jimmy. Anything's all right now."

The desperate McCarthy watched Nehf walk Cochrane, then replaced him with Sheriff Blake. Simmons greeted him with a hard single, Foxx followed suit, and Cochrane scored the tying run. McCarthy called upon Pat Malone but there was no stemming the tide. Malone hit Miller with a pitched ball, filling the bases. Dykes rammed a hard drive to left,

Stephenson leaped for it but it skidded off his finger tips for a double, driving in two more runs. Then, at last, the Cubs retired the side.

For sheer magnificence overcoming almost impossible odds, there is no inning in baseball history to match that rally.

The final game was a thriller, too, with the A's rallying for three runs in the ninth to win, 3-2. But it was almost an anticlimax after the demoniacal uprising that had preceded it. Again Philadelphia feted the Grand Old Man of baseball and he was accorded an honor such as never before or since was bestowed upon any one in the game. He was presented the Bok Award as the citizen who had done the greatest service for the city in 1929.

Mack quickly discovered all was not cakes and ale, however. His champions were hard to sign, especially Al Simmons, who remained in Hot Springs, Arkansas, all Spring while the A's trained in Ft. Myers, Florida. Connie continually insisted: "Al's all right; he'll be with us."

But the day before the season was to open, Mack called in the baseball writers for a surprising announcement: Simmons was not signed, after all. The next day, before the game, Connie sent for Al in a last effort at compromise. Simmons proved adamant and it was Connie who capitulated, to a three-year contract at a total of $100,000. Simmons signed, rushed to the dressing room, threw on his uniform and without even one batting practice swing, went up and hit a dramatic home run in his first turn at bat. He led the league in batting with .381.

The A's won almost as easily as the year before, but met sterner World Series opposition in the St. Louis Cardinals, just becoming known as the "Gas House Gang." The Macks were equal to it, and with the superlative pitching of George Earnshaw, they pinned down the Redbirds in six games. I asked Mack recently if anyone had ever pitched greater World Series ball for him than Earnshaw.

"No, sir," he answered emphatically. "George was terrific, especially against the Cardinals."

George certainly was. He allowed 13 hits and two runs in 25 innings.

Mack had often said: "A champion is not great unless he repeats." Now he said: "To be truly great, a champion must win three times in succession." His boys took the hint and rolled to another runaway victory in 1931, chalking up 107 victories for a percentage of .704, highest ever made by the team. It was Mack's ninth pennant. Grove had an astounding record of 31 victories and only four defeats. Simmons retained the batting crown with .390.

Again the Cardinals were the opposition and it was a chance for Mack to become the first manager ever to win three World Series in succession. But the Cards shut this door in his face.

"We were over-confident," Jimmy Dykes said recently. "We were getting fat and sassy and we thought nobody could beat us. We found out."

That was the year Pepper Martin got on a burning streak similar to that enjoyed by Hank Gowdy in the 1914 Series. The Macks finally managed to lasso the "Wild Horse of the Osage" in the last two games but much damage had been done. He batted .500 and stole five bases on the redoubtable Cochrane.

"What's he hitting?" Mack fumed at Earnshaw at one point.

"Everything I get near him," Earnshaw replied.

Despite Martin's pyrotechnics, the A's put Connie Mack in the seventh game of a World Series for the first time in his life. And he had no fears of the outcome with Earnshaw working the final game. The St. Louis fans shared his belief. Only 20,805 turned out for the deciding contest. But although the Cards made only one solid hit off Earnshaw in seven innings, they beat him, 4-2, with a bunch of bloopers and a home run by George Watkins.

The A's were still a magnificent team in 1932, but perhaps they were satiated with victory, or perhaps the Yanks had simply become a better ball club. At any rate, the Macks had to be content with second place. Their era had come to an end and soon they would be scattered to the winds. For years, both Philadelphia ball clubs had complained they were handicapped by being denied Sunday baseball. They were sure it would mean greater profits, more to spend for talent. They got the boon that season, but all it resulted in for the A's was the gradual break-up of the club.

Before that took place, though, Jimmy Fox nearly wiped out Ruth's home-run record of 60 in a season, and probably would have done so had not St. Louis picked that year to screen the front of its right-field pavilion. Jimmy hit 58 homers, and also hit that new screen about five times.

The nation was in the throes of a depression, the A's had a staggering payroll, and their attendance was declining again. Mack decided another unloading was in order. Most fans were convinced such a stripping of talent as Mack had engineered after 1914 never again would be witnessed, but they reckoned without Connie. In a few short years, he repeated the process all over again.

First to go were Simmons, Haas and Dykes, to the White Sox for $150,000. The A's slid to third in 1933 and at the end of that season, Mack sent Cochrane to Detroit and picked up another $100,000. By then, Tom Yawkey had obtained the Red Sox and was trying to buy up a pennant and Mack completed a series of sales to him. First he sent them Grove, Walberg, and Bishop for $125,000 and after the A's dropped to fifth in 1934, Earnshaw was shipped to Chicago for $20,000 more.

Again his first-baseman was the last to go. The Macks hit bottom in 1935, where they have been most of the time since. After that season, Jimmy Foxx, along with a young pitcher, Johnny Marcum, went to the Red Sox for $150,000. The last of the Mohicans had vanished.

Mack's seven-year sojourn in the cellar from 1915 through 1921 is unparalleled. But surely what followed was an even more dismal epoch. Nine times in 12 years the A's finished last, twice were seventh, and once tied for fifth. There is little to remember of that time except a monotonous succession of defeats, and a few more sales: Doc Cramer and Eric McNair to Boston, Pinky Higgins to Boston, Frank Hayes to the Browns.

Then, almost by magic, Mack assembled once more a team that stirred Philadelphia—and he did it almost as cheaply as that marvelous assemblage of nearly 40 years ago.

From Toronto, through a working agreement, he plucked two young pitchers, Phil Marchildon and Dick Fowler for $7,500 each. Old friends, former players, and well-wishers sent him, for little or nothing, pitchers Joe Coleman, Bill McCahan, Lou Brissie, Bobby Shantz, Carl Scheib. He drafted Ferris Fain from San Francisco for $7,500. Already he had an infielder drafted from Kansas City, Pete Suder. He made a deal with the Cardinals for Eddie Joost, who had twice failed in the National League. He took Hank Majeski off the Yankees' hands for the waiver price. Cobb had sent him a promising young outfielder before the war, Sam Chapman, a University of California athlete. From Palmerton, Pennsylvania, Connie picked up a young Czech, Elmer Valo, and he got Barney McCosky from Detroit for George Kell—a bad deal but McCosky did hit well. And from Cleveland, Connie obtained Buddy Rosar.

To say Mack visualized a topnotch team in this loosely assembled outfit is to take a great deal on faith. It looked more as if he was just going along as he had for years, picking up a cheap buy here, a cast-off there, in hopes there would be some improvement. But by one of those inexplicable combinations of circumstances that take place in baseball, this team suddenly galvanized into a winner. The young pitching staff looked like the best ever put together. Fain played first base like a fiend—and there is no better fighter in the game. The colorless Suder developed into a sterling second-baseman. Joost was positively brilliant at short and got the range of the left-field bleachers, Majeski became worth his weight in gold at third. Chapman hit many a long ball, Valo became a daring rightfielder, and McCosky batted over .300 and fielded acceptably in left. Rosar caught the best ball in the league.

This team gave the American League the fright of its life in 1947. It threatened into July before it ran out of gas and faded to fifth at the finish. Once more Philadelphians flocked to Mack's standard and many an enthusiast dreamed of a 1948 pennant. And again the team ran a terrific race. Truly, no team ever deserved more credit, for these A's got the last ounce out of their possibilities. They charged with the leaders until August but again hung in the stretch and finished fourth.

Contrary to general belief, this was not a young team. Only the pitching was youthful. If this miracle were to happen, it had to be quickly. It was not to come to pass, of course. And the club faded just a little sooner in 1949 and slipped back to fifth again.

By now, Connie Mack himself had been captivated by the will o' the wisp that danced ahead each Spring. For some reason, he had soured on Majeski, one of his most useful cogs, especially at driving in runs, and Connie traded him to the White Sox. But he shelled out a reported $100,000 to the Browns for Bob Dillinger in the belief he was the man he needed to supply the punch necessary for a pennant.

Meanwhile, though, a move had been made that evidently took away more strength than Dillinger ever could contribute. The A's fans were stunned in October of 1949 when the club released its two chief coaches, Earle Brucker and Al Simmons.

Mack announced with tears in his eyes that it had not been his doing, that the board of directors had made the decision. But the fans were becoming accustomed to sudden, sometimes calamitous moves. Only the season before, Mack had alienated many fans by an explosion of temper. He had taken back one of his former pitchers, Nelson Potter, from St. Louis, and Potter pitched some excellent relief ball for him. Then, because of one bad performance after a number of good ones, he lost a game. Mack fired him on the spot, right there in front of the dugout as Potter came off the mound.

Connie already had taken on the old Shibeshire favorite, Jimmy Dykes, as a coach and after the summary dismissal of Brucker and Simmons, he added Mickey Cochrane and Bing Miller. The Athletics organization prepared for Mack's Golden Jubilee Year with the whole country rooting for Mr. Baseball to get his "one more pennant."

The happily anticipated jubilee turned out to be a hideous nightmare. The magic touch Brucker had shown with the pitchers was sadly lacking and the staff disintegrated. Fate helped along by sidelining one pitcher after another with injuries. Phil Marchildon's arm had gone dead the year before and he was finally let out. Bill McCahan, perhaps the most promising of all the youngsters, ruined his arm after the 1947 season. Dick Fowler pitched as long as he could on his courage alone after bursitis crippled his arm, then was forced out. Others got sore arms— or forgot how to win. But for a rookie up from Buffalo, Bob Hooper, the A's would have fallen out of the league.

Dillinger helped not at all and soon was sold to Pittsburgh in an effort to salvage some of the expense. The rest of the lineup began to creak at the joints. The team fought a desperate battle to stay out of the cellar, then resigned itself to that fate and finished a bad last. Only the most faithful came out to view the bitterest disappointment of Mack's life. The Phillies, soundly rebuilt with youth by Bob Carpenter, developed even faster than their owner antici- pated and won the National League pennant. Philadelphia deserted its old shrine and followed the new champions.

As we have seen, the disintegration of the franchise was sudden after that. And in the end, only the public's fondness for Connie Mack caused any regret that the team was moved from the stadium which bears his name and transferred to Kansas City. Connie no longer serves them, except in an honorary capacity, but the Athletics, under manager Lou Boudreau and an aggressive new ownership, and playing be- fore big, enthusiastic crowds once more, soon may be able to recapture some of the glory that was theirs a quarter of a century ago.

THE DETROIT TIGERS

BY H. G. SALSINGER

Baseball history in the city of Detroit dates back, as far as the citizens are concerned, to an August day in 1905 when a skinny kid from Georgia joined the club. His name, Tyrus Raymond Cobb, meant nothing at the time. But within two years, he had established himself as the top player of the league and its leading genius, a distinction grudgingly admitted by contemporaries as he grew in stature with the passing years.

In Detroit, they are not concerned with what happened in the years B.C. (Before Cobb). I very much doubt whether 100 people in the city can name the individual members of the "Big Four" who won the pennant and post-season series in 1887. Probably not 20 among the city's population know that Charlie Bennett, one of the best catchers of all time and the man for whom the original American League playing field, Bennett Park, was named, was the first catcher who ever wore a chest protector outside his uniform. But they are fully acquainted with the city's baseball history during the last 49 exciting years.

They will tell you that four Detroit players won 18 batting championships between them; that five have been elected to the Hall of Fame at Cooperstown, New York; that Detroit had the greatest hitter and base-runner of all time;

157

that in 1921 every regular on the team with the exception of shortstop Emory Rigney hit better than .300 and the club batting average was .316, an American League record that still stands; that the Tigers boast the only third-baseman (George Kell) who ever won a batting championship; that two of their players (Cobb and Harry Heilmann) hit better than .400 in winning batting titles; that Sam Crawford made more three-base hits than any other player in history; and that the Tigers have finished last only once and that was in 1952.

They will tell you these things and many more, for Detroit has become one of the best baseball cities in the country in the last 40 years. During the Tiger-Cub World Series of 1908, a Saturday game at Bennett Park drew only 6,210 paying spectators. In 1945, the Tigers, playing only day games, drew 1,280,341, which was 398,496 more than the New York Yankees drew at home. For the last six years, the Tigers have drawn approximately 1,000,000 cash customers to Briggs Stadium each season.

Before the turn of the century, Detroit was a member of the National League for eight years. Although one of the great teams of the era represented the city, a team that won the "world championship" in 1887, attendance was so low that the league voted to drop the club. Byron Bancroft Johnson, the Cincinnati sports editor who had visions of launching a new major league, induced the city to join his new Western League, forerunner of the American League.

Johnson wasn't enthusiastic about his new acquisition, however. He wanted to shift the franchise to Pittsburgh, and would have made the shift except for the peace pact that ended the National-American League war. The pact, signed in 1903, provided that Johnson could place a team in New York provided he kept out of Pittsburgh.

Since the formation of the American League, five principal owners have guided the baseball destinies of the Detroit club. First, there was James D. Burns, the county sheriff and owner of a hotel bearing his name. He was installed as president and was in control of front-office policy under the direction and mandate of Johnson. George Tweedy Stallings, who later won fame as the "Miracle Manager" of the 1914 Boston Braves, managed the Tigers on the field. He also owned a large share of the club's stock. Burns and Stallings rarely saw eye to eye and Johnson, tiring of their bickerings, tossed them out of the league and turned the club over to Samuel F. Angus, an insurance man. Angus' bankroll was soon dissipated.

When he became head of the club, Angus installed Frank J. Navin, one of his employes, in the front office. Navin had attended law school and had also been a sheet-writer at the race tracks. He was an inveterate horse player and eventually owned a stable of thoroughbreds and a breeding farm in Kentucky. But at this time he kept the club's books and guarded the dwindling fortunes of Angus.

When it became certain that Angus would have to retire, Navin began looking for a purchaser. At the time, William Clyman Yawkey, the leading lumber baron of Michigan, was the richest man in the state. Navin began selling him the Detroit franchise, and the job of selling was near completion when Yawkey died.

When the lumber baron's will was executed, his son, William Hoover Yawkey, inherited $10,000,000. Navin convinced him that the Detroit franchise was a profitable investment, and young Yawkey purchased the club for $50,000 in 1904. Navin received $5,000 in stock for executing the deal, and another $2,500 went to Edward Grant Barrow, the team manager, who later became the strong man of the New York Yankees.

Navin went on to become a legendary figure in baseball. His stock holdings grew as he acquired additional shares each year. His influence expanded. He was the power behind the throne, the most influential individual in the game. Presidents of both leagues came to him for counsel and the late Commissioner Kenesaw Mountain Landis leaned on him for help. It is a matter of record that Landis called Navin on the long-distance telephone and asked his advice as many as 20 times in a single day. The Judge regarded him as the most astute man in baseball.

It was a strange relationship. Landis, the thunderous foe of horse racing, depending for guidance on Navin, the plunging horse player. It was his habit to take as many $1,000 bills to the track as there were races on the card and bet at least $1,000 on every race. At times, he bet as high as $25,000 on a single race, when he was certain that he had selected the right horse. He was one of the few plungers who kept ahead of the bookmakers.

Frank had the ideal "poker face," an inscrutable countenance that never expressed an emotion. He was cold, methodical, calculating. He did not smoke and rarely took a drink. He was parsimonious, watching every dollar very carefully, as his players discovered when it came time to discuss contract terms.

If Navin was frugal, he was no more so than William Hoover Yawkey, the chief stockholder and president of the club. Yawkey had inherited $10,000,000 from his father and when he died, in Ty Cobb's arms at Augusta, Georgia, at the age of 43, he had pyramided his inheritance into $40,000,-000. Most of his fortune was willed to his nephew and adopted son, Thomas Austin Yawkey, who used part of the money to buy the Boston Red Sox.

When Yawkey bought the club, he expected nothing less than a pennant. When the team went on a protracted losing streak, he decided it was time to act. Stalking into the clubhouse after a losing game, he announced that as soon as the players had changed into street clothes, they were to climb into a bus waiting outside. When they were all in the bus, Yawkey gave the driver orders to get started. The bus stopped at the first saloon. "All out!" shouted Yawkey. They all got out. He told them to step inside and line up at the bar. After everybody had a drink, he ordered them back into the bus. There were repeat performances at saloon after saloon until none of the players was able to stagger out of the bus.

The last stop was at a Turkish bath. Attendants helped carry in the players. They were given the full treatment and put to bed. At noon the next day, the bus came back and carted the Tigers to the ball park. Strangely enough, they won five games in a row.

As Yawkey's empire expanded and he had less and less time for baseball, he let Navin gradually acquire the remainder of the club's stock, paying for it out of his earnings. Eventually, he had complete control.

After several years of ownership, Navin decided it would be good public policy to have a few co-owners, so he sold 25 percent of his stock to John Kelsey, auto wheel manufacturer, and 25 percent to Walter Owen Briggs, auto body manufacturer, for $500,000. This was in 1920.

When Kelsey died, Briggs purchased his stock from the estate. Although owning the same number of shares as Navin, Briggs was a silent partner. He let Navin run the club as he saw fit and never interfered.

Navin and Briggs entered into an agreement which provided that in the event either died, the surviving partner had the right to purchase the remaining 50 per cent of the stock within six months, if he so desired. Navin fell off a horse and died of heart failure a month after the Tigers won their first World Series in 1935. A few months later, Briggs acquired the outstanding shares for something like $1,000,000.

Briggs, who had always dreamed of owning a ball club while he was acquiring his millions in the manufacturing business, finally realized his dream and made the best of it.

He spent more than $1,000,000 rebuilding the park that had first been Bennett Park, then Navin Field, and now became Briggs Stadium. He made it the finest and best maintained plant of its kind in the country, the only ball park that is given a fresh coat of paint each year, that has an underground watering system, and other features. He set new highs for salaries, paid big bonuses, poured more than $600,000 into one minor-league club alone. He was opposed to night baseball, but finally decided to install a lighting plant to accommodate workers who had no opportunity to see day games except on Sundays and holidays. Up to the time of his death in January, 1952, it was his only concession to the times.

Only one club, the New York Yankees, has won more games than Detroit in 50 years of competition. In the last 20 years, the Tigers have won four pennants and two World Series.

Their first manager, as already mentioned, was George Stallings. The Tigers finished third under Stallings and after the season Ban Johnson discharged him. Frank Dwyer managed the club in 1902, finished seventh, and was replaced the next year by Ed Barrow. He brought the Tigers home in fifth place and in the middle of the following season, 1904, left the club. Bobby Lowe took over. Lowe, an outstanding second-baseman with the Boston Nationals, and the first player ever to hit four home runs in one game, was finishing his career with Detroit. He had charge of the club during the remaining days of the 1904 season. In 1905, William R. Armour was installed as head man.

Armour is not remembered as one of the better managers, but it was he who changed the destinies of Detroit baseball. The Tigers trained at Augusta, Georgia, in the Spring of 1905, using the Augusta club's park for their practice field. Navin, now a stockholder in the club as well as general manager, went to Augusta to look over the players. As he entered the lobby of the Albion Hotel, long since burned down, he met Wild Bill Donovan, the club's ace pitcher, and Herman (Germany) Schaefer, second-baseman and the first of baseball's comedians. Schaefer told him:

"We've got a big laugh for you. There's a kid working out with the local club and he's a scream. Wait till you see this baby run. You'll laugh yourself sick. But don't let him see you laugh or you'll spoil all the fun. We've been having a swell time kidding him along. If you talk to him, tell him you think he's a great ballplayer."

Navin had his first look at Tyrus Raymond Cobb the next day. He was unlike any other player Frank had ever seen. He was extremely fast and had a remarkable quick start, going at top speed with his second step, but it was plain that he needed polish. He had raw ability and ran like a wild colt.

In lieu of rent, Navin promised William J. Croke, owner of the Augusta club, that he would loan him a player for the season and Croke promised Navin that the Detroit club could have the pick of the Augusta team at the end of the season for $700. Navin turned over Eddie Cicotte to Croke. At the time, Cicotte weighed 135 pounds, and Navin did not like little men for pitching. He wanted them big; the bigger the better. He always said that batters had no respect for little pitchers.

Augusta played Savannah in the opening game of the 1905 Sally League season. Cicotte was the pitcher for Augusta and Cobb played center field. Cicotte won, 2-1, and missed a shutout when Cobb, eating popcorn in center field, started late after a fly ball and missed catching it. The fluke hit drove in the only run Savannah got that day.

Andy Roth was catcher-manager of Augusta. He took a dislike to Cobb and, acting strictly on his own, sold him to Ed Ashenbach, manager of the Charleston club, for $25.

When Croke, the Augusta owner, heard about the sale, he immediately cancelled it. He appreciated Ty's latent ability. He paid him $90 a month at the start of the season and increased his salary to $125 after two months of play.

The Sally League season was in its second half when Croke asked the Tigers to select the player they wanted. He was afraid that Cobb would be drafted since a few of the high minor-league clubs, including Atlanta, were interested in him. The draft price for Sally League players was $350, just half of what Croke would get from Detroit.

One of Cobb's teammates was Clyde Engle, an infielder-outfielder, and Navin favored him. Bill Byron, who later won fame in the National League as the "singing" umpire, was calling plays in the Sally League in 1905, and he advised Armour to select Cobb. Armour took Byron's advice. He held out for Cobb, and Navin finally acquiesced, although not without misgivings. He could not forget the picture of Cobb in Spring training, the player who was regarded as a screwball.

Navin sent a check for $750 to the Augusta club, the extra $50 being for immediate delivery, and Ty made his debut in the big leagues on August 30, 1905, substituting for Dick Cooley, the center-fielder, who was ill.

Having sponsored Cobb and insisted upon selecting him over the protests of Navin, Armour felt compelled to keep Ty in the lineup. He played 41 games in the remaining weeks of the season and batted .240, the only time in his 24-year major-league career that he failed to hit .300 or better.

All this time, Navin was searching for a new manager to replace Armour. He finally decided on Hugh Ambrose Jennings, who had started earning his living in a Pennsylvania coal mine before he took up baseball. Navin bought Jennings' minor-league managerial contract for $1,500 and informed American League headquarters that Jennings would be installed as the Tigers' manager.

This brought immediate response from Ban Johnson. He barred Jennings, informing Navin that, "We don't want any of that Baltimore Oriole crowd in our league." This made Navin all the more determined. He told Johnson that Jennings would either manage Detroit or Bill Yawkey would withdraw his financial support from the club. Johnson grudgingly consented.

Jennings had played shortstop for the Baltimore Orioles when that team made baseball history. The Orioles were one of the roughest, toughest, and most resourceful teams of all. They changed the style of play, invented the hit-and-run, the squeeze and double squeeze, and other modern features of play. They produced more big-league managers than any other club. They won four consecutive National League championships and two Temple Cup series under the management of Ned Hanlon.

Jennings was redheaded, generously freckled, and had a perpetual grin that echoed, as Timothy Hurst once described it. He had been the most aggressive of the Orioles, specializing in getting hit by pitched balls to help in the scoring of runs. He was hit as many as three times in one game and 49 times in one season, a record that will probably never be matched since baseball rules now prohibit batters from getting hit intentionally. One time, in Philadelphia, Jennings was hit in the head in the third inning, played the game out, and then was unconscious for three days. He had played six innings by instinct.

Seeking a college education, he coached the Cornell University baseball team in exchange for his tuition in law school. One evening, he decided to take a swim. It was dusk and he didn't bother to turn on the lights in the natatorium. He took a dive off the high springboard and landed head first on the concrete floor of the empty swimming pool. He survived that, too. He had become accustomed to being hit in the head.

Jennings was the most colorful manager in the history of the American League. He managed the Tigers for 14 years, won three pennants, and made them the most spectacular club in the league. But his greatest achievement was that he enabled Cobb to develop into the greatest player of all time, a genius who revolutionized the game.

There probably never was a keener judge of baseball talent than Jennings. When he took over the management of the Tigers, he was eager for a look at Cobb, of whom he had heard much. What he saw delighted him and resulted in a resolution. He took Cobb aside one evening and told him:

"There isn't a thing about baseball that I can teach you. Anything I might say to you would merely hinder you in your development. The only thing for you to do is go ahead and do as you please. Use your own judgment. You can teach yourself better and get along faster than by the aid of any man I know. Just go ahead and work things out in your own way and do what you think best and I'll back you."

Jennings kept his word. He predicted at the time that within three years Cobb would be the greatest player the game had known. It took Cobb less than three years.

With Ty wrecking infields, the Tigers reached the Glory Road. The club had considerable talent, but prior to the arrival of Jennings, it lacked leadership. Jennings' enthusiasm and aggressiveness were contagious and, combined with Cobb's play, enabled the Tigers to climb from sixth place in 1906 to first place in 1907. They repeated in the next two seasons, winning three pennants in a row and losing as many World Series, causing Ban Johnson to remark: "We could win 'em until Navin hired that tramp from Baltimore to manage the Tigers."

Sam Crawford played right field on that rollicking team.

Sam had been a barber at Wahoo, Nebraska, before he entered professional baseball, therefore the nickname "Wahoo Sam" that he carried throughout his career. In Detroit, they still tell you that if Sam had been batting against the lively ball, he would have set a home-run record that would never have been approached by Babe Ruth or any other player. Crawford played four years with Cincinnati before jumping to Detroit, where he played for 15 seasons and set the all-time record for three-base hits—312.

Sam batted only against the dead ball. I have seen right-fielders, playing against the fence, catch five fly balls off Crawford's bat in one game, five fly balls that would have cleared the fence any time after the season of 1920, when the jackrabbit ball was introduced.

Crawford, the outstanding power hitter of the dead-ball era, made only 15 more triples during his lifetime than his teammate Cobb. Ty ranks second in the records, Honus Wagner third.

The 1907 pennant race was one of the memorable ones in big-league history. All Summer long, it had been a four-club struggle with Chicago, Cleveland, Detroit, and Philadelphia fighting for the lead. Chicago and Cleveland gradually dropped back in the stretch run and it became a two-team race with the Athletics in first place by half a game when the Tigers arrived in Philadelphia on September 27 for a three-game series.

Connie Mack had a great pitching staff including Rube Waddell, Chief Bender, Eddie Plank, and Jack Coombs, and a fine defensive team. Mr. Mack started Bender against Mullin in the first game and Detroit won, taking the lead by half a game. It rained the next day, the game was called off, and a doubleheader was scheduled for September 30.

Columbia Park, home of the Athletics at that time, had a seating capacity of 18,000, but 30,000 people jammed into the place. They stood and sat all over the outfield. Jennings nominated Wild Bill Donovan to pitch the first game and Mack countered by selecting Jimmy Dygert, one of the best spitball pitchers of the time. Mack had Eddie Plank ready but decided to save him for the second game. However, there was no second game. The first one went 17 innings and consumed three hours and 50 minutes of playing time. It was called on account of darkness and the second game was never played.

At the end of five innings, the Athletics were leading, 7-1. Jennings would have removed any pitcher except Donovan under similar circumstances, but Philadelphia was "Wild Bill's" home and Jennings let him continue, a sentimental gesture that paid off in the end.

The Tigers had chased Dygert in the second inning and he was relieved by Waddell, who stopped the rally cold by striking out two batters. He was less fortunate in the seventh when Detroit scored four runs and cut the Athletics' lead to two, but they got one in their half and were ahead, 8-5. The Tigers got another in the eighth and were trailing by two when they came to bat in the ninth.

Cobb came up with Crawford on base and none out and hit the ball over the right-field fence, tying the score at 8-8. Mack removed Waddell and rushed in Eddie Plank, who retired the side by striking out three batters in succession.

In the 11th, Cobb put the Tigers ahead again by hitting a two-bagger with Claude Rossman on base, but the Athletics scored one in their half and tied the score again at 9-9. Cobb reached third base in the 17th inning, but was left there. After the Athletics took their turn at bat without scoring, the game was called on account of darkness.

The Tigers left Philadelphia leading the league by half a game. They had two series left, one each with Washington and St. Louis. The Athletics likewise had two series left, with Cleveland and Washington, but they never got back into the lead. The Tigers finished in front.

Years later, Cobb said: "I experienced about every thrill that can come in baseball that afternoon."

Baseball analysts, telling how a pennant was won, generally point to one series and say it was the crucial and deciding one, but you can go deeper than that. You can point to one game and, more than that, to one pitched ball. The 17-inning tie game that enabled Detroit to win the pennant in 1907 is an illustration. Victory was snatched from the Athletics in the ninth inning on a home run by Cobb with a man on base. It was made possible because Cobb outguessed Waddell, one of the best left-handed pitchers of all time, illiterate but cunning, with great physical powers, a remarkable curve ball, and speed. Connie Mack used him in relief, sure that he could handcuff the Tigers, clinch a victory for the Athletics and return them to the league lead. A few years later, I asked Waddell how Cobb happened to hit the score-tying home run off him and he told me:

"Up comes this Cobb and I feed him a fast ball on the inside, where he ain't supposed to like 'em. I always figured that if this fellow had a weakness it was on a ball pitched tight, close in. The way he stood up there made him shift too quick for him to get a good hold of the ball.

"I throws the first one over the inside corner and he don't even look at it. The umpire calls it a strike but he don't pay no attention. I figgure he's lookin' for a certain ball and is sure I'll feed it to him on the next pitch, or the one after that. He's got an idea I'm going to work on him. I see my chance to cross him up. I says to myself, 'I'll feed this cuckoo another one in the same spot and get him in a hole, then let him guess what's coming.'

"I aims another one for the inside corner an' the second I let go o' the ball I know I make a bum guess. This Cobb, who didn't seem to have noticed the first one, steps back like he had the catcher's sign, takes a toe hold, and swings. I guess the ball's goin' yet.

"After the season, I meets this Cobb an' says to him: 'It's all over an' everything and there ain't no hard feelin's or nothin', so tell me why you don't swing on that first ball I throws inside to you but swings on the next one in the same spot. You're all set when I repeat the pitch. Did you get the catcher's signs or somethin'?'

"An' he says, 'Why no, Rube, I don't get no catcher's signs. I figures if I lets the first one pass an' make out like I don't notice it, you're sure to figure out I'm lookin' for somethin' else and cross me up by slippin' me the same pitch again. I feel so sure it's the same pitch that when the ball leaves your hand I jump back, take a toe hold, and swing. An' sure enough, it's the same pitch, like I figure.'

"I says to him: 'Kid, you had me doped 100 percent right.' An' sure enough, the lucky stiff did."

The Tigers lost the World Series to the Chicago Cubs, the last great team that Frank LeRoy Chance guided. In the previous October, the Cubs had been beaten by the Chicago White Sox, still referred to as the "Hitless Wonders," after setting an all-time record by winning 116 games. But they had their revenge in 1907, and the Tigers were the victims.

The Tigers won again in 1908 but had to wait until the last day of the season to clinch the pennant. Donie Bush, destined to become the best of all Tiger shortstops, joined the club at the end of August, replacing Charlie O'Leary. He arrived too late to be eligible for the World Series, but he was in time to give considerable help in the stretch run for the flag.

Bush was the most aggressive of all Tiger infielders. One writer described him as an "Injia rubber ball," after Kipling's Gunga Din. He covered "acres of ground," as they say in the trade, and had uncanny timing in throwing to first base.

Jennings also added a right-handed pitcher to his staff

that year, Eddie (Kickapoo) Summers, and a catcher, Ira Thomas, who was later traded to the Athletics.

The 1908 race is still remembered as one of the tightest of all time. Three Western clubs—Chicago, Cleveland, and Detroit—were in a virtual tie on the last day of the season. The Tigers were scheduled to play the White Sox and Jennings was counting on his ace, Donovan, to start against Big Ed Walsh, master of the spitball and winner of 40 games that year. But the day before the game, there seemed little chance that Donovan could pitch, due to a rheumatic condition that had developed in his right arm. All that night, the club trainer nursed Bill's arm, applying mustard plaster and steaming hot towels. Donovan not only pitched, but he held the White Sox to two hits while shutting them out, 7-0. Cobb made three hits that day and Crawford got four.

They played the Cubs again in the World Series and managed to win the third game, Mullin beating Pfeister, 8-3. But that was the only game they could take in the series.

Cobb did well against the Cubs making seven hits in 19 times at bat, scoring three runs, batting in three, stealing two bases, and finishing with a percentage of .368. He had hit .324 during the season, winning his second consecutive batting championship.

There were changes in the lineup in 1909. The veteran infield of Rossman, Schaefer, O'Leary, and Coughlin, that had won two pennants, was followed by a new combination. Tom Jones replaced Rossman at first base. Jim Delahanty, a brother of the immortal Ed, was the new second-baseman. Donie Bush had clinched the shortstop position, and George Moriarty, an aggressive third-baseman whom Detroit secured from the New York Highlanders, was Coughlin's successor.

The new lineup was eight games better than the old one that had gone to the last day of the season to win the previous year. This time, the Tigers won by a comfortable margin and met the Pittsburgh Pirates in the World Series.

The Pittsburgh-Detroit series went seven games and I still recall the mail-carrier in Pittsburgh, who won so much money that he was able to retire. This mail-carrier never attended ball games and cared nothing about baseball, but there was so much baseball talk in Pittsburgh just prior to the World Series that he became interested. He made inquiries, and one of the persons he talked to was a practical joker who told him:

"This series is all fixed. The Pirates will win the first game, the Tigers the second. They'll keep alternating, with the Pirates winning the seventh game and the series. But don't tip off a soul."

The mail-carrier tipped off no one. He drew out what money he had in the bank and bet on the Pirates to win the first game. He bet the whole wad on the Tigers in the second game and kept alternating, each time wagering his entire winnings on the next game.

I recall no other seesaw series like it. Fred Clarke, the Pittsburgh manager, surprised everyone by starting Babe Adams, a recruit. He beat Mullin in the opening game, 4-1, George Cobb spoiling his shutout by stealing home.

Bill Donovan beat Pittsburgh in the second game. Maddox won the third for the Pirates, Mullin the fourth for Detroit. Adams scored his second victory in the fifth game and Mullin scored his second in the sixth. Adams came back in the seventh game and shut out the Tigers, 8-0, clinching the title with his third victory.

Mullin, who was sold to Washington for the waiver price in 1913, is still credited with a number of Tiger pitching records. He won 29 games in 1909, a total equalled only by Hal Newhouser, in 1944. He set four Tiger records in 1904 when he started 44 games and completed 42, pitched 387 innings, and lost 23 games. He added a high mark in 1905 when he walked 140 batters.

The Tigers finished third in 1910 and second in 1911.

The next two years, they were sixth, but they remained the best drawing team in the league. I was talking with Connie Mack one day in the Summer of 1914. His team had won the pennant and World Series in 1913 and seemed a cinch to repeat. I remarked that the Athletics looked unbeatable.

"Yes," agreed Mr. Mack, "I'm pretty sure we'll win again. We have the best team in baseball, we are the world champions, and still we're being outdrawn at the gate, 3-1, by Detroit, a team in sixth place."

I asked Mack how he explained the fact that Detroit drew three times as many cash customers as his team, and he replied:

"The answer can be found in center field."

Ty Cobb was the answer. He had made the batting championship his exclusive property. After hitting .324 in 1908, he zoomed to .377 in 1909, .385 in 1910, .420 in 1911, .410 in 1912, .390 in 1913. He hooked together nine championships before Tris Speaker broke his run in 1916, but he was back on top in 1917 and went on to add three more titles.

A few other players probably had more mechanical ability than Cobb, could field better, could throw better, could hit the ball farther. But none matched him for speed of mind and limb, for aggressiveness and daring, for ingenuity and flaming competitive spirit. He has been called the greatest competitor that any sport ever knew.

His wide edge over the field was mental. He thought faster than his rivals and put his mechanical ability to more uses than they did. Many of his hits were attributed to superior speed, but that explanation does not hold water since several other players were just as fast. They did not cause fielders to hurry, to fumble, and to make wild throws the way Cobb did. They did not upset infields in the Cobbian manner.

Ty studied infielders, outfielders, pitchers, and catchers.

He made mental notes of their individual playing habits. Nothing escaped him. The mechanical moves of an infielder, the peculiarities of an outfielder, the unconscious giveaway signs of a pitcher or catcher were all known to Cobb. He knew more about most players than they themselves knew, and he used his knowledge to his own advantage.

In running bases, Cobb's lightning brain worked faster than his legs. He continuously crossed up infielders. He would break unexpectedly and fail to break when they expected him to run. Every move he made was carefully planned. Going into a base, he knew what the infielder would try to do and suited his own actions to counteract the infielder's. He was not a natural hitter, and when he came up to Detroit, he could not hit a loud foul off a left-hander. But within a few years, he hit left-handers better than right-handers, due to tireless practice. He could not slide when he started playing professionally, but he became the most expert and spectacular slider in history.

Ty led the league in total hits for seven years and tied for the lead in 1919. In nine seasons, he made more than 200 hits per season. When he batted .420 in 1911, he collected 248 hits. From 1910 to 1913, inclusive, his batting average was .401.

They flocked to the ball parks to watch Cobb, and since he batted third, they were in their seats at the start of the game. He never let them down. He played the string out in every game, never relaxed, never coasted. Where Babe Ruth appealed to the eye, Cobb appealed to both the eye and mind.

"The greatest thrill I ever got out of baseball," said Everett Scott, the durable shortstop, "was seeing Cobb come tearing down the base line. He always reminded me of a great thoroughbred streaking for the finish line."

He has been accused of deliberately going into infielders with spikes high, trying to cut them down, but this is best disproved by his base-stealing record. In his 24 years of major-league competition, he stole 892 bases. He did not steal them by going into infielders but by sliding away from them. He invented the hook, fallaway, and fadeaway slides.

From 1909 until 1934, the Tigers came near winning another pennant only once. That was in 1915, when they won 100 games, 10 more than in 1908, when they finished on top. But the Boston Red Sox won 101, and beat Detroit out.

Harry Heilmann joined the club in 1914, and while it took him five years to get into the .300 division, he won four batting championships and finished with a lifetime average of .342.

Bob Veach, Absolam (Red) Wingo, Bob (Fats) Fothergill, Heinie Manush, and other hefty belters roamed the Tiger outfield. Some of them did not rate tops as fielders, but they could all hit.

Unable to get pitchers, Jennings resigned after the 1920 season when the club finished seventh for the second time in three years. Cobb succeeded him as manager. He had no managerial ambitions but took the job at the behest of Navin, who believed that Cobb's agressiveness would be the inspiration needed to return the Tigers to the Promised Land.

Cobb, who has the highest lifetime batting average on record (.367), proved that he could teach hitting as well as hit himself. In his first managerial year, every regular on the club hit better than .300 with the exception of shortstop Emory Rigney. Heilmann, who had never hit higher than .320 before, finished the season with an average of .394 and the American League batting championship, for which he gave due credit to Cobb's coaching. The Tigers had a team average of .316, an American League record that still stands. But with all the batting power, unmatched as it was, the club finished sixth.

The Tigers did not hit as well the next season, but they finished three notches higher, in third place. The year following, Cobb brought them in second, the best showing the club made in the six years that the fiery Georgian served as its manager.

They say that no great ballplayer can ever be a great manager. Cobb did better than the average with one second, two thirds, one fourth, and two sixth-place finishes, but that was contrary to Cobb. He had to be first. He could stand anything but defeat. His main fault was his own excellence. He was always a play or two ahead of his opponents. He expected his players to be the same. He gave them the plays but he did not realize that only he could execute them.

In his defense, it must be said that he, like Jennings, lacked pitching. He developed hitters but he could not develop pitchers. The material was not there.

Cobb won his 12th and last batting championship in 1919 and now Heilmann, his star pupil, was taking over. While Cobb won in successive years, Heilmann won only in odd years. After finishing on top with .394 in 1921, Heilmann finished behind George Sisler in 1922, Sisler matching Cobb's 1911 average of .420. Heilmann won again in 1923 by hitting .403, missed the next year when Babe Ruth led with an average of .378, and bounced back in 1925 by hitting .393. The next year, his outfield mate, Heinie Manush, took the title with an average of .378. But in 1927, Heilmann landed in front again with an average of .398.

Cobb had retired as manager after the 1926 season and George Moriarty, one time Tiger third-baseman and later an American League umpire, was installed as manager. He held the reins for two years, in which the Tigers finished fourth and sixth, respectively.

Under Moriarty, the Tigers were distinguished for their ability to powder the ball, but not for much else. However, the club found unexpected strength at second base. Charles

Leonard Gehringer, from the nearby village of Fowlerville,
had joined the club, and he gave every indication of impend-
ing greatness. He developed into one of the four or five
best second-basemen of all time. Only Nap Lajoie ever
matched him for sheer grace. He had poetry of motion and,
like Lajoie, made every chance look easy.

Bucky Harris succeeded Moriarty in 1929 and continued as manager for five years during which the club
never finished higher than fifth—but it was not much of a
club. David Dale Alexander, a giant, was the team's first-
baseman. He was as awkward as he was big and one of the
two weakest fielding first-basemen in the league's history.
Detroit traded him to Boston, along with outfielder Roy
Johnson, in mid-June of 1932, and Alexander finished the
season with an average of .367, which made him the league's
batting champion. He could hit, but his bad fielding cost
more runs than he was able to drive in.

In the Summer of 1933, Thomas A. Yawkey, who had
purchased the Boston Red Sox franchise, came to Detroit
and asked Navin whether he had any objections to his signing Harris. Navin replied that if Yawkey could offer Harris
more salary than Detroit was paying him, he was free to
negotiate.

Harris signed a Boston contract and Detroit was without a manager. The Tigers had lacked an aggressive catcher
since the days of Charlie Schmidt, and the most aggressive
catcher in the league was Mickey Cochrane of the Athletics.
Walter Briggs had always liked Cochrane and wanted him,
but up to that time Connie Mack had shown no inclination
to put Mickey on the market.

After the 1933 season, Mr. Mack needed money. Also,
he believed that Cochrane, as well as Robert Moses Grove,
his ace left-hander, was near the end of the major-league

trail. He offered Grove and Cochrane as a battery for $200,000 cash.

Navin had been flattened financially by the depression. He wanted Cochrane but he did not want Grove, since he believed that Lefty was near the end of his career. If he could get Cochrane to manage the team as well as catch, he would like to make a deal for him alone. He suggested the purchase of Cochrane to Mack and Connie finally agreed to let Detroit have the catcher for $100,000 and a player.

Would Cochrane agree to manage? Navin sent an emissary to interview Mickey. Yes, he would be very glad to manage.

Now all that Navin lacked was the $100,000. He submitted the proposed purchase to Briggs. His silent partner heartily approved and gave him the needed cash. The deal was soon closed.

Navin made another deal. The year before, he had traded Earl Whitehill, the left-handed curve-ball pitcher, to Washington for Fred (Firpo) Marberry and Carl Fischer. Now he traded outfielders with Clark Griffith, sending Jonathon Stone to Washington for Leon (Goose) Goslin.

Cochrane, making his debut as a manager, announced in Spring training that the Tigers would win the pennant. Navin scoffed at this, saying, "In no other sports does form run as true as it does in baseball. We finished fifth last year and the year before. With Cochrane catching and Goslin supplying added batting punch, we should be a bit stronger this year and, with luck, finish fourth. Forget this talk about winning a pennant. If the club lands in fourth place, I'll be perfectly satisfied."

Navin, one of the keenest students of baseball, was wrong—and Cochrane was right.

As a field leader, Cochrane probably never had an equal. No other playing manager was ever able to lift a team the way Cochrane could. His aggressiveness was contagious. Under his leadership, the Tigers soon developed into a fiercely competitive club. He had the inspirational touch.

The Tigers met the St. Louis Cardinals, still remembered as the Gas House Gang, in the World Series, and it was one of the most riotous ever played. Dizzy Dean beat Alvin Crowder and the Tigers in the first game, and Rowe beat the Cardinals, 3-2, in 12 innings in the second game. The Cardinals got only one hit off the Schoolboy in the last nine innings. Paul Dean beat Tommy Bridges in the third game but Elden Auker won the fourth and Bridges came back to win the fifth.

With the Tigers leading, 3-2, in games, the teams returned to Detroit to finish the series. Cochrane had Rowe ready to clinch the title. He had had four days' rest and, considering how effective he had been in the second game, it seemed a foregone conclusion that he would win. But when Cochrane entered the clubhouse that day, he found Rowe seated on a trunk, nursing his right hand. It was swollen. It was doubtful whether he could pitch.

What actually happened to Rowe's hand has not been determined to this day. He told four different stories, none of which was credited. However, he pitched the sixth game, opposing Paul Dean. He threw with difficulty and lacked the stuff that returned him the winner in the second game. At that, the score was only 4-3 against him.

The series was now tied, and in the seventh game, Dizzy Dean came back to clinch the title. Three days before, Dean had elected himself as a pinch-runner and was hit in the forehead by a thrown ball, getting in the way of Rogell's relay on an attempted double play. Dizzy was knocked out and carted off to a hospital, where it was announced that he had a probable fracture and was through for the series. However, it was only a concussion, which meant little to Diz. He proved it by shutting out the Tigers, 11-0, on six hits in the seventh and final game.

The Tigers won the pennant again in 1935, and this time they met the Chicago Cubs in the World Series. It was the same team that had won the year before and lost the World Series in seven games, but this time it was different. The Tigers finally conquered their World Series hoodoo and beat the Cubs in six games. The sixth and final game is still well remembered. It was one of the most dramatic ever played in Detroit.

The Tigers had a 3-2 lead in games as they went into the sixth contest. Tommy Bridges worked for Detroit, Larry French for Chicago. Going into the ninth inning, the score was 3-3. Stan Hack, leading off for the Cubs, hit a booming triple. Bridges struck out Billy Jurges, the next batter, threw out French at first after bluffing Hack back to the bag, and retired Augie Galan on an outfield fly.

In the bottom half of the inning, Cochrane was on second with two out when Goslin singled him home, winning the game and giving the city its first World Series title.

Hank Greenberg broke his wrist in the second game of the series when he collided with Gabby Hartnett. Owen was shifted from third to first base, where he set a record by making four assists in one game.

A month after the series, Frank Navin died suddenly, and before another training season arrived Walter O. Briggs was the sole owner of the club. One of his first acts was to pay the Chicago White Sox $75,000 for the veteran outfielder, Al Simmons. But the purchase did not help the Tigers repeat, although it marked the beginning of a wild spending era to improve the quality of Detroit baseball. The Tigers finished second in 1936 and again in 1937, and it was on May 25, 1937, that Cochrane's playing career was suddenly terminated at Yankee Stadium. A fast ball pitched by Irving

(Bump) Hadley crashed against his temple and fractured his skull.

As a playing manager, Cochrane was without equal, but he was a failure as a bench manager and in August of the following year he was replaced by Del Baker, who was serving as a coach. Baker had previously managed the Detroit farm club at Beaumont in the Texas League.

The Tigers finished fourth in 1938 and fifth in 1939, but in 1940 they won the pennant after a ruling by Commissioner Landis had wrecked their farm empire. In January of that year, Landis emancipated 91 players owned by the Detroit club and at the same time indicted Jack Zeller, general manager, for practices outside the laws of baseball.

"I did the same things that Frank Navin did when he was running the club," said Zeller.

There was a difference as far as Landis was concerned, between Navin doing something and Zeller doing the same thing. He leaned on Navin for advice and guidance and closed his eyes to any sharp practices, such as covering up players, on Navin's part. He had no such obligation toward Zeller.

That Landis was grateful for the help Navin gave him was apparent in his ruling. The first announcement included pitcher Paul (Dizzy) Trout, and when Dizzy read his name in the list of the emancipated, he began debating the size of the bonus he should demand as a free agent. He already had two offers by noon the next day when Landis issued a correction. Trout was not a free agent. Further inquiry revealed that he still belonged to the Detroit club.

Rudy York's name was not included, and Rudy wondered why. By 1940, he was established as one of the leading sluggers in baseball and he believed that as a free agent he could demand $50,000 to sign a contract.

What Trout and York did not realize was that they had been covered up by Navin and that Landis was protecting the memory of his friend and advisor. None of the players Navin had covered up was set free—only those Zeller had shifted illegally.

None of the players on whom the Tigers counted was among those set free by the Landis edict. The club had strengthened its lineup by trading Rogell to the Chicago Cubs for Dick Bartell. Auker, Jake Wade, and Chet Morgan were traded to Boston for Michael (Pinky) Higgins, veteran third-baseman, and Archie McKain, a pitcher. Beau Bell was shipped to Cleveland in exchange for outfielder Bruce Campbell.

Rudy York, once described as part Indian and part first-baseman, had been tried out as a catcher and left-fielder. He fitted neither position. For that matter, he had never played either before. His only spot was first base and Greenberg was on first.

Zeller reached a happy solution. He induced Greenberg to switch to left field, making it possible to use York on first, thus giving the Tigers the best one-two batting punch in the league. Greenberg, batting fourth, hit 41 home runs and batted in 150 runs, and York, hitting fifth, knocked out 33 homers and batted in 134 runs.

Greenberg can be used as a model for any aspiring ball-player. He was flatfooted and awkward and had none of the natural physical ingredients associated with athletes. He made himself into one of the top players of the game by study and practice. He worked for many hours to develop batting and fielding skill, and while he was not the greatest first-baseman of all time, he was certainly well above the average. When he was converted into an outfielder, it was a similar story.

Hank came up the hard way, being prepped at Hartford, Raleigh, Evansville, and Beaumont, Detroit farm clubs. He developed into one of the game's leading sluggers. In the four years before he entered the Army in 1941, he hit 172 home runs, 58 of them in 1938 when he came within two of tying Babe Ruth's all-time record.

With York looking after first base, the veteran Gehringer at second, Bartell covering the short field, and Higgins playing third, the Tigers had a first-rate infield. Greenberg played left field, Barney McCosky was in center, and Campbell in right. The catchers were Bill Sullivan and George (Birdie) Tebbetts.

Heading the pitching staff was the voluble Louis Norman (Bobo) Newsom, whom the club had acquired the year before from St. Louis in a 10-player trade. Bridges and Rowe, stalwarts of the 1935 championship team, remained. Freddie Hutchinson, Hal Newhouser, Dizzy Trout, Al Benton, John Gorsica, and Archie McKain had been added to the staff.

Simmons had been sold to Washington for $15,000 after wearing a Tiger uniform for one year. Fox was now a reserve outfielder, as were Tuck Stainback and Earl Averill.

In the last week of the season, the race had settled down to a contest between two clubs, Detroit and Cleveland. The pennant would be decided in a three-game series at Cleveland, the last on the schedule. Bob Feller, then at his peak, was announced as Cleveland's starting pitcher for the first game. Baker countered by nominating Floyd Giebell, a slender right-hander who was virtually unknown to the large crowd. He had joined the club a few days previously, coming up from Buffalo, then a Detroit farm.

It was a precarious spot for a youngster, making his big-league debut in the largest baseball amphitheater in the country, in full view of more people than he had ever seen before—all of them rooting for his downfall and a pennant hanging on the outcome. But a miracle happened. The stranger in the gray road uniform of the Detroit club shut out Feller and Cleveland with six hits. The score was 2-0. the result of a home run by York with Gehringer on base.

The victory clinched the pennant for the Tigers, but in

the World Series with Cincinnati, their old hoodoo overcame them. Newsom, pitching heroically, won the first and the fifth games. In the seventh, he opposed Paul Derringer and the big Reds' pitcher beat old Bobo in a tough one, 2-1.

In June of the following year, the Detroit owner set a new all-time record when he signed Dick Wakefield, a sophomore at the University of Michigan, for a bonus of $52,000, a custom-built automobile, and a few other gifts. Wakefield at the time was the most sought-after player in the intercollegiate field, although he had played only one season of college ball. His father had been a major-league catcher until his arm went dead and he had taught his sons how to play ball from the time they were able to toddle. Young Wakefield had started as a catcher and had been converted into an outfielder. He was inept at both positions, but he could hit.

It was apparent that Wakefield needed further prepping in the minor leagues but talent was scarce and all the clubs were scraping the bottom of the barrel. Wakefield played in every game in 1943, made 200 hits (leading the league in that respect) and finished with an average of .316. The Tigers limped home fifth despite his hitting.

Before the next season opened, Wakefield was in the Navy, in Officers Training School. Early in July, he was temporarily released and rejoined the Tigers. At the time, they were in the second division without any hope of getting anywhere. Wakefield picked them up. He began hitting at a terrific clip. He ignited a fire that shot the Tigers into the first division. In the last week of the season, it seemed certain that they would win their seventh American League pennant. They were in first place with one series left. Their closest rivals were the St. Louis Browns. The Eastern clubs were finishing the season in the West that year. The Tigers' last games were the Washington Senators, while the Browns had a four-game series with the New York Yankees.

It seemed a foregone conclusion that the Yankees would trip the Browns while the Tigers would roll over the Senators, but that wasn't the case at all. The Browns swept the four-game series with the Yankees while the Tigers were beaten by Washington on the last day of the season, with Emil (Dutch) Leonard doing the pitching for the Senators. The Browns won their first and only pennant by the margin of a single game.

Wakefield owed the Detroit club nothing after the season. He had carried the club from the second division to within one game of the championship. In the 78 games he played in the last half of the season, he made 98 hits, including 12 home runs, scored 53 runs, batted in 53, and finished the season with a batting average of .355.

The following season, 1945, was probably the all-time low for major-league baseball. The war had enrolled nearly all the top talent and the clubs were compelled to fill their rosters with stale veterans and minor-league players. The Tigers were no exception but they got a break when Greenberg was discharged from the Army and rejoined the club at mid-season. He signalled his return by hitting a home run and a veteran baseball writer remarked:

"Well, it looks like the pros are about to take the game back from the amateurs and semi-pros."

With Greenberg's potent bat exploding regularly, the Tigers got up there again. The team to beat, strangely enough, was Washington. The Senators had finished last the preceding year but now, with a few days left, they had a grand chance to finish first. They ended their season with a record of 84 games won and 69 lost, closing their schedule one week early so that Clark Griffith could rent his park to the Washington Redskins, a professional football club.

While the Senators were idle, fairly confident that they would win out, the Tigers were fighting desperately to overcome them. It settled down to the final game of the season, in St. Louis. The Tigers had to win to finish first. It rained that day and ordinarily the game would have been called off. The skies were so heavily overcast that there was no chance for clear weather the remainder of the afternoon, and it kept on raining, but because of what was at stake the game was played.

Going into the ninth inning, the Browns were leading, 3-2. Hubby Walker, Skeeter Webb, and Doc Cramer got on base, bringing up Hank Greenberg. He took a full swing at a pitch and connected. The ball landed in the left-field bleachers, four runs scored, and the Tigers were American League champions for the seventh time.

The Cubs won the National League pennant and the two clubs met once again in the World Series. There never was another like it and those who love baseball hope there never will be. Never before or since has so much bad baseball been crammed into a championship series. It went seven games. Hank Borowy, whom Larry MacPhail had sold to the Cubs at mid-season for a reported $90,000, was Chicago's mainstay. He had been a Tiger nemesis ever since he had made his big-league debut. (The Detroit club bought him from Pittsburgh this year). Borowy beat the Tigers twice but in the end, in the seventh game of the series, he opposed the left-handed Hal Newhouser, who that season had won 25 games for Detroit and had beaten Borowy in the fifth game after being beaten by him in the first. Borowy had won the sixth game two days previously and was too tired to be a match for Newhouser, who beat the Cubs, 9-3, despite bad fielding support. After the game, one of the press-box pundits remarked:

"Well, we saw a new record set today. Newhouser beat two clubs, the Tigers and Cubs, in the same game."

The Tigers finished second in 1946 and again in 1947. After they came home fifth in 1948, Steve O'Neill was released as manager.

The club had lost its batting punch. York was traded to Boston for Eddie Lake in January of 1946, and the following January, Hank Greenberg was sold to the Pittsburgh Pirates after wearing a Tiger uniform for 12 years, during which he hit 306 home runs and batted .319.

The Tigers got a break in May, 1946, when Connie Mack brought his Athletics to Briggs Stadium for a series. He visited the front offices and inquired whether they needed a third-baseman. They had been looking for a third-baseman ever since Higgins had left. Mr. Mack said he needed an outfielder and would trade his third-sacker, George Kell, for one of the Detroit outfielders. He was given his choice of six and selected Barney McCosky.

Mack had given up on Kell. He considered him to be too slow ever to become a good fielder because he had "bad" legs, and he despaired of him ever developing into a big-league hitter. In 1943, with Lancaster in the Inter-State League, Kell hit .396, the highest average in organized baseball that year. On the strength of that, Mack bought him. After two years with the Athletics, Kell had an average of .270, and when he did not hit in the first four weeks of the 1946 campaign, Mack decided to trade him.

All Kell had to do to become a hitter was put on a Detroit uniform. He finished the 1946 season hitting .322, hit .320 the next year, dropped to .304 in 1948, when he missed 62 games because of various accidents, but in 1949 hit .343 and won the batting championship, the first American League third-baseman ever to finish on top. His margin was a fraction of a point better than that of the great Ted Williams, whom he overtook on the last day of the season.

After O'Neill was released, a dozen candidates were considered to succeed him. Spike Briggs, son of the owner and vice-president of the club, believed it was not necessary to go outside the organization to hire a manager. His candidate was Robert (Red) Rolfe, one-time third-baseman of the conquering New York Yankees and for the last year manager of the Tiger farm system.

Rolfe took over in the Spring of 1949. It took him more than four months to get the team properly organized, but in the last six weeks the Tigers were the hottest club in the league. They finished a strong second, three games behind the Yankees.

Rolfe performed a managerial miracle. He had only one sound infielder, Kell at third. He converted Don Kolloway, a second-baseman who had been tossed off by the Chicago White Sox, into a first-baseman. Wertz, who had shown little in the previous two seasons, suddenly developed into one of the power hitters of the league and finished third in runs-batted-in, behind Williams and Vern Stephens of the Red Sox. Evers, shifted to left field, improved all around.

After trying to bring Wakefield back to his pre-war efficiency and getting nowhere, Rolfe traded him to New York for Dick Kryhoski, a first-baseman. Gerry Priddy was purchased from the St. Louis Browns for $100,000 and the Tigers were set for the 1950 season as well as it was possible to be set. Everybody knows by now how they acquitted themselves under Rolfe's sterling leadership.

Actually, it might have been better for Rolfe if he hadn't done quite so well in his first year as manager. For in 1951, with Art Houtteman in the army, Hal Newhouser virtually useless and Hoot Evers peeling a whopping 99 points off his batting average, the Tigers sank to fifth place. Whereas the season before they had won 95 games, in '51 the best they could do was 73 victories. They ended up 25 games behind the Yankees. In July, '52, with the Tigers unable to untrack themselves at all, and the fans becoming steadily more depressed over the big trade that had sent the beloved Kell to

Boston along with Evers, Dizzy Trout and Johnny Lipon in exchange for Walt Dropo, Johnny Pesky, Fred Hatfield, Bill Wight and Don Lenhardt, Rolfe was fired and Freddie Hutchinson appointed his successor.

After the discouraging last-place showing in '52, the first in the club's history, the Tigers moved up to sixth the following season. Rookie Harvey Kuenn, a shortstop from the University of Wisconsin, and third-baseman Ray Boone, a failure in Cleveland, were the important figures in an exciting late-season drive. Manager Hutchinson, making steady and successful use of kid outfielders Al Kaline and Bill Tuttle, moved Detroit up to fifth in '54. Things were apparently looking up for both Hutchinson and the Tigers when the manager and the ball club suddenly parted. Denied a two-year contract but offered another one-year term, Hutch announced he was returning to his native Seattle to handle the city's Coast League team. The Tigers picked a man who knows his way around Briggs Stadium to carry on where Hutchinson left off. Bucky Harris, manager of the Tigers from 1929 through 1933, has come back to prove there is a lot of fight left in the Tiger.

THE BALTIMORE ORIOLES

BY BOB BURNES

The good people of Baltimore would prefer to remind you that 60 years ago the old Baltimore Orioles were tearing up the National League, winning three championships in a row, than they would that today's Orioles used to be Browns and lived in St. Louis for more than a half century, or until the franchise was transferred in 1953. Actually, as we shall see, a Baltimore fan can find something to brag about in the history of the predecessors of the modern Orioles and plenty to stir up a lively baseball conversation. For the Browns were alternately good, bad, pathetic and inspiring. They were seldom just plain dull.

Even the Baltimore fan steeped in the tradition of Ned Hanlon's belligerent Oriole teams of the 1890's will be pleased with parts of the Browns' record. There will, of course, never be another outfit like the original Orioles. They are still used as a synonym for the tough, spike-throwing, spit-in-your-eye type of baseball that, fortunately, has gone out of fashion. A hapless umpire of that day, referring to Wee Willie Keeler, Steve Brodie, Hughie Jennings, John McGraw, Kid Gleason, Wilbert Robinson and others on the Baltimore team, once said they ate gunpowder and warm blood for breakfast on the day of a game. Whatever it was, it made them battle like a pack of wildcats.

But the original Orioles, like the more recent Browns, had their ups and downs. They were a dismal 12th in 1892, which is four places lower than the Browns ever finished. We won't deny, however, that in 52 seasons in the American League the Browns presented an interesting study in futility. Before they were rescued by Clarence Miles and his associates and hustled to their big sprawling new home in Baltimore, the Browns spent only 12 years in the first division. They were about as familiar with eighth place as they were with the first four. They won a single pennant and had two near misses.

People made bad jokes about the Browns. The St. Louis counterpart to the famous Washington chant of "first in war, etc.," was "first in booze, first in shoes and last in the American League." Others used to say that "the Browns spend more time in the courts than they do in the first division."

If nothing else, the Browns were a turbulent organization and they had their moments. It seemed as if they were always suing somebody or being sued, that they were selling ballplayers, or obtaining others past their prime. But they were not without claims to greatness.

From the time they entered the American League in 1902 until approximately 1926, the Browns more than held their own. They were the favorite team in St. Louis and the Cardinals were the poor relations who were always broke and generally in the second division.

But in 1926 the Cards won their first National League pennant and after that, except for the brief reign of Luke Sewell during which they finished first in '44, the Browns were the other team in St. Louis, playing a constant and discordant second-fiddle to the high-flying Cardinals. Even the one pennant came under a shadow. While they were winning with a great finish, the Cards loafed to victory. That's the way it went for the Browns.

When the Browns' George Sisler was hitting at a tremendous clip in the American League, Rogers Hornsby was doing equally well for the Cardinals. When the Browns brought up Bobo Newsom in the Thirties, the Cardinals had Dizzy Dean who was a little more colorful and a better pitcher.

Since 1926, the Browns hired various men who, as players, coaches or managers had achieved success with the Cardinals, hoping that the great talent they had shown on the other side of the fence would work for them, too. Hornsby, Bill Killefer, Gabby Street and Jim Bottomley all had a try at resurrecting the Browns. None succeeded.

More recently, Marty Marion was unable to lift the Browns out of their rut in a two-year try as manager.

The one man who reversed the procedure, who went from the Browns to the Cardinals, is more responsible than anyone else for exchanging the fortunes of the two St. Louis clubs. Branch Rickey came to the Cardinals from the Browns in 1917.

He had been replaced by Fielder Jones. The work of Rickey did not produce big results until a decade later when his farm system policy began to pay dividends. But in his first year with the Cards Rickey made another important contribution to the club's growth.

He organized the Knot Hole Gang.

His idea of admitting youngsters into the bleachers and, later, into the left wing of the grandstand free of charge helped account for the difference in attendance between the two St. Louis teams in post-war years. The Knot Holers of 20 and 30 years ago are solid Cardinal customers today. Those fans who grew up with the Cardinals liked what they saw and Bill Veeck nor anyone before him on the Browns could persuade them to change their affiliations.

Yet right up to the Browns' last gasp you could hear fans say "St. Louis is a Browns' town." It was said in the face of attendance figures which showed the Cardinals playing to a million or more customers while the Browns were drawing an average of approximately 350,000. The year they both won a pennant, 1944, the Browns outdrew the Cardinals at Sportsman's Park by about 21,000.

It was only natural then that during their last years in St. Louis, Brownie fans took refuge in the past glories of the team which goes back to 1869.

Fire Chief Henry Sexton organized a club called the "Empires," which was the best in the vicinity. In September of 1869, the famed Cincinnati Red Stockings played and defeated the Empires in St. Louis, 31-9. A day or two earlier, the Red Stockings had walloped the Empires' bitter rivals, the "unions," 70-9.

In the mid-Seventies, the team changed its name to the Brown Stockings and moved to Sportsmans Park, located, as it is today, on North Grand at Dodier Street. The park is the oldest in virtually continuous use in the majors. No one is sure how it was named, or why it was ungrammatically called "Sportsman."

In 1876 and 1877, the Brown Stockings played in the newly-formed National League, with pitcher George Bradley, who contributed an early no-hitter, as its ace performer. Membership in the league was confined to those two years. When St. Louis returned to the National League in 1885, it was with different personnel.

The Brown Stockings went on playing independently until 1881 when they were sufficiently improved to turn the tables on Cincinnati's Red Stockings, this time by a 15-8 score. Another game that season marked one of the important milestones in the history of the organization. The Dubuque Rabbits came to Sportsmans Park for a game and were defeated by the Browns, 9-1. The visitors' first-baseman, a tall, lanky individual who displayed real agility around the base, made such an impression on fans here that he was persuaded to stay on.

His name was Charles Comiskey. He quickly rose to captaincy of the famed Browns' team which won four successive American Association pennants in 1885, 1886, 1887 and 1888, plus world championships the first two years. From the Browns, Comiskey moved to Chicago and eventually took complete control of the Chicago American Leaguers, an organization which remains in his family today.

Comiskey's arrival with the Browns was practically simultaneous with that of one of the most fabulous characters baseball has ever known—Chris Von Der Ahe, "Der Poss President," as he termed himself.

Chris financed the ball club; Comiskey ran it. That was the general idea but it never worked that way. Von Der Ahe wasn't built to sit in the background or out of the limelight.

He had a variety of interests but it was as a saloon keeper that he became aware of baseball. His saloon was a block South of the ball park and he discovered that when games were played, he had more and thirstier customers. His bartender, Edgar Cuthbert, an itinerant outfielder who had played with Chicago and occasionally filled in for the Browns, suggested that business would pick up if Von Der Ahe could bring the beer to the fans. The best way to do this was buy an interest in the team and supply beer on the spot.

Thus, in partnership with W. W. Judy and newspaperman Al Spink in 1880, he bought into the ball club, which by now was in the six-club American Association. On this team, which won four successive pennants, there were some great players—Comiskey, pitchers Dave Foutz and Bobby Carruthers, Tip O'Neill in the outfield and Arlie Latham at third.

Like others on the team, Latham lived in one of Von Der Ahe's boarding houses. Being close to the players, Chris tried to take a more active part in operating the club. This led to the Browns' undoing. Comiskey insisted that the captain (or manager) must have complete control. In addition, Von Der Ahe's love of high living was getting out of hand and his fortune was dissipating. In 1889, he sold Latham, Foutz and Carruthers to other clubs without consulting Comiskey. The latter, incensed, left for Chicago after the season. By that time, the ball club had disintegrated.

Until 1902, there were no Browns in St. Louis and Sportsmans Park lay idle. The National League Maroons were operating a few blocks away, but fans were tired of watching baseball only as a sideshow to fireworks displays and band concerts.

Ban Johnson, who with the Spink family, was trying to organize a new major league, wanted to put a team in St. Louis. No sponsor could be found in the city but Johnson eventually located the man he wanted, Robert Lee Hedges, a Cincinnati carriagemaker. He persuaded Hedges to move the franchise operated in Milwaukee by Matt and Tim Killilea to St. Louis. Hedges was dubious at first but, with a promise of firm backing, he agreed.

On April 23, 1902, in refurbished Sportsmans Park, the Browns had an auspicious American League opening before 8,000 fans, defeating Cleveland, 5-2.

True to his promise, Johnson produced players to give manager Jim McAleer a capable team. He did this by taking the cream of the Maroons, or Cardinals: outfielders Jess Burkett and Emmett Heidrick, shortstop Bobby Wallace, catcher Joe Sugden and pitcher Jiggs Donahue. The latter hurled the opening victory, Burkett got two hits and Wallace smashed a home run in a five-run fourth inning.

The Browns finished second their first year in the league with 78 victories and 58 defeats, five games back of the champion Athletics. That was the high mark of McAleer's eight-year regime and in fact, the team's best finish for 20 years. The next three seasons saw the Browns end up in the second division. They dropped to the cellar in 1905. The following year, 1906, the club moved up to fifth and had its first batting champion in outfielder George Stone, who hit .358.

Stone, perhaps, is the least-known batting champion in American League history. Poor health plagued him during a good part of his career, so he never again reached the heights he attained that season. Stone was also one of baseball's silent men. "He's so quiet," McAleer once told friends, "that we always go looking for him when we're getting off a train. If we didn't lead him off, they mightn't find him for weeks."

Despite the in-and-out performance of the club on the field, president Hedges was making money at the box office, and in 1908, he poured the profits back into the ball club. Sportsmans Park was rebuilt and the capacity was increased to almost 18,000. In February of 1908, Hedges bought pitcher Rube Waddell from the Athletics after Connie Mack had given up on him.

The Rube was as much of a problem with the Browns as he had been with the Athletics, but he was sure box-office material and Hedges found a quick return on his investment. The first time that Waddell pitched for the Browns in Philadelphia that season, a crowd of 24,000 turned out. On July 29, he fanned 16 Philadelphia batters in a game. Waddell wound up with a record of 19 victories and 14 defeats, helping the Browns to a fourth-place finish. The four Western clubs battled down to the wire with Detroit, Cleveland and Chicago preceding the Browns in the race.

Considering that the club finished in the first division only twice in his eight years as leader, it was surprising that McAleer held on as long as he did. He was popular with the fans and with the players—too popular, in fact, for his easy-going disposition led to his downfall. As long as the club made money, Hedges agreed with the status quo.

When McAleer was dismissed, catcher Jack O'Connor, a native of St. Louis and a popular figure, was named to replace him. In quick succession, the Browns had three managers in as many years, O'Connor, Bobby Wallace and George Stovall. Two, O'Connor and Stovall, were dismissed on league orders. O'Connor's trouble developed on the final day of the 1910 season as the Browns were finishing an inglorious last. Their opponents were the Cleveland Indians whose second-baseman, Nap Lajoie, was in a furious battle with Ty Cobb for the league batting crown.

Lajoie went to bat nine times in the twin bill and hit safely on his first eight trips, many of them slow rolling taps or plain bunts down the third-base line. The third-baseman was rookie John (Red) Corriden. Despite the succession of tricklers in his direction, he persisted in playing an unusually deep position. On his final appearance at the plate, Lajoie hit a ground ball to shortstop Bobby Wallace, who fumbled the chance. The official scorer called it an error but a few minutes later, a message came to the press box, signed by coach Howell, stating that if the scorer saw his way clear to calling it a hit, he would receive a suit of clothes.

The scorer stuck by his guns and it cost Lajoie the batting championship, ousted two men from baseball and hampered the career of the third one. Cobb edged out Lajoie by a fraction of a point (although it was so close an auto manufacturer awarded cars to both of them) and president Hedges, informed of the message by the scorer, went immediately to Ban Johnson.

After hearing a report of the affair, Johnson banned manager O'Connor and coach Howell from baseball for life and took the matter of Corriden "under consideration." Corriden, a rookie who had simply been taking orders from superiors, went back to the minors.

Hedges replaced O'Connor with Bobby Wallace but the

latter, a great fielder and popular with everyone, just wasn't cut out to be a manager. He knew it better than anyone else and begged off in the middle of his second season. Stovall finished the campaign and started the next one but he, too, was ousted by official order when he spewed tobacco juice all over an umpire while protesting a called third strike.

Infielder Jimmy Austin, who was to linger with the Browns for many years, finished out the season as manager but before the campaign had ended, Hedges had another pilot lined up for 1914. He remembered a second-string catcher who had warmed the Browns' bench a few seasons earlier. Hedges admitted he was the worst catcher he had ever seen, but he was impressed by the man's clean-cut appearance and habits and his sharp knowledge of how the game should be played. After unhappy experiences with his three previous managers, Hedges wanted someone who would cause no official trouble. So he sent out a call for Branch Rickey, a lawyer and part-time baseball coach at the University of Michigan.

Rickey made one important contribution to the Browns. He enabled the Browns to obtain the greatest player the club ever has had, the incomparable George Sisler.

It was an important acquisition for baseball, too. Sisler was not procured easily and a long and bitter court battle was waged over his services. The decision that brought him to the Browns led to the dissolving of the "Three-man Commission" and, indirectly, to the installation of Judge Landis as supreme commissioner of the game.

Sisler's hitting and pitching prowess at Akron (Ohio) High School attracted attention in 1910 and the Akron club of the Ohio-Pennsylvania League signed him to a contract. Instead of reporting, he played independent ball for a year at Barberton, Ohio, then enrolled at the University of Michigan, where he was a standout for four years and where, incidentally, he was coached by Rickey.

Akron sold his contract to Columbus of the American Association, which in turn delivered it to Pittsburgh in 1913. Sisler, unaware of these behind-the-scenes maneuvers, went on playing college ball at Michigan and when he had completed his career there, his old coach, Branch Rickey, was waiting for him, contract in hand.

Sisler came to the Browns primarily as a pitcher and his first three seasons, 1915, '16 and '17, he divided time between the mound, first base and the outfield. After that, he was exclusively a first-baseman, perhaps the finest fielder the position has ever seen. Only Hal Chase has challenged his defensive greatness. His hitting, of course, was superb, reaching its peak with his magnificent .420 in 1922. Failing eyesight ended his career too soon.

Sisler was painfully shy and retiring, so much so that it led to a false impression that he was something of a college sophisticate. This impression, unfortunately, was enhanced by his eye trouble. Often he passed friends and acquaintances without recognizing them. Those who knew Sisler then and know him now will tell you that George was, and is, quiet, sincerely unassuming and modest to a fault. He had a burning competitive spirit which few, even on the ball field, recognized at all times.

One incident, in particular, illustrates Sisler's character. It occurred on September 11, 1922, at Sportsmans Park with the Browns making a desperate fight against the Yankees for the pennant. Sisler was threatening two of Ty Cobb's records, both established in 1911. Cobb had batted .420 that year and had hit in 40 consecutive games.

On this September afternoon, Sisler had a good chance to equal or pass that .420 average, high batting mark of the American League. More important, he had hit in 38 consecutive games, only two away from Ty's record. The Browns, with every game important, were trailing the Tigers, 4-3, in the ninth. With two out, Chick Foster beat out an infield hit and brought Sisler to bat.

As far as Cobb, then managing the Tigers, and Sisler knew, George hadn't had a hit all afternoon. Actually, a lenient official scorer had credited him with a hit on a pop fly in the sixth inning which Bobby Veach reached but couldn't hold.

For two reasons, Cobb couldn't walk Sisler. It would put the tying run in scoring position and move the winning run to base. In addition, Cobb, the holder of the consecutive-game record, couldn't risk criticism of walking a man and withdrawing his last chance to keep a rival streak alive.

So Cobb gambled. He called Ira Flagstead, a good defensive outfielder, off the bench and substituted him for Bob Fothergill in right field. He motioned Flagstead to deep right center and stationed himself only about 15 yards to Flagstead's right. It was a big challenge for one of the greatest place hitters the game has ever known. Sisler could have pulled the ball down the line or hit into the yawning gaps in left. Instead, he took Cobb's dare.

Sisler hit Howard Ehmke's first pitch on a line between Cobb and Flagstead in right center. It went for a triple and a moment later, Marty McManus singled Sisler home to win the game. Three days after that, Sisler broke Cobb's record by hitting in his 41st game.

Before Sisler joined Rickey in St. Louis in 1915, the Browns had experienced much travail. Rickey had many problems of his own. Branch joined the Browns at the time the United States League, and then the Federal League, were competing with the two major circuits. Federal League operators placed a team in St. Louis and found several local business men interested in the project. When the warfare was settled, these men still were eager to stay in the game while

Brownie president Hedges, in ill health and tired from the years of battling, wanted out. His interest in the Browns was sold to a syndicate held over from the Federal League and headed by Phil Ball, millionaire ice machine manufacturer and operator of cold-storage plants, and St. Louis brewer Otto Stifel.

Irascible is probably a good one-word description of Ball. He had a low boiling point and was apt to fly off the handle at matters that seemed trivial. There was the time, for instance, in the late Twenties when the Browns and Red Sox, both imbedded in the second division, wanted to call off a game one afternoon at Sportsmans Park. It had been raining all day. Willie Johnson, the Browns' road secretary, called Ball for permission, pointing out that no one would come to a game on a day like this. "I'm coming," Ball said. "Open the gates."

For the benefit of Ball and a couple of his friends, two or three-dozen fans and vast expanses of empty seats, the teams wallowed through the affair in a steady rain.

It should be remembered that Ball was one of the first baseball executives who came to the game after making a fortune elsewhere. Well aware of his lack of baseball knowledge, Ball intrusted running of the team to Bob Quinn, who was general manager during the club's greatest days.

Ball's disputes with his players were frequent but often they had a humorous side to them.

An early air enthusiast, Ball once flew into Detroit to watch the team play. In company with secretary Johnson, he entered the dining room of the hotel, eager to visit with the players. There were no players present. Ball asked where they were.

"We give them five dollars a day for meal money, Mr. Ball," Johnson answered, "so they go to the hamburger shop on the corner, spend 75 cents there and pocket the rest." In high dudgeon, Ball immediately ordered players to sign dining room checks, a practice adopted generally around the majors until the second World War when food shortages and high prices brought a return to the old system.

Progress was slow at first. Under Jones in 1916, the Browns finished fifth and dropped to seventh in 1917. There were a couple of highlights in that season. On May 5 and 6, pitchers Ernie Koob and Bob Groom pitched no-hit games for the Browns against the Chicago White Sox, although they were not in succession. Groom's effort came in the second game of a twin bill on May 6.

Jones gave up the following season and Jimmy Burke, a North St. Louis product, took over as manager in 1920. The club was beginning to move up. Quinn, an astute judge of baseball talent had begun to assemble the team which was to make its great bid in 1922.

Right-fielder Johnny Tobin, one of the greatest bunters of all times, was the first important acquisition. He was plucked off the sandlots of St. Louis in 1914 to join the Federal League club, moved to the Browns when the transfer was made and never played an inning in the minor leagues.

Sisler and catcher Hank Severeid arrived a year later, the latter coming up from Louisville. Outfielder Bill Jacobson came up in 1915, too, but went back to the Little Rock for more seasoning before returning to stay in 1917. Throughout his major-league career he was known as "Baby Doll," a nickname hung on this rawboned Iowan by Negro fans who frequented the bleachers in Little Rock. Shortstop Wally Gerber, even then a veteran, was plucked from Columbus in 1917, third-baseman Gene Robertson was signed off St. Louis sandlots in 1918 and in 1919, the Browns came up with a real prize in outfielder Ken Williams, purchased from Portland for $4,500.

Next to Babe Ruth, this lanky, left-handed hitter, who bore quite a physical, if not facial, resemblance to the present Ted Williams, was the league's outstanding home run slugger.

Burke brought the Browns home in fourth place in 1920 but his easygoing, placid disposition seemed reflected in the play of the ball club. So in 1921, Lee Fohl, who had piloted Cleveland for five years, was given the job.

The Browns were almost ready that year but they lacked depth in the pitching staff. Urban Shocker, obtained from the Yankees in 1918, won 27 games. Dixie Davis and Elam Vangilder, brought up from Louisville and Tulsa, respectively, in 1919, were the only other dependable pitchers. The Browns finished a creditable third in 1921 and hopes were high as the team prepared for 1922.

Those hopes were nearly realized even though they suffered several setbacks. Sisler was hurt on numerous occasions, pitchers Davis and Pruett were plagued by arm trouble. Shocker hurled 348 innings that year even though he disappeared for a week and missed two vital turns on the mound.

Despite these setbacks, the club battled all the way. They were involved in one of baseball's strangest games early in the season. It was played against the Yankees at the Polo Grounds. This was the one the Browns won in the clubhouse, so to speak.

Sad Sam Jones led Shocker, 2-1, going into the ninth. With two out, two pinch-hitters reached base, bringing up John Tobin. He hit an easy roller to Wally Pipp whose throw to Jones beat Tobin to the bag. The crowd swarmed down on the field and many players were in the clubhouse before anyone realized that the plate umpire, on Fohl's protest, had reversed the decision. He had seen Jones juggle the ball. The players returned and Jones lost his stuff. The Browns pounded out six runs, climaxed by Jacobson's grand slam homer, after the third out apparently had been recorded.

By late August, it was obvious that the next three-game series with the Yankees in St. Louis would probably determine the pennant winner. The games were played Saturday, Sunday and Monday and Sportsmans Park was packed each day. Standing room on the field was permitted for the first game, but after center-fielder Whitey Witt of the Yankees was beaned by a pop bottle in the ninth inning, spectators were barred for the rest of the set. Blood was streaming down Witt's face as he was carried off the field and newspapers were besieged with calls that night. Most fans thought he was killed or seriously injured. But he was back in action the next day and eventually struck the most telling blow of the series.

Bob Shawkey hurled against Shocker in the Saturday opener and out-dueled him, 2-1. Sisler, bothered by a shoulder injury, hit into a double play to end the game. Hopes rose again on Sunday when Pruett exercised previous magic against the Yanks, beating them, 5-1. Williams smashed a homer and kept ahead of Ruth. That afternoon the Babe, who always had a lot of trouble with Pruett's screwball, gained his only hit against Shucks, a home run.

The third game still is discussed in St. Louis. It wound up in heavy managerial strategy in the ninth inning. Most Browns' fans to this day contend that manager Lee Fohl outguessed himself. Going into the ninth inning, Dixie Davis had a four-hitter working and not one of the safeties had left the infield. The Browns held a 2-1 lead. Opening the ninth, Wally Schang smashed a hit off Davis' glove. Elmer Smith batted for Everett Scott and Davis cut loose a wild pitch, sending Schang to second. Fohl moved into action. He came out to the mound and the entire Browns' infield moved in. They huddled there for more than five minutes while Pruett came in to replace Davis. Mike McNally batted for Smith and bunted. Severeid slipped going after the ball, threw high to third and everybody was safe. A pass loaded the bases and brought in Shocker to the relief of Pruett. Witt then cracked a single to center, scoring two runs and giving the Yanks the ball game, 3-2, and a lead in the pennant race.

The race ended up with the Browns sweeping three games in Chicago from the White Sox, but the Yanks held their lead.

Dissension hurt the club which dropped to fifth place in 1923. Pitcher Dave Danforth, whose tricky deliveries had put him in a suspicious light before, ran afoul of American League umpires again who accused him of doctoring the ball. His teammates drew up a petition defending him but Fohl refused to sign it. A week later, Fohl was dismissed (although it was said the two events had no connection) and Sisler replaced him.

Like other great players who turned to managing George felt himself unequal to the task. Despite this, he brought the team home fourth in 1924 and third in 1925. Once again Ball's hopes rose. So optimistic was he that he enlarged the seating capacity of the park from 18,000 to its present 34,000 by doubledecking the grandstand to the ends of the foul lines.

There was a World Series at Sportsmans Park in 1926 all right but the Browns were just onlookers. Their tenants, the Cardinals, won the National League pennant. The Cardinals had been renting there since 1920 when their own Robison Field burned. To the very finish it was a peaceful occupancy only on occasion. Ball once tried to evict the Cardinals because they were 24 hours late with the rent. More recently, the DeWitt brothers tried to evict the Cardinals on a technical violation of the contract. Both times the Cardinals won from the Browns.

As the Cardinals gained in prestige and power from 1926 on, the Browns sagged lower and lower. Dan Howley, who succeeded Sisler after George gave up because of eye trouble, got the team into the first division in 1928 and 1929 but it wasn't enough. In Howley's last year at the helm, Phil Ball made one final effort to help the ball club. He acquired the first "bonus player," although the term is used a bit loosely.

Commissioner Landis had made Rick Ferrell of Columbus a "free agent." Ball obtained Rick's services by paying him $25,000, not a great figure by present standards but astounding at that time.

Bill Killefer replaced Howley in 1930 but he left in mid-season of 1932 with the Browns a payment behind in his salary. Ball, in ill health and fighting the depression, lost interest in the club. In the early Thirties, the Browns hit rock bottom. In desperation, they accepted Sam Breadon's offer of Hornsby as manager. Rog had returned to the Cardinals that year as coach and pinch-hitter. The Browns grabbed him.

It was not a happy choice. Hornsby was the same hard-bitten manager who had driven the Cardinals to a flag but this was not the same kind of a ball club. The Browns were a dispirited second-division team.

Hornsby tried everything. He fired Debs Garms and Blaeholder because he found them laughing in the clubhouse after a particularly horrendous defeat. There were a few good players on the club: a fire-balling youngster named Louis (Buck) Newsom, who pitched as good a game as he talked; a colorful, eccentric catcher, Rollie Hemsley; and a pepper-pot shortstop, Red Kress.

Newsom pitched a no-hitter for the Browns for nine innings against Boston in September of 1934—and lost. That's the way the Brownie fortunes were going in those days. The game was tied, 1-1, after nine innings, the Sox run coming on a walk and an error, and then Newsome yielded a hit in the 10th and was beaten, 2-1.

Phil Ball died in 1933 and the ball club was a ship

without a rudder. There was no one in the organization to re-place him, no one in his family who had anything more than a mild interest in baseball. Louis B. Von Wiese was trustee of the Ball estate and he tried to take charge. But he was out of his element and knew it.

The club went from bad to worse in 1934 and 1935 and the family was interested only in disposing of the Browns. In desperation, Von Wiese went across the hall and asked Branch Rickey if he had any interest in buying it. Rickey, then at his peak as operator of the Cardinal farm system, said he had no interest but would try to find a buyer. Listen-ing in on the conversation was Bill De Witt, who had climbed from a vendor at the park to assistant to vice-president Rickey. Rickey suggested that De Witt find a buyer.

That's how Don Barnes entered the picture and it was purely by accident, as Bill De Witt recalls today.

"Mrs. Barnes and my wife were good friends," he said, "and the Barnes were at our house for dinner a couple of nights later. Just to make conversation, I mentioned the Browns' story and Don said he was interested in getting into baseball. It floored me. I knew him only as a fan. It had never occurred to me that he might want to buy in."

Between the 1935 and 1936 seasons, control of the Browns passed from the Phil Ball estate to the syndicate headed by Barnes and De Witt. The Ball family, however, retained title to the ball park and both the Cardinals and Browns rented the property until 1947 when Richard Muck-erman, who succeeded Barnes as president, bought historic Sportsmans Park. When he sold out to the De Witt brothers, the ball park was included in the package.

The new owners looked with bright hope to the future, but they had six rough years ahead of them before they were to reach the first division. Hornsby was retained as manager, a matter which occasioned some surprise.

But the Browns stumbled home in seventh place and

when they didn't look as if they would improve on that record in 1937, Hornsby, whose predilection for playing the horses was under official scrutiny by Commissioner Landis, was dismissed and Jim Bottomley, the old Cardinal favorite, now finishing out his career at first with the Browns, replaced him.

But the ball club just didn't have it. Gabby Street, who produced two Cardinal champions in 1930 and 1931, tried his luck in 1938 with no more success, even though Bobo Newsom, back for a second hitch with the Browns, won 20 games. Fred Haney tried his luck as manager after Street departed and wasn't much of an improvement.

In 1940, the Browns were league spoilers. They were helpless against Detroit, which won the pennant, but took great delight in walloping the Yankees and Indians, the Tigers' closest opponents. The Browns swept a doubleheader with the Indians in Cleveland on Labor Day, jolting the Tribe's flag hopes. The final week of the season, they won another important game in Cleveland. Even more devastating, however, was the three-out-of-four pasting the Browns handed the Yanks on their last visit to St. Louis.

In 1941, the Browns stumbled at the start and when the club hit bottom in June, Haney was ousted and the Browns' man of destiny, James Luther (Luke) Sewell was pulled from the coaching ranks at Cleveland and given the job.

People sympathized with Luke and couldn't understand why he gave up his comfortable post at Cleveland for the "suicide job" in St. Louis. That's what they were calling it. In six years of the Barnes-De Witt regime, Sewell was the fifth manager. But quiet, business-like Sewell accomplished what no other manager in Brownie history had been able to do—he produced a pennant.

Even today, only six years after it happened, most baseball observers are inclined to write off the Browns' 1944 performance as a wartime accident. It was scarcely that. The

Browns were third in 1942, and even though they finished sixth in 1943, they were only three and one-half games out of the lead on July 4 when a series of unfortunate episodes hit the club. They snapped back the next year to win.

Much of the credit must be given to Bill De Witt who smartly collected players who looked like they would not be lost in the draft. Sewell did a remarkable job. He knew how to handle pitchers. He refused to coddle them. There were no histrionics when a pitcher was removed. Luke just waved them off the bench.

Going into the final week of the season, the Tigers and Browns were deadlocked for the lead. It looked like a cinch for the Tigers. They had tailenders Washington and Philadelphia to play. The Browns had to face fourth-place Boston and third-place New York.

Until Thursday, the two clubs matched games. That afternoon, Newhouser blanked the Athletics, 4-0. The Browns were rained out, and the game was set back to Thursday evening. At game time, it was still pouring but Sewell ordered the canvas off the field. Workmen spread dirt and sand until the umpires appeared. Manager Joe Cronin of the Red Sox met Sewell at the plate. In front of the umpires, he said: "Luke, call it off. Take your chances on that half game. You know how it is when a team is forced to play when it doesn't want to. I'd love to see you win the pennant but Luke, so help me, I know we're going to beat you if we play in this rain."

Sewell shook his head. "No, Joe," he said. "The boys don't want it that way and neither do I. We've gone this far. We're gonna win it or lose it on our own." Cronin nodded, muttered a "good luck" and walked away. Cronin knew whereof he spoke. Pinky Woods beat the Browns that night, 4-1, and they trailed by a game with four to play. They almost had to sweep the series from the Yanks in order to win.

Friday night they were back in a first-place tie. They had whipped the Yankees twice, 4-1 and 1-0 behind stout pitching by Kramer and Potter. Borowy pitched a two-hitter in the second game but Potter beat him. The Tigers split with Washington.

Saturday both Detroit and the Browns won. That left the result hinging on the final day and if that didn't settle it, a one-game playoff was set for Detroit on Monday.

It wasn't needed. Dutch Leonard and Stan Spence combined their talents to beat Detroit for Washington.

The Detroit game was over early. By the time the Browns came to bat in the fourth inning, they knew that a victory would clinch it. At the moment, it didn't look too good. The Yanks had picked up two early runs and held a 2-0 lead over Sig Jakucki, who was a surprise, and almost a desperate choice by Sewell, although he had every man on his staff in the bull pen.

In the fourth, Kreevich singled to left, the first blow off Mel Queen. Chet Laabs, often a Brownie disappointment, smashed a drive into the leftfield seats and the score was tied. Kreevich and Laabs came up again in the fifth and repeated their performance, Mike with a single and Chet with a blast against the scoreboard back of the bleachers. Vern Stephens hammered out another run in the eighth but it wasn't needed. Jakucki kept firing the ball in and when McQuinn raced to the Yankee bullpen for a tumbling catch of Oscar Grimes' foul, the Browns had won, 5-2, and the day for which thousands of St. Louis fans had waited 44 years had come to pass. The Browns had won a pennant at long last.

For once, the Cardinals had been forgotten. They had been too good. The 1944 pennant was one of the easiest to win in National League history. The Cardinals won 73 of their first 100 games, and were 21 games in front at one time before they relaxed and coasted home.

The Cardinals felt the World Series would be a breeze. They were rudely shocked when Denny Galehouse bested hard-luck Mort Cooper in the opener, 2-1. The Browns made only two hits but they were placed back to back in the fourth inning when Gene Moore singled and McQuinn, who was to have a .438 series, homered.

They scared the daylights out of the Cards in the second contest and but for brilliant relief pitching by Blix Donnelly, might have made off with it. The Cards gave Max Lanier an early 2-0 lead but the Browns tied it in the seventh. When Kreevich led off the eighth with a double, Donnelly was hauled in and retired the side without incident. In the 11th, McQuinn led off with a double but Donnelly leaped on Christman's bunt and retired McQuinn at third. Then the Cards won against Muncrief with hits by Ray Sanders and Ken O'Dea.

Again in the third game the Browns moved in front with a 6-2 victory behind Kramer's stout hurling. It was their last gasp. Brecheen won the fourth game from Jakucki, Cooper turned the tables on Galehouse in the fifth game and Wilks, with a great relief job, closed it out in the sixth.

The Browns, however, had had their moment of glory. That was what really counted.

Two years later the Browns were back in familiar surroundings—seventh place—and even the persistent and frequently spectacular efforts of Bill Veeck, who took control of the club in 1951, could not change their unhappy lot. Veeck certainly tried hard enough. The Browns became the topic of nationwide conversation when a three-foot seven-inch midget named Eddie Gaedel batted in their lineup in the first game of a doubleheader on August 19, 1951. Gaedel walked and was lifted for a pinch-runner and league president Will Harridge promptly issued an order banning midgets. Veeck tried a variety of new stunts to attract customers, hired famous Rogers Hornsby as manager and fired him after less than two months of the '52 season had passed, traded players and stirred up controversies—but the Browns were still the Browns.

After losing $396,000 in the operation of the club in 1952, Veeck tried desperately to move the franchise, first to Milwaukee and then to Baltimore, in March, 1953. Shortly before the National League approved the shift of the Boston Braves to Milwaukee, Veeck's plea to take the Browns to Baltimore was rejected by American League club owners. So the Browns and St. Louis suffered through another dreary season.

On September 29 the league did what it had refused to do six months earlier and the sale of the Browns for $2,475,-000 to a Baltimore group led by attorney Clarence W. Miles was approved.

The 1954 Baltimore Orioles were really the same old Browns, as their seventh-place finish proved, but what a difference in the treasury! More than a million fans paid to see the team that had drawn 297,238 in St. Louis the year before. The club made a profit of $942,153.

President Miles and his associates immediately put the revenue to work in an effort to improve the club. Manager Jimmie Dykes was dismissed and Paul Richards, whose keen baseball mind and original strategy attracted a lot of attention in Chicago, was hired as general manager and field manager. Richards' early trades were reminiscent of the Browns' star-peddling deals in some respects. But there was a noticeable difference: The Orioles, with a big first-year profit and a city bubbling with baseball enthusiasm behind them, were building for the future.

THE CLEVELAND INDIANS

BY GORDON COBBLEDICK

One thing about the Cleveland Indians: They may, in the words of a once-popular song, have been a headache, but they never were a bore.

They were born of the turmoil and strife that attended the launching of the upstart American League, back when the century was a yearling, and they have made strife and turmoil their business ever since. They have fought among themselves and brawled magnificently with opponents and spit in the eyes of everyone who didn't like it. They have spawned and nurtured a breed of fans beside which Brooklyn's legendary rooters seem models of sanity and prim decorum. They have been loved and hated, ridiculed and flayed, praised and reviled and scorned. And they have earned it all.

They are the Cleveland Indians of Tris Speaker and Lou Boudreau, of Ray Chapman and Wes Ferrell and Robert William Andrew Feller, of Earl Averill and Bob Lemon and Mel Harder, of Sunny Jim Dunn and Alva Bradley and Oscar Vitt and Cy Slapnicka, whose knack for getting into trouble was matched by his ability to spot baseball talent before even its owner was aware that it existed. They are the Indians of the screwball genius, Bill Veeck, and his successor in the front office, Hank Greenberg.

Through the years, they have won and held the loyalty

213

of a sprawling territory that embraces all Ohio, including the backyard of the Cincinnati Reds; that reaches into western Pennsylvania and New York State; that even bulges over into Michigan, where the Tiger prowls. But it is loyalty like that of the man and wife who fight each other until the neighbors call the cops and then pool their muscles to repel the peacemakers. The territory reserves and exercises the right to call the Indians all manner of bad names, but resents bitterly any slurs cast upon them by outlanders.

Each summer Sunday when the Indians are at home, special trains, buses and chartered airplanes disgorge their cargoes of thousands at the gates of Municipal Stadium. For the Indians are not merely Cleveland's baseball team; they are the core of a tight little duchy whose citizens are united in a common madness. They are Akron's Indians and Canton's Indians and Sharon's Indians as surely as they are Cleveland's.

The Indians haven't commanded that allegiance by winning pennants. They waited 20 years for their first one and sweated out 28 more for their second. They have disappointed and disgusted and enraged their perennially hopeful followers times without number. But they haven't been dull.

Baseball writing in Cleveland has never been a mere matter of reporting the outcome of ball games and the events leading up to same. In no other city are the activities—athletic, social and personal—of a hired ball club the subject of so much Page One newspaper space as the Indians are allotted in the three Cleveland dailies. The letters-to-the-editor columns on the editorial pages, which are devoted in saner communities to such weighty matters as the Marshall Plan and the eternal conflict between capital and labor, are largely concerned in Cleveland with attacks upon the defenses of the Indians' manager of the moment.

The territory of which Cleveland is the hub is not quite normal where the Indians are concerned. It has always been so in greater or less measure, but since Bill Veeck's explosive arrival upon the local scene in 1946, the madness has reached unprecedented heights—shrewdly nourished by the astute Veeck and his successors of the new and current administration, headed by president Ellis Ryan and general manager Hank Greenberg.

When the Indians have won, the city has celebrated as no other city has ever celebrated a baseball championship. When they have lost—as they did with a team that was expected to win in 1949—it has been capable of the supreme Veeckian jest of a mock funeral, complete with frock coats and mourners, and the burial of the pennant.

The cherished flag may rest in peace, but the wacky spirit of baseball in Cleveland lives on.

The history books will tell you that Byron Bancroft Johnson, that implacable fighter, was the father of the American League. And, in truth, it was Johnson who had the idea and the combativeness to carry it out. But Johnson's enterprise would have gone the way of all other attempts to muscle in on the National League's ancient monopoly (and there had been several before him) if it hadn't been for Charlie Somers. A young and handsome Clevelander, Somers had the bankroll and the faith. It was his money that not only founded the Cleveland club but that also made possible the infant league's successful invasions of Chicago, Philadelphia and Boston.

Somers and Jack Kilfoyl, his original partner in Cleveland, had no manager, no players and no ball park. League Park, with its old wooden stands, was owned by Frank DeHaas Robison and M. S. Robison, owners of the St. Louis National League club. They refused to lease it to the American League rivals.

"All right," said Ban Johnson, "if they want to fight, we'll fight. Two-thirds of the players in the National League are ready to jump to us. We'll bring the Robisons to terms."

His threat was made good within a few days. The National League called a quick meeting in Cleveland on March 3 and agreed to the installation of a franchise in Cleveland. Shortly thereafter, the Robisons leased League Park to Somers and Kilfoyl for a flat annual rental of $12,000. Johnson agreed that the new league would not claim major-league status that year.

But still the young men had no team and no manager. Jim McAleer, who had been a great outfielder for the Cleveland National League club, was living in retirement in nearby Youngstown. He was induced to undertake the recruiting of a team and to manage it when and if. It was an excellent stroke of business. McAleer, in his own particular field, was to become nearly as prominent as Somers in the expansion of the new circuit, especially in inducing established National Leaguers to throw in their lot with the American.

In the first raid on National League personnel, Cleveland landed third-baseman Bill Bradley, pitcher Ed Scott and outfielder Jack McCarthy from the Chicago Cubs and a good catcher, Bobby Woods, from Cincinnati.

Somers' confidence and Somers' money had launched the American League but it hadn't done much for Cleveland. The city's entry in the infant organization finished seventh. McAleer, of course, was fired as manager. However, better days loomed just ahead.

When Napoleon Lajoie, an ex-cabbie out of Woonsocket, Rhode Island, jumped to the Athletics from the Phillies, it occasioned no great consternation in National League ranks. But after he had hit for an amazing .405 for Mack in 1901, John I. Rogers, president of the Phillies and an able lawyer, awoke to the realization that he had lost something valuable. He went before the Pennsylvania Supreme Court and obtained an injunction restraining Lajoie from playing for any team other than the Phils.

Mack sent Lajoie and Bill Bernhard, another Phillie, across the river to Camden, New Jersey, to escape the Pennsylvania process servers. There they sat for a month, until Somers, seeking help for his team, directed a plea to Mack. Connie, remembering that Somers had put up the money which established him in Philadelphia, agreed to turn both Lajoie and Bernhard, a first-class pitcher, over to Cleveland. The Phillies' president countered by suing to prevent the pair from playing with Cleveland, but his petition was denied. However, the injunction forbidding them to play in Pennsylvania with any team other than the Phillies was upheld and for two years the Bronchos, as they were then called, were obliged to appear in Philadelphia without the two stars. It wasn't until 1903 that the federal court in Cleveland dissolved the injunction and Lajoie and Bernhard were free at last.

Lajoie, a 200-pound six-footer of pure French stock, is remembered for two things: his matchless grace in the field and his almost incredible batting power. A line-drive hitter rather than a home-run leader, he was a menace to the lives and limbs of third-basemen and a terror even to shortstops.

As a second-baseman, Lajoie never made a difficult play, which is to say that he never made a play look difficult. Never seeming to hurry, he glided with consummate grace over a vast territory. Once he went far to his left for a sharp ground ball that barely eluded the fingertips of Charley (Piano Legs) Hickman, his first-base teammate. Scooping it up with one hand while the batter was still 20 feet from first base, he turned to throw only to find Hickman gaping in open-mouthed wonder an equal distance from the target.

"If you just want to watch this ball game," Larry growled, "you ought to pay your way into the park."

The Bronchos were in eighth place when Lajoie joined them in early June, 1902. They finished fifth, largely because the Frenchman batted .369. Bernhard, his fellow fugitive from the Phillies, contributed a substantial bit in the form of 18 victories against five defeats.

Another contribution came from a tall, rail-thin pitcher who had been purchased that spring from Toledo. His name: Adrian C. (Addie) Joss. In his first start for Cleveland, he pitched a one-hit game against the St. Louis Browns, though the Bronchos who are living today still insist angrily that the Browns' lone hit, a short fly to center which the umpire ruled had been trapped, was legally caught.

Joss was only 31 years old when he died in 1911, a little more than two years after he had pitched a perfect no-hit no-run, nobody-reach-first game against the great Ed Walsh. But before his untimely passing, he had engraved his name indelibly in the hearts of all Cleveland fans.

How tightly the team was built around Lajoie, however, can be judged by the outcome of a 1903 newspaper contest to choose a new nickname for the team. The Blues of 1901 had derived their name from the fact that they wore the same blue uniforms that had been affected by their National League predecessors, the Spiders. The players themselves picked the name of Bronchos a year later, but it never gained popular acceptance—chiefly, it is likely, because it didn't lend itself to a convenient contraction calculated to please a hard-pressed headline writer. The name chosen by the fans, who knew and cared nothing about the technical problems involved in telling a headline story, reflected the common feeling that when one thought about the Cleveland team one thought, inevitably, of an individual—Napoleon (Nap) Lajoie. By popular acclaim, the Bronchos became the Naps. They remained the Naps for the duration of Lajoie's glorious career in Cleveland.

The foundation of Cleveland's reputation as a graveyard for managers was laid early. Jim McAleer, unable to win with an admittedly inferior team in 1901, was fired. His successor, Bill Armour, struggled through two full seasons, finishing fifth and third, but the home press generally ignored him. Lajoie, his field captain, was regarded as the actual leader.

It was natural, therefore, that when the Naps, who had been picked in a nation-wide poll of sports editors to win the 1904 pennant, played only .500 ball, Armour should turn in his resignation to Somers. It was equally natural that Lajoie should be appointed to succeed him. He lifted the team to fourth in the final month, but 1904 remained a disappointing season. The campaigns of 1905, 1906 and 1907 were launched on a note of high promise and ended in blank frustration. Then came 1908. This was to be Cleveland's year. The Naps were solid. Their infield of George Stovall, Lajoie, Terry Turner and Bill Bradley was conceded to be the best in the game. And they had the incomparable Addie Joss.

One of the few who could claim to be Addie's equal was Big Ed Walsh, the big White Sox spitballer of whom someone (it must have been Ring Lardner) said he was the only man in the world who could strut sitting down. By dint of working four or five times a week, Walsh won the fantastic total of 40 games that year. Joss, who was not physically strong, won 24, but Clevelanders argued that in any duel between the two they would take a ticket on Joss.

They had met many times before, but the duel of duels was held on October 2. The race had narrowed to a three-team affair coming down to the wire, with Detroit, Chicago and Cleveland all owning a chance to win. When the White Sox came into Cleveland in that early fall day, it was recognized that this was the series that could determine the winner, and 10,598 fans were in the stands at League Park.

Only three days before, on September 29, Walsh had

pitched and won both ends of a doubleheader against Boston. Nevertheless, he was the choice of Fielder Jones, the White Sox manager, for this game of games. Lajoie nominated Joss—who else?

Addie, his fadeaway pitch functioning beautifully, causing the Sox to beat the ball into the dirt, retired man after man. So did Walsh—until the third inning. Pitching to leadoff batter Joe Birmingham, he tried to fire a fast ball past the right-handed hitter. It was what Birmie had hoped for. He swung and drove a single to right center. He stole second cleanly and scampered to third as the ball caromed off first-baseman Frank Isbell's shoulder into center field. Then, after Walsh had retired the next two batters, he uncorked a fast ball which tore through the catcher and rolled to the grandstand. Birmingham scored the only run of the game, the only run Addie Joss needed.

Other Cleveland pitchers had fashioned no-hit games before and others have done it since—Earl Moore, Dusty Rhoades, Wes Ferrell, Bob Feller, Bob Lemon, Don Black. Feller has done it three times. Joss himself was to notch another no-hitter in 1910. But this one—his perfect game against Walsh—was perhaps the pitching classic of all time.

It could have meant Cleveland's first league championship, but it didn't. The next day, with the city humming about Addie's perfect game, the Sox, with Walsh pitching masterfully in relief, won, 3-2. That, to all intents and purposes, eliminated Cleveland. Detroit won the pennant.

Joss had rather a poor year in 1909, but started the 1910 season with his second no-hitter. This also was against Chicago and the score again was 1-0. Never in robust health, he was ill much of that season. In 1911, he made the spring training trip with the Naps and accompanied the team as far as Chattanooga on its northward journey. There he fainted on the field, was revived and sent home. He teammates never saw him alive again. On April 14, two days before the opening of the season, the quiet man who had written one of the brightest chapters in baseball history died at his Toledo home of tubercular meningitis.

Early in September of that year, Connie Mack was fighting for a pennant and felt that one established outfielder would put his Athletics over the top. After looking over the field, he decided that the man he must have was Briscoe Lord of Cleveland. Somers countered Connie's trade proposal with a suggestion, based on a tip from a New Orleans friend, that the A's turn over to the Naps a young outfielder whom they had on option with the Pelicans. Mack agreed readily enough. He had tried the player twice and recognized his promise, but hadn't been able to keep him happy. For Shoeless Joe Jackson was chronically homesick for the North Carolina woods, and that was why the man who may have been the greatest natural batter baseball ever saw became a member of the Naps. In 20 games for Cleveland that fall, he batted .387. The next year, his average climbed to .408. A season later, it was .395. The barefoot kid who could neither read nor write but who could hit a baseball as no more than half a dozen others ever have hit it, had arrived.

Denton True Young was no stranger to Cleveland when, in 1909, Charlie Somers made a deal with the Red Sox that returned the greatest pitcher of his or any other day to the city he had called home. Young was just short of 42 at the time and Boston had supposed that his usefulness was at an end. Boston was mistaken. The grand old master won 19 games for the Naps that year, one of them a two-hit shutout victory over his old Red Sox mates. He had come off his father's hill farm in Tuscarawas County in 1890 to pitch for the Canton team of the Ohio & Pennsylvania League. That was where he earned the nickname of Cyclone, which was promptly shortened to Cy.

Young's first pitching assignment for the Spiders was

against Anson's Colts. He held them to three hits, fired his fast ball past Anson for a third strike, and won his game, 3-1. It left him with only 510 victories to go for a record that has never been approached and probably never will be. Only 44 pitchers in all history have won 200 games in their lifetimes. Only 12 have won 300. Only one other, Walter Johnson, won 400. Young won 511 in a career that spanned 22 seasons!

Old Tuscarawas' return to the Naps in 1909 and his early demonstration that he could still pitch baseball with the best of them, once more made Cleveland the pennant favorite. But, as was to happen so many times in later years, something went wrong with the script. A sportswriter suggested the name "Naps" be changed to Napkins—"the way they've folded up." Lajoie was roundly criticized for his handling of the shaky pitching staff. He became increasingly short-tempered with his players and rebellious sounds began to issue from the dugout.

The big Frenchman hung on until mid-season and beyond, but on August 17 he stalked into Somers' office and offered his resignation. "I don't want to leave Cleveland," he said. "I'd like to stay on as a player. But I think you'd better get a new manager. I've done all I can with this club and it isn't good enough."

Jim McGuire, a coach, became the fourth Cleveland manager in nine years of membership in the new league. George Stovall, the popular first-baseman, was named field captain. The great Lajoie submerged himself in the ranks. Freed of the burden of managing a disappointing team, his batting eye, which had seemed to be on the wane in 1907 and '08, regained its sharpness. He hit .384 in 1909. It was his highest mark as a Cleveland player.

The team that had missed by a hair in 1908 missed by a mile in '09, finishing sixth. Obviously McGuire didn't have the answer. Neither did Stovall, who succeeded him in mid-

1911. Neither did Harry Davis, Connie Mack's old first-baseman, who took over in 1912 to the tune of loud grumbling by the players, who wanted Stovall to continue. Neither did Joe Birmingham, to whom the unhappy Davis relinquished the reins in August of that year.

In 1914, the tide went out and the team under Birmingham suffered Cleveland's first and only last-place finish. Lajoie had slipped badly and had become difficult for Birmingham to handle. What was perhaps more significant, Somers' fortune had faded, too. His bankers first advised, then urged, and finally demanded that he get out of baseball.

Kilfoyl already was out. He had been a rabid fan to whom every close game was torture and every defeat a heartbreak. The 1908 race was too much for him. His nerves shattered and his health undermined, Jack had been forced to step out. Somers was soon to follow him.

Sunday baseball in Cleveland was outlawed until 1911 and the Naps, denied the use of their own ball park, sometimes journeyed to Columbus and Dayton for Sabbath games. On repeated visits to the state capital, Somers had become acquainted with the young sports editor of the Columbus *Dispatch*, Ernest Sargent Barnard. Impressed by his knowledge of baseball and his enthusiasm for the game, Somers engaged him as travelling secretary in 1904. After Kilfoyl's retirement and Somers' elevation to the presidency, "Barney" became vice-president and general manager. It was at his urging that Somers inaugurated baseball's first chain-store venture and established a modest farm system.

But nothing helped. In 1916, Somers found himself nearly $2,000,000 in debt. He had been forced to sell Joe Jackson to Chicago for $15,000. His creditors gave him no peace. Reluctantly, he yielded to the insistence of his bankers that he get out of the baseball business and give full attention to his coal-mining interests. It was up to the league to find a buyer for the Indians (that name had been adopted after the inevitable newspaper contest when Lajoie, nearing the end of his career, was sold to the Athletics at the conclusion of the 1914 race).

Ban Johnson found the buyer at a convivial gathering in Chicago. James Christopher Dunn, called Sunny Jim, was a railroad contractor. When he admitted that he could lay his hands on hardly more than $15,000 in cash at the moment, Johnson agreed to lend him $100,000 on behalf of the league. Charley Comiskey, whom Somers had helped establish in Chicago, came through with another $100,000. Dunn's friends in Chicago and Marshalltown, Iowa, his birthplace, subscribed to the remainder of the $500,000 needed to complete the purchase.

The Saturday before the opening of the 1916 season, Ed Bang, sports editor of the Cleveland *News*, glanced at a routine dispatch from Boston and leaped to the telephone. The story was simply that Joe Lannin, president of the Boston Red Sox, was disgusted with Tris Speaker's holdout fight.

To Bob McRoy in his League Park office, the sports editor said:

"Get hold of Jim Dunn and have him get in touch with Lannin. We can get Tris Speaker. Lannin will sell anything for enough money."

The next day, Cleveland bought the greatest outfielder baseball has ever known for $55,000 and two players—Sad Sam Jones, who was to become one of the best and most enduring of pitchers, and Fred Thomas, a rookie infielder. By a threat that he wouldn't report to the Indians unless his demand was met, Speaker forced Lannin to pay him $10,000 of the purchase price.

Tris accepted the sale reluctantly. He said flatly that he considered Cleveland a bad baseball town with a bad ball club. That it became the holder of virtually all the attendance records in the book is owing in no small part to the man they called the Grey Eagle. With Tris Speaker's arrival on the scene, Cleveland's baseball fortunes took a sharp upturn.

The Naps had finished last in 1914 and the Indians had landed seventh the following year. Not even Speaker's presence could lift them higher than sixth in his first season in a Cleveland uniform, though the 28-year-old Grey Eagle hit .386 and ended Ty Cobb's nine-year reign as batting champion.

In 1917, two things happened: The Indians began the climb that carried them to their first pennant and world championship in 1920—and the United States entered the first World War.

Lee Fohl was a stolid, colorless manager who had none of the qualities of which popular heroes are made. Nevertheless he had earned a reputation as an astute developer and handler of pitchers. By 1917, Barnard's farm system had begun to produce something for him to develop and handle. Stan Coveleskie and the first Jim Bagby came up that year, and for the first time since 1908, the Cleveland club had solidity and balance, with good batting power, fair and rapidly improving pitching, and a catching staff, headed by Steve O'Neill, that was widely recognized as the best. The Indians finished third that year and in 1918 zoomed to second in a season abbreviated by the "work or fight" order of Secretary of War Newton D. Baker.

By the spring of 1919, the nine members of the Cleveland team who had gone into the military service were back and the Indians were ready to make their first serious pennant challenge since 1908. Fohl and Speaker, who had assumed the position of a sort of assistant manager without portfolio, told Dunn they could win if he got them a third-baseman and a bit of outfield help. Sunny Jim obliged. In a deal with Connie Mack, he obtained Larry Gardner, an old Boston teammate of Speaker's, and Elmer Myers, a right-handed pitcher, in a swap for Bobby Roth, the Indians' regular right-fielder.

Speaker, who sat in on the conference with Mack despite the fact that he had no official standing, suggested that it would be nice if Connie threw in Charley Jamieson, a waiver-price outfielder he had obtained from Washington. With no more than the standard amount of hemming and hawing, Connie agreed. Gardner was good. He helped the Indians mightily in their pennant fight. Myers was fair. Jamieson was brilliant, then and for a dozen years thereafter. The man whom Connie Mack threw in in a gesture of generosity is Cleveland's all-time left-fielder.

On July 18, 1919, with startling suddenness, Tris Speaker became manager of the Indians.

When first approached, Speaker said, "I don't want the job. I'd rather be a player. I believe I'd be more useful to you that way. But I'll take it on one condition. Lee Fohl has to ask me to."

Fohl did just that and the Grey Eagle took over. In confirmation of his own fears and misgivings, his batting fell off to .296, but he steered the Indians into second place, three and a half games behind the White Sox—the team that was to live in infamy as the Black Sox.

Baseball has never seen another year like 1920 (for which baseball is duly thankful) and Cleveland was submerged to its ears in the torrent of rumors and events, exciting and sordid, joyous and starkly tragic, that set that season apart.

On September 28, a Cleveland grand jury returned indictments against eight White Sox players charged with conspiring to "throw" the 1919 World Series to the Reds. The lid was off!

It might have been supposed that the scandal, which shook the faith of millions in the integrity of baseball, would have killed public interest in the Indians' fight for their first pennant. It seemed to have the opposite effect. The newspapers castigated "the crummy Chicago thieves" and rallied the fans to the support of Speaker and his Tribe. In the final week, the Indians opened a gap of two games between themselves and the riddled remnants of the White Sox. The 20-year famine was broken! There was dancing in the streets!

The Black Sox scandal was forgotten, but the Indians' joy in their victory was incomplete. Ray Chapman wasn't there to share it. Chapman, a .300 hitter, a brilliant baserunner and a dazzling fielder, was perhaps the most popular of all the Indians—with his teammates and with the resident fans. Dynamic and intensely aggressive, he was one of those eye-compelling athletes who were born to be heroes. On August 16, the Indians were leading the race by a game and a half over the Yankees as they moved into the Polo Grounds for another in an interminable succession of crucial series. Pitching for the Yankees was Carl Mays, the "submarine pitcher" whose underhand delivery seemed to whip the ball plateward from the grass tops.

In the fifth inning, as Chapman took his characteristic crouching stance, his toes nearly touching the plate, his head thrust into the strike territory, Mays fired a fast ball. Chapman turned his head slightly to the right. It was the only move he made. The ball struck him squarely on the left temple. A doctor, summoned from the grandstand, ordered him removed to a hospital. A delicate brain operation was performed that night but Chappie died at five in the morning without having regained consciousness.

Within five days the Indians, their interest in the pennant race buried with their friend and teammate, surrendered first place to the Yankees. But they bounded back. They picked up a pint-sized collegian out of the University of Alabama to fill in at shortstop. His name was Joe Sewell and he went on to hit .329 for the season, field superbly and establish himself as Cleveland's shortstop for the next ten years.

Three tremendous pitchers formed the backbone of Speaker's pennant-winning staff. Jim Bagby, Sr. won 31 games. Stan Coveleskie won 24. Ray (Slim) Caldwell, dropped by the Yankees and Red Sox as a problem child, notched 20, including a vengeful no-hitter against the Yankees. Then Speaker had Dunn buy an erratic southpaw named Walter (Duster) Mails, from the Pacific Coast League. He won seven in a row after September 1 to aid the Indians' stretch drive.

Brooklyn, under Uncle Wilbert Robinson, won the National League pennant by a seven-game margin, but the Indians, loaded as they were with .300 hitters, were favored to take the world championship in the best-five-out-nine series. Though Bagby had been his biggest winner, Speaker thought of Coveleskie as his ace pitcher and there was no surprise in Cleveland when the big Pole was nominated to pitch the opening game of the World Series, played in Brooklyn. He defeated Rube Marquard, 3-1.

But in the next two games, Burleigh Grimes bested Bagby, 3-0, and Sherrod Smith edged Caldwell, 2-1. The odds favoring Cleveland dropped to even money as the teams moved into League Park to continue the series. Four games were scheduled there, and the eighth and ninth, if they were necessary, were to be played in Brooklyn. But Brooklyn never saw its heroes again that year. The Indians took four straight in their own ball park and Cleveland's cup of joy ran over.

Coveleskie racked up his second Series victory by outclassing Leon Cadore in the fourth game, 5-1, to even matters at two games apiece. The next day, Sunday, found 26,684 fans jammed into a park that normally held only

22,000. They saw a game that will be talked about as long as baseball is played.

Elmer Smith, the Indians' right-fielder, became the author of the first grand-slam homer ever hit in Series play. Jim Bagby slammed the first home run ever credited to a pitcher in the Series. And to top it all off Bill Wambsganss, the Indians' second-baseman, completed an unassisted triple play. It was a memorable day for Indian fans.

The sixth game was a tight one, but the brilliant Mails nosed out Sherrod Smith, 1-0, and the Indians needed only one more victory. The Dodgers' manager, Wilbert Robinson, had intended starting Marquard in the seventh game, but by that time the Rube was in disgrace. He had been arrested as a ticket scalper, the charge being that he had tried to peddle a set of box seats for $350. The cops didn't hold him, asserting piously that it would have been unsportsmanlike. But if he didn't go to jail, he was placed under equally effective restraint in Uncle Robbie's dog-house. Grimes was called upon to pitch with only one day's rest, but Coveleskie defeated him, 3-0, and joined the short roster of pitchers who have won three games in one World Series.

Jim Dunn died in the early spring of 1922 and the club passed into the hands of his widow, with Barnard as its operating head. The Yankees, loaded with the best talent from the Red Sox, had become a dominant factor in the league, and the Indians' fortunes declined steadily until 1926. That season, in the death struggle of a once-mighty team, they finished a good second to the Yankees. Then they were done. Tris Speaker, in December of that year, announced his retirement to enter business in Cleveland.

Jim Dunn's widow, now Mrs. George Pross, had no wish to be the owner of a ball club and Barnard had been given to understand that he would be the new president of the league when and if he could break away from his

Cleveland connection. Barney's loyalty to Mrs. Dunn kept him on the job, but he allowed it to be known that the Indians could be bought. A syndicate of millionaires headed by John Sherwin, a banker and one of Cleveland's wealthiest men, announced the purchase of the team on November 17, 1927. The price was about $1,000,000 or approximately double what Dunn had paid a little more than ten years earlier. Alva Bradley, whose financial interest was considerably smaller than that of Sherwin and several other stockholders, was named president—on the theory, as he smilingly explained, that he knew less about baseball than any of his associates.

Since, by his own admission, he knew nothing about baseball, and since he was losing Barnard, Bradley began to cast about for a general manager. The field of his search was narrowed by his determination to make this an all-Cleveland operation, but his choice was universally acclaimed as a good one. Billy Evans resigned two other jobs to become executive head of the Indians. He was the star of the American League's umpiring staff and also sports editor of the Newspaper Enterprise Association, an important feature syndicate whose offices were in Cleveland. Now the new owners had a ball club and a man to run the business end of it. They still lacked a manager and, though they didn't know it, also lacked competent players at nearly every position. Speaker was gone, Joe Sewell had slowed up, and Charley Jamieson was showing the ravages of age. George Uhle and George Burns, the only other survivors of the 1920 champions, were near the end of the line.

But before Bradley and Evans could concern themselves with the playing personnel, they had to find a manager. Still desirous of choosing a native son, they thought of Roger Peckinpaugh, who was then on the White Sox roster as an infielder. Peck had jumped directly from Cleveland's Eash High School into the Naps' 1910 lineup, playing a few games at shortstop as keystone mate of the great Lajoie. Later he had been traded to the Yankees and from there had moved to Washington, where he established himself as one of the greatest defensive shortstops the league had ever seen.

As a neophyte manager, Peck inherited all the problems of his predecessors, though for two years life looked rosy enough. Nothing was expected of the Indians in 1928 and nothing was what they delivered. But before a new season rolled around, Evans, armed with a limitless bankroll, had gone into the minor-league market and brought home a package containing Earl Averill and Dick Porter, two .300-plus hitters. He had also recalled from the Three-Eye League a 21-year-old pitcher named Wesley Ferrell, who was to win 20 games or more in each of his first four seasons as an Indian.

Then Peckinpaugh found himself with a lap full of new problems, for the roof caved in on the world of business and finance in the fall of 1929. Bradley and his directors, hard hit in the market crash and pinched by the depression that followed, decreed a general tightening of the purse strings just when the Indians, who had leaped all the way from seventh place to third in the two years of their ownership, might have been built into a formidable team by some judicious expenditures. Chiefly through the efforts of Averill, Porter, Ferrell, Joe Vosmik and Mel Harder, they remained a first-division club for seven successive years, but they never seriously challenged for the pennant.

Peckinpaugh was relieved of the managerial reins in June, 1933, after somewhat more than five years of struggle and disappointment. Cleveland's reputation as a graveyard of managers, dormant through Speaker's long tenure, was about to take on new luster. Not until Lou Boudreau took over years later were the Indians to have a leader who could survive more than three seasons.

The choice of a successor was made against the judgment

and advice of Billy Evans. Bradley, the baseball fan, had long been an admirer of Walter Johnson, the pitcher. He felt that the Big Train, probably the most honored player the game had produced, would reduce the heat on the front office.

He was mistaken. As a pitcher, Johnson had been popular with friend and foe alike. As a manager, he was cordially hated by his own men. They said he was a nagger, that he couldn't administer a bawling-out and then forget about it but harped on the subject for weeks on end.

Johnson cooked his own goose early in 1934 when, while the Indians were in Philadelphia, he suspended and sent home two veteran players, Willie Kamm and Glenn Myatt. The charges against the latter were never made very clear, but Kamm was accused of undermining the manager. Young players, despairing of ever getting Johnson's ear when they had a problem to discuss, had formed the habit of taking their troubles to Kamm. There was no evidence that the old third-baseman encouraged the practice, but it persisted and Johnson resented it bitterly.

Johnson survived until August 5, but he had received his notice a week earlier. Once more the public was firing a manager who had been hired by Alva Bradley and this time there was no doubt about it. Bradley still liked and admired Johnson, but the people would have none of him. With eight weeks of the season remaining, Steve O'Neill became the third manager of the Bradley regime. Under him the Indians found new life and finished a respectable third.

But when Billy Evans resigned as general manager at the conclusion of the 1935 season, having taken one deep salary slash after another, and when Cyril C. Slapnicka was appointed to the new office of assistant to the president a long smouldering resentment against the Indians' front office came to a head.

At the time he moved into the front office, the Indians

had two highly promising young outfielders on their New Orleans farm. Against the advice of Larry Gilbert, the New Orleans manager, Slapnicka recalled Roy Weatherly at the end of the 1936 season but sent Tommy Henrich to Milwaukee, though the latter was clearly the superior ballplayer. Henrich immediately registered a complaint with Commissioner Landis that Cleveland was keeping him in the minor leagues beyond the legal span of years. Landis agreed and Henrich was made a free agent.

Bradley was fully aware of his new assistant's penchant for getting into hot water and of his growing unpopularity, but he said, "You have to give Slap credit; he knows how to make money."

The fans and the writers took a different view. They called Slapnicka a penny-pincher.

Slapnicka wasn't the only ivory-hunter who recognized the rare talent of 17-year-old Robert William Andrew Feller. But the others were city slickers and Bill Feller, Bob's father and early baseball mentor, didn't thoroughly trust them. Slapnicka talked to him of the prospects for a good corn crop and the price of pork on the hoof, and Bill Feller saw that here was a man to whom he need have no hesitancy in signing away his big son's future. Baseball law forbade the signing of a sand-lot player by a major-league club, but Slap was never one to allow the law to fetter him, as he had demonstrated in the Henrich case. Besides, he signed Feller to a New Orleans contract, which made everything legal. Then, because Bill Feller had heard that the metropolis of the bayous was a sink of iniquity, he agreed to transfer the boy's contract to Fargo-Moorhead, another Cleveland farm in the Northern League. But Feller never pitched for Fargo-Moorhead.

The St. Louis Cardinals, the old Gashouse Gang, came to League Park for an exhibition game on July 6, 1936. George Uhle, then a coach, pitched the first three innings for the Indians. Feller was assigned to pitch the middle three, with manager O'Neill as his catcher. As Frankie Frisch, the Cards' manager, watched him warming up, his eyes grew wide, then narrowed. To Buzzy Wares, one of his lieutenants, he said, "Ease over there and ask that kid if the Indians have got him signed. If they haven't, tell him to do nothing till he hears from me." To Lynn King, a reserve outfielder, he said, "You ever played second base?" King replied in the negative. "You're playing next inning if that wild man pitches," Frisch assured him. "The old Flash is taking no chances."

One saw what he meant. Bob Feller kicked his left foot high and let fly with the most blinding fast ball the game had seen since Walter Johnson began to fade. But there was a difference. Johnson knew where his pitches were going; Feller didn't. Some of them shot over O'Neill's head. Some plowed up the dirt in front of the plate. One splintered a chair in the grandstand. But enough of them were over the plate to result in eight strikeouts in three innings.

With all pennant hopes gone, O'Neill started Bob in his first championship game on August 23. He struck out 15 St. Louis Browns. Three weeks later, he faced the Philadelphia A's and fanned 17, tying Dizzy Dean's one-game strike-out record.

But Slapnicka was in trouble again. Judge Landis was examining the evidence relating to the juggling of those New Orleans and Fargo-Moorhead contracts. It was freely predicted that the commissioner would rule Feller a free agent, and speculation as to the size of the bonus he could command for signing with another club was on every sports page in the land. Guesses ranged from $100,000 to $250,000. Bib Falk, scouting for the Red Sox, smiled when he was asked what Boston would pay.

"I've got a blank check in my pocket," he said. "My only orders are to get him."

Landis' decision, when it was handed down three months later, proved to be a strange compromise by that hard, uncompromising old jurist. He ruled that Cleveland should pay $7,500 to the Des Moines club, for no better reason than that Des Moines was in Iowa, but that Feller should remain the property of the Indians. People in position to know said the verdict was based not on law but on Landis' conviction that a battle of bankrolls centering around the greatest teen-age baseball prospect of all time would have been bad for the game.

Feller went on to set a new single-game strikeout record of 18 and, after four years of war service, much of it in the Pacific combat zones, he fanned 348 batters in 1946 to shatter the season standard set by Rube Waddell in 1904—when everything favored the pitcher over the hitters!

Slapnicka was not one of O'Neill's more rabid admirers, and so, as the books were closed on the 1937 season, "the public" fired O'Neill. Bradley went shopping for a new manager and found him in the Yankee chain.

Oscar Vitt was a bouncy, toothy, little pepper-pot who had played third base for Detroit a good many years before. In 1937, he had managed the Newark club that had won the International League pennant by the incredible margin of 25 and one-half games over the runner-up.

Vitt promised that the Indians would be a fighting team, and so they were. But not in the way he had meant the phrase. By mid-1939, the players were at the point of open rebellion against his authority. In fact, sentiment against the effervescent pilot had so crystallized that, as an eastern trip neared its end, the Indians had all but determined to demand of Bradley that Vitt be fired forthwith. The trip ended with a Sunday doubleheader in Yankee Stadium and, much to their surprise, the Indians won both games. This threw off their timetable but didn't alter their purpose. It was evident that, with Cleveland bubbling over with enthusiasm as the result of the double victory over the hated Yankees, they couldn't tell Bradley that it was impossible for them to win under Vitt. So they waited.

In late May, 1940, they embarked on another swing through the East, and by this time they were ready to demand Vitt's scalp even if they won every game. It was strongly suspected that in this purpose they were being encouraged—or at any rate that they were not being counseled against it—by Slapnicka, who despised the little manager with an intensity that equaled, if it didn't surpass, the feeling of the players.

In Boston, on the morning of the last day of that fateful trip, I noted something strange about the lobby of the Kenmore Hotel. Bags had been packed and dispatched to the Huntington Avenue Station, where the team was to board the train for Cleveland immediately after that afternoon's game. But there wasn't a ballplayer in sight in the hotel. To anyone who has ever travelled with a ball club and is acquainted with the players' fondness for lobby-sitting, that would have been a strange circumstance. Its strangeness was emphasized when, suddenly, two dozen players appeared from nowhere. It meant only one thing to this suspicious mind, already alerted by the feeling that something ominous had been brewing for days. Obviously there had been a meeting of the players.

I asked questions and, from one of the team's stars, got a complete set of answers. When the Indians arrived in Cleveland the next morning, Mel Harder, as senior member of the club and one of the most respected players in the business, would telephone Alva Bradley and request a nine o'clock appointment. He would be accompanied to Bradley's downtown office by a large delegation. They would lay their case before the president in, substantially, these words: "Get rid of Vitt and we'll win the pennant. Keep him and we'll probably blow it."

They would present their charges in detail, but that would be the ultimate demand: "Fire Vitt!"

The meeting with Bradley was held on the morning of June 13, 1940. That was the day Paris fell to Hitler's legions, but when the *Plain Dealer* appeared the next morning, the most tragic war news of the century was subordinated to the Indians' unprecedented rebellion. The players accused Vitt, among other things, of ridiculing them in public, of using them for laughs in his persistent clowning before enemy dugouts. The charges sounded convincing enough when stated orally by the enraged athletes, but they didn't read well. Around the country the papers boiled down the bill of complaints to this: Vitt had criticized his men; therefore they wanted him removed. From Maine to Southern California, the Cleveland Indians became the Cleveland Crybabies, and as the Crybabies they suffered through the most miserable half-season to which any team has ever been subjected.

In every city in the league, they were showered with overripe fruit whenever they made their appearance on the field. A dozen times or more games were interrupted while ground crews with shovels, brooms and wheel-barrows cleaned up the debris. On one trip to Detroit, they were met at the Michigan Central Station by a mob estimated at 2,000, and were pelted with eggs, tomatoes and rocks as they marched from the train to the taxicab stand.

The Indians hung on grimly until September. They went into the final month of the campaign leading the race by six games. Then they collapsed. They lost the pennant to Detroit on the first day of the last series of the season when an unknown rookie named Floyd Giebell outpitched Feller, 2-0.

Vitt was released at the end of the season after three stormy years as manager. Roger Peckinpaugh was engaged to replace him. A year later, Slapnicka "resigned" as assistant to Bradley and Peck moved into the front office as vice-president and general manager. He was succeeded as field leader by Lou Boudreau, a 24-year-old shortstop who had been in the major leagues only a little more than two years, in professional baseball less than four.

Boudreau and his second base partner, Ray Mack, joined the Indians August 7, 1939. Before that season was over, Boudreau had taken charge. He was a natural leader, and the team's veterans, far from resenting the rookie, seemed content to lean on him. They accepted him as unofficial captain. When the managerial post was vacated by Peckinpaugh's promotion to the office, Boudreau asked Bradley for the job. The president believed he was too young, but was persuaded by George Martin, a director of the club, to give the appointment to the youthful University of Illinois athlete.

For four years, Boudreau managed an undistinguished wartime team. Then, as the army and navy veterans came back in 1946, Cleveland baseball reached its most significant turning point. Bill Veeck, a war-damaged ex-marine, hit the town with the explosive force of a hydrogen bomb.

Thirty-two years of age, son of a former president of the Chicago Cubs, ex-owner of the Milwaukee club, the younger Veeck had determined while still a patient in various naval hospitals that he was going to get back into baseball. With Harry Grabiner, retired general manager of the Chicago White Sox, he investigated the possibilities of buying into Pittsburgh and Cleveland. For a variety of reasons, they picked the latter.

Several of Alva Bradley's millionaire associates in the 1927 purchase of the Indians had died and their heirs were anxious to get out of a business that had been neither pleasant nor especially profitable. Bradley himself wanted to stay, but the banks almost literally sold the club out from under him. Veeck became president and principal owner on June 22, 1946.

The Indians were in sixth place and drawing at the rate of about 750,000 fans for the 77-game home season—an average that would have been sure to decline as it became apparent that the team was without hope. They finished sixth and drew more than 1,000,000 customers for the first time in Cleveland history. In '47, they jumped to fourth and played to more than 1,500,000. In '48, they won the pennant and world championship and set an all-time attendance record of 2,620,000!

Veeck had built the team by a series of shrewd trades and purchases. He obtained Joe Gordon from the Yankees and, as an offshoot of that deal, got Gene Bearden out of the Yankee farm chain. He signed Larry Doby, first Negro ever to play in the American League. Shortly thereafter he received a laconic telegram from Kansas City: "Am available. (signed) Satchel Paige." He gave the venerable relic of the Negro leagues his chance in the big show. He paid the St. Louis Browns $100,000 for Sam Zoldak, a $15,000 pitcher.

On the evening of Labor Day, 1948, the Indians were four and a half games behind the pace-setting Red Sox. On the morning of the last day of the season, they were a full game in front. But they lost to Detroit on that final day and the Red Sox downed the Yankees. The pennant race had ended in a tie.

But it was a tie in which everything favored Boston. A toss of a coin several days earlier had determined that a playoff game, if one were necessary, should be played in Fenway Park where the Red Sox were as nearly unbeatable as any team has ever been. Besides, Boudreau had no pitcher ready. Feller had worked the losing game on Sunday. Bearden had thrown a brilliant shutout at the Tigers on Saturday. Bob Lemon, overworked in the stretch drive and obviously tired, had pitched Friday. Bearden, a surprise choice, came through brilliantly and the Indians won breezing, 8-3.

Two days later, still in Boston, they opened the World Series against the Braves. It was an anti-climax. The Indians had reached their goal in that playoff and then had collapsed in a heap. They played listlessly in the Series, but still won by four games to two. Bearden pitched a shutout against the Braves and saved the last game.

The final game was played in Boston. The next morning, the Tribe returned to Cleveland to run head-on into the wildest celebration the city had ever seen. It was Armistice Day in Paris. It was V-J Day in New York. It was all days of hysterical rejoicing rolled into one.

The Indians were favored to win again in 1949, but Bearden's magic was gone and Boudreau, Gordon and Keltner, the batting stars of the pennant year, fell flat on their faces. Even Veeck seemed to have lost much of his dynamic quality. He shrugged off repeated defeats as the Indians ran a bad third. Throughout that season, rumors that the club was for sale persisted in spite of official denials. In November, it happened. A Cleveland group headed by Ellis Ryan, an insurance executive, bought the Indians for a price in the neighborhood of $2,500,000.

An era had ended but a new one had begun. Hank Greenberg, whom Veeck had brought in as vice-president after his retirement as a player, became general manager under the new regime. When Lou Boudreau was given his release, a storm of criticism broke over the heads of Ryan and Greenberg, but the 1951 accomplishment of the new Indian manager, Al Lopez, stilled, once and for all, every dissenting voice. Al brought the club in a strong second.

The 42-year-old Lopez, a major-league catcher for 19 years, accepted his first big-league post with relish. A bright-eyed, alert and popular fellow, Lopez was a natural to become a manager. He hadn't even finished his first season at Indianapolis when they were talking about him as a first-rate prospect to pilot a major-league club. But it was generally supposed that he was next in line for the Pittsburgh Pirate job.

Under Lopez the Indians were soon showing the most impressive pitching in the majors. Bob Lemon, Early Wynn, Mike Garcia and the veteran Bob Feller gave the Indians a starting group that was more than a match for any other quartet in baseball. But despite the pitching advantage and the power hitting of Al Rosen, who led the league in homers and RBI's in 1953, the Tribe couldn't catch the Yankees. Cleveland won 93, 93 and 92 games in the seasons 1951 through 1953—and finished second each time.

But in 1954 the Indians nearly ran out of sight of everyone in the league, including the Yankees. In first place for 134 days of the season, they won a record 111 games and finished eight in front of New York. The smashing victory was the result of sound performance at every position. But among the individual standouts were: Bobby Avila, who won the batting title; a spirited Larry Doby; old faithfuls on the pitching staff, Lemon, Garcia, Wynn and Feller, plus newcomers Ray Narleski and Don Mossi.

The American League pennant came with ease to the Indians but the World Series with the Giants was something else again. To the astonishment of everyone, the Indians proved tame opponents and the National Leaguers made short work of them. Only the slugging of Vic Wertz, who batted .500, and the fact that the record gate receipts enabled them to take home $6,712.50 each gave the Indians any satisfaction. Otherwise, they might have done better to rest on their laurels at the end of the season.

Just as the song said, they may have been a headache but they never were a bore.